# MAL

THE INTERNATIONAL JO̶̶̶̶̶̶̶̶̶̶ AGGRESSION

Volume VIII                                          1984-1985

REINHOLD AMAN

EDITOR

MALEDICTA PRESS
WAUKESHA
WISCONSIN

Library of Congress Catalog
Card Number 77-649633

ISSN 0363-3659

ISBN 0-916500-28-4

*First Edition*


**NIHIL + OBSTAT**

**R** 23 September 1985 **A**


Printed in the United States of America

# CONTENTS

## VOL. VIII · 1984–1985

*Pseudonym

## DEPARTMENTS

**Frequently used abbreviations:**

MAL = *Maledicta*
MJ = *Milwaukee Journal*
NL = *National Lampoon*
WF = *Waukesha Freeman*

# WORDS CAN KILL
## THE ANATOMY OF A MURDER

## Reinhold Aman

Every day around the world, tens of thousands of people are killed, injured, jailed, fined, fired, demoted, humiliated, or commit suicide because of insults, slurs, curses, threats, blasphemy, vulgarities, and other offensive words. Such events emphasize the importance of this type of language and cry out for more research on verbal aggression and its effects.

We will keep on documenting this destructive power of maledicta. But I can report only those events that make the news: those few cases that I read in the two local newspapers, and those sent to me by helpful readers who read their papers with an eye for such news. There are countless other ones recorded more fully in criminal and civil court proceedings, in depositions and legal opinions dealing with evictions, assaults, traffic accidents, torts, libel, slander, fighting words, and many others instances where frustration led to anger, anger to offensive words, and offensive words to some negative result for the user or target of such "bad words." How many volumes of *Maledicta* we could fill with such fascinating documentation if our readers who are lawyers or judges would send photocopies of the relevant pages of cases they are involved in!

To illustrate, I will present such an event as reported in the *Milwaukee Journal* (20 April 1985, pp. 1 and 6). The news story lacks important details about the target and the actual offensive words spoken, but that is typical in newspaper reports. Relevant information may appear in a follow-up story months or years later (see the slur about Henry Kissinger in **ELITE MALEDICTA**).

In capsule form, here are the essentials proving that *offensive words caused death* in this situation:

1. **WHO?** (maledictor, the person(s) speaking or writing offensive words): Derrick Mayer, 19, of Menasha, Wisconsin.
2. **AGAINST WHOM?** (target, victim(s) of verbal abuse): An automobile driver and a passenger.
3. **WHAT?** (offensive words uttered or written): "Angry words."
4. **WHY?** (cause of verbal abuse): Drunkenness and anger.
5. **WHEN?** (time): 19 April 1985, ca. 10:30 p.m.
6. **WHERE?** (place): Milwaukee, Wisconsin; ca. 29th Street and Wisconsin Avenue.
7. **CONSEQUENCES** (results for maledictor and target): Maledictor Mayer killed with three gunshots into his back and upper right chest. Target fled.
8. **BACKGROUND** (additional useful information): See below, 1–6.

Some of these essentials seem to be too detailed, but all bits of information given are clues from which the reader can infer what really happened and why. The news report gave additional information, most of which is irrelevant to our concern.

1. The *name* of the maledictor is important in this case: I speculate that Derrick Mayer was white (not reported by the newspaper). His *age* is important: an older white male probably would not have yelled offensive words at big-city blacks cruising in a new luxury car. His *home town* is important: Menasha is a city of 14,752 inhabitants with few or no blacks; thus Mayer either may have disliked blacks or, being naive, may not have been familiar with this type of dangerous "Northern Urban Black."

2. The targets were not described, but I speculate that they were male and black. It is this newspaper's civil-minded policy not to identify the race of persons involved; the reader must deduce it from names, street addresses, or other evidence ("After having shot the police officer, he went to a watermelon stand to eat."). The race of the target is important, as it narrows down what the "angry words" were that caused Mayer's death. That news story was also incomplete by not reporting whether the driver and passenger were male or female. As Mayer's two drinking buddies (white males from Neenah, Menasha's twin city) were near Mayer when he was killed, they saw the driver and passenger, both of whom got out of the car. The driver and the passenger could be a male pimp and his whore (possible, because of time and place and type of automobile), two females (unlikely, as they would not attack an obnoxious drunk and his two male friends), or two males (most likely; perhaps two pimps or drug dealers, or just two fellows cruising for "foxes"). They were most likely blacks, the most common type of person cruising in a "late-model, four-door, brown Oldsmobile or Cadillac" on a Friday night at 10:30 p.m. on Wisconsin Avenue and about 29th Street, and having a handgun in their car. It is unlikely that two well-to-do whites would cruise, armed with a gun, in their new Cadillac on Wisconsin Avenue and 29th Street at this time and day. Most whites are either in some bar or in their homes.

3. The most important piece of information, the actual "angry words" shouted by Mayer at the driver, is not reported. But what would a young, white, angry, drunk fellow yell at two blacks cruising by in a new Caddy? Most likely "Niggers!" or some other racial slurs.

4. Why did Mayer shout at the driver? Because he was drunk and angry. The news story reported that he had been at a Milwaukee Brewers–Texas Rangers baseball game,

where he had drunk five bottles of beer. Later, he went to the Leprechaun Lounge on Wisconsin Avenue and 27th Street and drank one more bottle. Drunkenness was the prime reason, but there was also anger. Yet if he had been just angry, he probably would not have done what he did. Mayer and his two friends quarreled with several patrons at the tavern and were ejected. They returned and became involved in a fistfight with other patrons of the tavern, during which Mayer's shirt was torn off. The three then were on their way back to their motel on Wisconsin Ave. and 30th Street when Mayer, drunk and angry, began to shout at several passing cars. Other drivers ignored Mayer, but the driver of the luxury car pulled over and parked. Meyer walked up to the car. Now the driver and passenger got out. "Angry words" and punches were exchanged. Mayer allegedly struck the driver in the face. The driver walked back to his car, got a gun, fired once in the ground, and then shot Mayer in the upper right chest and two more times (apparently as Mayer was fleeing) into his back. The driver and passenger then fled in their car. They are still at large.

5. and 6. The time (10:30 p.m.) and place (West Wisconsin Avenue at 29th St.) are important for clues about what kind of person would cruise at this time and place in a late-model luxury car.

Some of the preceding material is speculation based on the information provided by the newspaper. As it turned out, Mayer was indeed white, as shown by his photograph in a follow-up story in that newspaper (22 April 1985, p. 2). In order to obtain more facts, I called the Milwaukee Police Department, but the officer would not give me any information over the phone. He advised me to inspect the "Open Records" in Milwaukee. When I arrived there (a fifty-mile roundtrip), the police refused to let me see the Open Records and refused to tell me the actual "angry words," claiming that it was against policy to reveal such information as long as the case is still pending. I pleaded with the officer to tell me just the "angry words," the only information I was interested in, but he would not. I asked whether Mayer had called them "niggers." No answer. To get some idea of what the "angry words" were, I asked if he could tell me whether racial slurs were involved. Again no information.

The officer did provide me with a single-sheet report containing one important fact, backing up my earlier speculation: the targets were indeed two black males ("two unidentified black male suspects"). It also revealed that Mayer was shot three times, not twice, as the paper reported: he died of "three gunshot wounds — one above the right nipple and two to the right side of mid-back."

To find out the actual "angry words," I could have called Mayer's parents, but I would never invade their privacy and grief (as reporters are wont to do). Thus I called the Milwaukee Chief of Police who sympathetically explained that Open Records are confidential while a case is pending, basing his policy on a court case of his department versus a local newspaper. He suggested that I contact the District Attorney who advises the police on such matters. An attorney at the D.A.'s office promised to look at the record to see whether he can release the "angry words" to me. After checking his own files, he found no record of the words. Thus we will have to wait until someone is charged with the murder, so that the police officers can reveal the fateful "angry words."

# DIALOGUE GRAFFITI

The following chain of graffiti, most of them written by different hands, was copied verbatim from the men's room (third floor) in the Life Sciences Building at the University of California, Berkeley, 2 August 1985:

The sultry bitch with the fiery eyes
*The bulky bitch with thunderous thighs*
The horny bitch who goes for guys
*The topless bitch who digs French fries*
The unwashed bitch who attracts flies
*The romantic bitch with the lonesome sighs*
The executive bitch w/ the striped ties
*The ugly bitch who nevertheless tries*
The not-cooking bitch who makes my bread rise
*The sleezy bitch who the prudes despise*
The robot bitch you computerize
*The oriental bitch w/ slanted eyes*
The rich bitch who always buys
*The feminist bitch who will circumcise*
The micro bitch who seduces flies
*There's not a hitch to this misogynist kitsch*
The transvestite bitch to the mensroom hies
*The racist bitch for redneck guys*
The post-doc bitch who ain't so wise
*The starry-eyed bitch w/ warehouse eyes*
The vampire bitch who never dies
*The gorgon bitch who petrifies*
The prostitute bitch who her trade plies
*The warm-fronted bitch w/ the overcast skies*
The falsy-topped bitch whose outline's a lie
*The dead bitch who grossly putrifies*
The AIDS tainted bitch was my slow demise
*The Nympho-bitch w/ the orgasmic cries*

(Contributed by Professor Rudolf Schmid, Botany Department, University of California, Berkeley.)

# ALL ABOUT MERKINS

## Roger W. Phillips

### 1. LEXICOLOGY

Few words in the sexual vocabulary beyond the most basic have had such a variety of meanings and applications over the centuries as *merkin*. Today the chief definition of *merkin* is that of imitation pubic hair for women, although in earlier British times, when a variant spelling was *mirkin*, it referred to the pudendum itself and the natural hair that garnished it. The present usage crops up in the early 17th century, and by 1796 and the third edition of Francis Grose's *Classic Dictionary of the Vulgar Tongue* we have what amounts to today's denotation: "counterfeit hair for women's privy parts." The current edition of *Oxford English Dictionary* cites this; *Webster's New International* (third edition) gives "false hair for the female genitalia." Richard A. Spears in *Slang and Euphemism* (1981) calls it "false female pubic hair" after giving the above-noted obsolete meanings, but is rather far off the mark in placing this as "British, late 1700s-1800s," since, as shown by the quotations below, this sense was clearly established by the time of Shakespeare's death.

Numerous other meanings of the word are in evidence. Charles James's *New and Enlarged Military Dictionary* of 1802 defines *merkin* as "a mop to clean cannon." Among the meanings given in Farmer and Henley, *Slang and Its Analogues*, are that of "fur" in general and, as thieves' cant, "hair dye," the latter also noted in Eric Partridge's *Dictionary of Underworld Slang* (1961). In various editions of his *Dictionary of Slang and Unconventional English* (the latest of which appeared just last year), Partridge defines it as "an artificial vagina for lonely men"; this sense also appears in the most recent *OED* supplement.

The etymology of *merkin* is more than a little uncertain, but *OED* considers it an apparent variant of *malkin*, which was originally a diminutive for the name *Maud* and is dialectal for a number of things: "untidy woman, slattern"; "a pole with a bundle of rags attached for cleaning out ovens"; "scarecrow"; "cat"; "hare." It can be seen easily enough that not all the senses of the two words jibe.

As pubic wigs, merkins were later also called *bowsers*. The etymology here is also uncertain, although it might be conjectured that the word in this sense (while related in others to *booze*) is an offshoot of *bursar* (treasurer), which is derived from Latin *bursa*, lit. "purse," "a bodily pouch or sac," whence the connection with the female genitalia.

## 2. SOME INSTANCES OF USAGE
## FROM EARLIER LITERATURE

John Taylor, known as the "Water Poet" (1578-1653), employs the word in his *Trauells in Bohemia* (ca. 1617; collected works 1630), in iambic pentameter lines apropos of an enormous wine vat he had seen in Prague: *Or had Cornelius but this Tub to drench / His clients that had practis'd too much French / A thousand hogsheads then would haunt his Firkin / And Mistris Minks recouer her lost Merkin*. A partial loose translation: there's enough wine in such a tub to put the hair back on a woman's pussy.

In a 1660 periodical, *Mercurius Fumig*, appeared a notice that a merkin had been lost in Covent Garden.

John Wilmot, second Earl of Rochester (1647-80), in a letter apropos of his play *Sodom, or the Quintessence of Debauchery*, says that some people might as well "wear some stinking Merkin for a beard."

In *The History of the Lives of the Most Famous Highwaymen* (1714), Alexander Smith describes how one such rascal obtained a merkin, dried and combed it out well, and then presented it to a cardinal as St. Peter's beard.

Bishop Thomas Percy's *Reliques of Ancient English Poetry* (1765) includes some bawdy songs and ballads, among them one from ca. 1620 "wishing good health to all Ladyes that never used a Merkin." This is a little ironic since a woman wouldn't have needed to use one if she had been healthy in the first place. See the notes below.

### 3. GENERAL HISTORICAL NOTES

Merkins were in fairly common use in the 17th and 18th centuries due to loss of hair from the frequent smallpox epidemics. Naturally, the fashion fell off rather sharply after the introduction of vaccination. But there had been earlier precedents for the cosmetic attention paid to that area of the female body, as well as later manifestations. In 16th-century France it was considered an elegant thing for aristocratic ladies to pomade their pubic hair and adorn it with colorful bows and ribbons, while letting it grow as long as possible. Such fashions come and go: witness the recent fad for shaving the pubes altogether (if we can believe what's reflected in the proliferation of skin mags on this theme!), or, especially in the late 60s, cutting it into various symbolic forms, e.g. the heart shape.

The word under discussion has never been particularly well known or understood by the general public. This situation is interestingly underscored, I think, by its sly usage in proper names in a couple of British films that appeared within the last twenty years. In *Dr. Strangelove, or How I Learned How to Stop Worrying and Love the Bomb* (1964), the President of the United States, played by Peter Sellers, is Merkin Muffley. Then there's a 1969 bit of fluff directed by Anthony Newley and boasting the likes of Milton Berle,

George Jessel and Joan Collins, entitled *Can Hieronymus Merkin Ever Forget Mercy Humppe and Find True Happiness?* But the last laugh here is that there really are people in the world named Merkin, and more than a few. You'll find seven in the current London phone book, as well as five in Chicago and over forty in New York!

[*Editor's Note:* For more information on *merkin*, see Aman's "Offensive Words in Dictionaries" in this volume.]

"I assume you don't want to put a wreath
on the front door either."

# A MEDICAL CHRISTMAS SONG

On the twelfth day of Christmas,
The E.R. sent to me:
Twelve interns flailing,
Eleven blades a-cutting,
Ten grodies scratching,
Nine crocks a-moaning,
Eight appies waiting,
Seven psychs a-screaming,
Six stabs a-swearing,
Five P.I.D.'s,
Four D.O.A.'s,
Three flail chests,
Two horse O.D.'s,
And a gomer in the D.T.'s.

## Glossary *by* Richard O. Barton

**Appies** appendectomy patients. **Blade** surgeon. **Crock** hypochondriac.
**D.O.A.** dead-on-arrival patient. **D.T.** *delirium tremens*; violent tremors
suffered by alcoholics. **E.R.** emergency room. **Flail chest** patient with
rib fractures and paradoxical breathing. **Gomer** usually a male patient,
often confused, disheveled; frequently alcoholic; practices poor personal hygiene; has a demanding, argumentative personality. **Grodies**
street people, often infested with lice (pediculosis). From "Valley-
Speak": yucky, terminally disgusting. **Horse** heroin. **Interns**, esp. new
ones, in emergency situations often flail about excitedly but are of little
help. **O.D.** overdose. **P.I.D.** pelvic inflammatory disease, often gonorrhea in females. **Psych** patient needing psychiatric care. **Stab** person wounded in a knife fight; often swears and curses his assailant.

15

# DISEASE CURSES

## Reinhold Aman

Modern English has few "disease curses," a genre of malediction very common in other languages. Dutch and Yiddish have many; German has a few. In using these curses, one wishes an illness or disease upon the opponent. Examples from Dutch, German, and Yiddish are:

**Krijg de mazelen!** "May you get the measles!"

**Die Scheißerei sollst du kriegen!** "May you get the shits!"

**A kholerye af im!** "May he get cholera!"

While reading in a physicians' magazine about the side effects of Zantac and Reglan tablets (stomach medications), I came up with the following "disease curses" a tad more sophisticated than the run-of-the-mill type. Richard Barton, a California medical man, informed me that the possible (but rare) side effects of drugs have to be couched in technical terms so that "the average layman would not be scared shitless."

**May you suffer from involuntary facial grimacing!**

**May you suffer from rhythmic protrusion of your tongue!**

**May you get symptomatic gastroesophageal reflux!** (heartburn)

**May you suffer from an oculogyric crisis!** (rolling eyeballs)

**May you suffer from dyskinesia!** (impaired or uncoordinated movements)

**May you get gynecomastia!** (a benign but often painful enlargement of a male's breasts)

**May your pyloric sphincter refuse to relax!** (stomach won't empty)

These curses can also be transformed into the *I need you (it) like* ... formula. Example: **I need you like I need Peyronie's disease!** This disease is a possible side effect of Trandate, a blood pressure control medication. It causes a painful, curved penile erection.

# AGEIST LANGUAGE

## Frank Nuessel

Elders in our society are a heterogeneous group.[1] Membership in this sector of our society is unrestricted as to gender, race, religion, national origin, and handicap. In fact, Matthews (1979:68) has observed that "old age is not a social category with a simple definition or an obvious membership. It is a social category with negative connotations, but, because of the ambiguity surrounding membership, to whom negative attributes may be imputed, is unclear." In practice, assignment to this category of society is usually defined by an arbitrary chronology, physical appearance, and patterns of behavior. Participation in this open-ended group is normally viewed as highly undesirable and unpleasant. This explains why some people tend to lie about their age or conceal it. Moreover, the social stigma attached to aging accounts for the ever-increasing number of cosmetic products (hair dye, skin discoloration ointments, etc.) designed to mask the superficial signs associated with the aging process. The related upsurge in surgical procedures (facelifts, hair implantation, etc.) is a more radical example of such gerontophobia.

The expression "ageism" was first coined by Robert N. Butler, former Director of the National Institute on Aging, in 1967 (Butler, 1969, 1975). Verification of the lexicalization of this notion is confirmed because this neologism now has a separate entry in *The American Heritage Dictionary of the English Language* where the term is defined as "discrimination based on age; especially discrimination against middle-aged and elderly people" (Morris, 1979:24).

The lexicon of ageist language is substantial (Nuessel, 1982). Such maledictology provides an excellent domain for the empirical verification and confirmation of Aman's (1973, 1977) prototypical onomastic questionnaire for eliciting data on deviations from the norm, shortcomings, and flaws. The present study constitutes a preliminary inventory of ageist terminology in the English language.

The difficulty associated with defining who is an elder is also manifested in the complexity of selecting a suitable term for describing this group. Ward (1979:165) reports ten terms (**senior citizen, retired person, mature American, elderly person, middle-aged person, older American, golden ager, old timer, aged person**, and **old man/old woman**) for this sector of the community. Many of these are euphemisms, i.e., they involve the substitution of a supposedly innocuous phrase for one which is considered patently offensive.[2] The sheer number of such expressions constitutes a linguistic record and indictment of society's phobic reaction to inclusion in this classification.

Humorous labels for elders are numerous: **geriatric generation, Geritol generation**, and **Lawrence Welk generation**. The activist political organization (Consultation of Older and Younger Adults) founded by Maggie Kuhn and popularly known as the **Gray Panthers** is yet another appellation with half-menacing, half-comic overtones. Even the adjectivally-derived noun **elderly** is stigmatic because this word has been employed by media reporters who have traditionally portrayed this social subdivision in a negative and derisive fashion. Another euphemistic term is **agèd** (also used adjectivally). At present, the emerging, acceptable lexical item for this diverse group is **elder**.

Ageist language comprises two separate categories. One domain includes words whose specific denotation refers to elders. The other component includes lexical items whose connotation or intensional meaning is normally associated with elders.

Many ageist words are particularly pernicious in their deprecatory impact because they denigrate people on the basis of both age and gender (Matthews, 1979; Sontag, 1972). **Beldam(e), biddy, crone, granny, gremalkin, hag, trot** (archaic), and **witch** relate to women who possess unpleasant physical attributes or who comport themselves in a socially unacceptable manner. **Bag, bat,** and **battle-ax(e)** allude to women with major personality defects. Although the latter terms are not age-specific, these words are frequently prefixed by the adjective **old**. These hybrid syntagms, consequently, reinforce the disparagement of female elders. The semantically neutral **maid** in conjunction with **old** and the term **spinster** combine unflattering ageist and sexist references. Likewise, **little old lady** suggests impotency based on age and sex. In this same vein, an old wives' tale, is idol gossip engaged in by elder idle females.

Disparaging terminology marked for age and sex exists for males also. **Codger, coot, gaffer, geezer,** and **greybeard** all portray this group wrongfully by attributing unacceptable behavior to its membership. **Old goat** and **dirty old man** invoke perceptions of lecherous men with misguided sexual inclinations. The acronym **D.O.M.** (*Dirty Old Man*) is frequently employed. To this repertoire of ageist words may be added the following distasteful colloquialisms:[3] **baldy, back number, bottle-nose,** and **mummy**. In addition to this list, labels preceded by the descriptor **old** are also negative: **cornstalk, crank, fart, fool, fossil, fuck, fuddy-duddy, fussbudget, grouch, grump, guard** (a collective term), **miser,** and **reprobate**.

All of these phrases allude to repugnant and antagonistic idiosyncracies. **Oldster** and **old-timer** are currently considered unacceptable designations. The term **dotard** (see *dotage, dote*) is unspecified for gender yet marked for age.

**Decrepit, doddering, frail, infirm, rickety,** and **superannuated** are all specific ageist designations for physical decline. **Antediluvian, obsolete, old-fashioned,** and **outmoded** are qualities that normally refer to objects or ideas. Their more recent application to elders reflects society's disdain for this group of people. Many other qualifying adjectives are not age-related but are commonly linked to elders: **cantankerous, constipated, cranky, crotchety, eccentric, feebleminded, flabby, frumpy, fussy, garrulous, grouchy, grumpy, over-age** (a relative term), **peevish, rambling, silly, toothless, withered, wizen, wizened,** and **wrinkled.** Each one of these epithets is an objectionable or unattractive physical, mental or behavioral trait.

In fact, few favorable expressions exist to allude to elders. Positive, age-specific attributions are indeed exiguous (e.g., **august, experienced, mature, mellow, sage, seasoned, veteran, well-versed, wise**). In fact, many of the adjectives that refer to age in an auspicious sense carry favorable connotations only when applied to objects (alcoholic beverages, certain foods, and various handicrafts). Thus when *old* refers to wine or lace, this is a good property. Likewise, *aged* ascribed to brandy, cheese and wood is an excellent characteristic. Yet when assigned to people, these two terms (**aged, old**) are normally pejorative.

In addition to the denominations for the collective membership of elders, the terminology for the state of being aged is numerous. Many of these phrases — **anecdotage** (a blend of *anecdote* plus *dotage*), **declining years, second childhood, over the hill, twilight years** — imply decadence, decline or foolish activity. Words of Latin derivation such as

**longevity** and **senectitude** seem to be neutral. Other Latin derivatives for this status are **anility, caducity, debility, decrepitude, dotage, infirmity**, and **senility**. Again, most of these de-adjectival nouns which contain the same negative allusions as their derivational sources. The fact that they are erudite terms fails to conceal their euphemistic intent.

A few other ageist phrases are noteworthy. **Generation gap**, a neologism of the 1960s, focuses on the polarization of young and old people in our youth-oriented society (see note 3). **Convalescent center** is a frightening euphemism for a segregated concentration camp for elders. The pleasant and euphonic descriptive names (**Friendship Manor, Pine Tree Villa, Tendercare**) for these urban ghettoes conceals the fact that such sites are the penultimate repositories of their charges. Even the term **geriatric ghetto** has been employed to describe this form of virtual incarceration.

Even a few verbs may be considered ageist in their intent. The admonition **to act one's age** is a warning to elders to behave in a customary manner expected (even demanded) by society. The verbal expression **to show one's age** is sexist because it normally requires a [ + female] subject. This expression refers to the overt manifestations of the normal aging process (wrinkles, so-called age spots, etc.).

In summary, ageist language is insidious and nefarious because such parlance distorts or degrades its victims. The lexicalization (i.e., standardization of clichés about this group) facilitates verbal abuse of elders. Eventually, such maledictions can lead to far more serious mistreatment as evidenced by the current media accounts concerning the mistreatment of elders by their own children and by nursing home personnel.

# NOTES

1. Holmes (1983:116-17) cites Rose (1965) who suggests that the aged may be considered a clearly identifiable subculture because of patterns of interaction, and common interests and problems. Levin and Levin (1980:95) also take the position that elders are a minority group because they are victims of ageism. Many sociologists dispute such a categorization. In this regard, Matthews (1979:60) states that "except for a few obvious correlates of old age, such as collecting pensions and social security, there are few behavorial prescriptions that apply specifically to the aged and not to adults generally. At the same time, however, age is an attribute that has social meanings and is taken into account in social interaction." Streib (1965) also concurs that the aged do not comprise a minority group.

2. Fischer (1978:94) states "...praise words invented for old people... such as *senior citizen* are often laden with a heavy freight of sarcasm."

3. Fischer (1978:91-92) observes that many of the terms of elder abuse (*gaffer, fogy, greybeard, old guard, superannuated*) were simply redefinitions of earlier non-offensive lexical items. Moreover, the increasing number of such opprobrious phrases in the late 19th and early 20th centuries reflect urban and industrial society's tendency to favor the young (Holmes, 1983:171; Sokolovsky, 1983:117).

# REFERENCES

Aman, Reinhold. 1973. *Bayrisch-österreichisches Schimpfwörterbuch.* Munich: Süddeutscher Verlag.

———. 1977. "An Onomastic Questionnaire," *Maledicta* 1:83-101.

Butler, Robert N. 1969. "Age-ism: Another Form of Bigotry," *The Gerontologist* 9, 243-46.

———. 1975. *Why Survive Being Old in America.* New York: Harper and Row.

Fischer, David. 1978. *Growing Old in America.* Expanded Ed. Oxford: Oxford University Press.

Holmes, Lowell D. 1983. *Other Cultures, Elder Years: An Introduction to Cultural Gerontology.* Minneapolis: Burgess Publishing Co.

Levin, Jack and William C. Levin. 1980. *Ageism: Prejudice and Discrimination Against the Elderly.* Belmont, CA: Wadsworth Publishing Company.

Matthews, Sarah. 1979. *The Social World of Old Women: Management of Self-Identity.* Sage Library of Social Research, vol. 78. Beverly Hills, CA: Sage Publications.

Morris, William (ed.), 1979. *The American Heritage Dictionary of the English Language*. Boston: Houghton-Mifflin Co.

Nuessel, Frank. 1982. "The Language of Ageism," *The Gerontologist* 22:3, 273-76.

Rose, Arnold M. 1965. "The Subculture of Aging: A Framework in Social Gerontology." In: Arnold M. Rose and Warren A. Peterson (eds.), *Older People and Their Social World*. Philadelphia: F.A. Davis Co.

Sokolovsky, Jay. 1983. *Growing Old in Different Societies: Cross-cultural Perspectives*. Belmont, CA: Wadsworth Publishing Co.

Sontag, Susan. 1972. "The Double Standard Again," *The Saturday Review* (September 23), 29-38.

Streib, Gordon. 1965. "Are the Aged a Minority Group?" In: Bernice Neugarten (ed.), *Middle Age and Aging*, 35-46. Chicago: University of Chicago Press.

Ward, Russell. 1979. *The Aging Experience: An Introduction to Social Gerontology*. New York: J.P. Lippincott Company.

## AN AGEIST LEXICON

Definitions in this glossary are from three sources: (1) numbers only in parentheses refer to Morris (1979); (2) parenthetical references with Fischer and number refer to Fischer (1978); and (3) those glosses with no parenthetical references are the author's creation.

**act one's age** *v.* to behave as suitable for (13)

**agèd** *n., adj.* contemporary euphemism for *old* or *elders*

**anachronism** *n.* anything out of its proper time (46). Meaning extended to elders to indicate that this group of people is out of step with current society.

**anecdotage** *n.* garrulous old age or senility (used humorously) (49)

**anile** *adj.* of or like an old woman (52)

**anility** *n.* the state of being anile

**antediluvian** *adj.* very old; antiquated; primitive (55)

**back number** *n.* an anachronistic old man (Fischer, 92)

**bag** *n.* an unattractive woman (slang) (99)

**baldy** *n.* a person whose age is evidence by loss of hair

**bat** *n.* an ugly or nagging woman; shrew (112)

**battle ax(e)** *n.* an overbearing woman; virago (slang) (113)

**beldam(e)** *n.* an old woman, especially one who is loathsome or ugly (120)

**biddy** *n.* a garrulous old woman (slang) (130)

**bottle-nose** *n.* an alcoholic old man (Fischer, 92)

**caducity** *n.* the frailty of old age (186)

**cantakerous** *adj.* ill-tempered and quarrelsome; disagreeable; contrary (198)

**codger** *n.* an old man (informal) (258)

**constipated** *adj.* reference to a supposed chronic condition of elders

**convalescent center** *n.* a warehouse for elders (euphemism)

**coot** *n.* a foolish old man (292)

**crank** *n.* a grouchy person; an eccentric (304)

**cranky** *adj.* ill-tempered, peevish; odd, eccentric (309)

**crone** *n.* a withered, witchlike old woman (315)

**crotchety** *adj.* capriciously stubborn or eccentric; perverse (316)

**debility** *n.* the state of abnormal bodily weakness; feebleness (340)

**declining years** *n.* old age (euphemism)

**decrepit** *adj.* weakened by old age, illness, or hard use; broken down (344)

**decrepitude** *n.* the state of being decrepit; weakness, infirmity (344)

**dirty old man** *n.* lecherous aged male

**doddering** *adj.* feeble-minded from age; senile (387)

**D.O.M.** *n.* acronym for DIRTY OLD MAN

**dotage** *n.* second childhood; senility (392)

**dotard** *n.* a senile person (392)

**dote** *v.* to be foolish or feeble-minded, especially as a result of senility (392)

**eccentric** *adj.* departing from or deviating from the conventional or established norm, model, or rule (411-12)

**fart** *n.* a mean, contemptible person (vulgar slang) (476)

**feeble** *adj.* lacking strength; weak; especially frail or infirm (481)

**feebleminded** *adj.* mentally deficient; subnormal in intelligence; dull-witted; stupid; foolish (481)

**flabby** *adj.* lacking firmness; loose and yielding to the touch; lacking force or vitality; feeble; ineffectual (497)

**fogy** *n.* a person of old-fashioned habits and outmoded attitudes (508)

**fogyish** *adj.* having the attributes of a FOGY

**fogyism** *n.* having the traits of a FOGY

**fool** *n.* one who shows himself, by words or actions, to be deficient in judgment, sense, or understanding; a stupid or thoughtless person (511)

**foolish** *adj.* lacking good sense or judgment; silly (511)

**fossil** *n.* one that is outdated or antiquated; especially a person with outmoded ideas; a fogy (518)

**frail** *adj.* having a delicate constitution; physically weak; not robust (521)

**fuddy-duddy** *n.* one who is old-fashioned and fussy (531)

**fussbudget** *n.* a person who fusses over trifles (535)

**fussy** *adj.* given to fussing; easily upset; insistent upon petty matters or details; fastidious (535)

**gaffer** *n.* an old man or rustic (537)

**galoot** *n.* a clumsy, uncooth, or sloppily dressed person (540)

**garrulous** *adj.* habitually talkative; loquacious (544)

**geezer** *n.* an eccentric old man (547)

**generation gap** *n.* reference to supposed philosophical and ideological differences between young and old (divisive term)

**geriatric generation** *n.* elders as a group (derisive)

**geriatric ghetto** *n.* home for elders (*Maledicta* 5:340)

**Geritol generation** *n.* elders as a group (derisive). Geritol is a patent medicine marketed for this age group.

**goat** *n.* a lecherous man (564)

**golden age** *n.* a period when a nation or some wide field of endeavor reaches its height (565). Euphemism for OLD AGE.

**goose** *n.* a silly person, a simpleton (568)

**granny (grannie)** *n.* a grandmother; an old woman; a fussy person (Southern) (573)

**graybeard** *n.* an old man (576)

**Gray Panthers** *n.* Political organization (Consultation of Younger and Older Adults) founded by Maggie Kuhn. This is a humorous journalistic title for the organization.

**grimalkin** *n.* a shrewish old woman (579)

**grouch** *n.* a habitually complaining or irritable person (581)

**grouchy** *adj.* inclined to grumbling and complaint; ill-humored; peevish (581)

**grump** *n.* a cranky, complaining person (583)

**grumpy** *adj.* fretful and peevish; irritable; cranky (583)

**hag** *n.* an ugly, frightful old woman; termagant; crone; a witch, sorceress (592)

**infirm** *adj.* weak in body, especially from old age; feeble (674)

**infirmity** *n.* lack of power; bodily debilitation; frailty (674)

**Lawrence Welk generation** *n.* elders as a group (derisive). A reference to their supposed musical preferences.

**little old lady** *n.* a negative term, suggestive of impotency and frailty

**maid** *n.* a girl or unmarried woman; a virgin (786)

**miser** *n.* one who deprives himself of all but the barest essentials to hoard money. A greedy or avaricious person (838)

**mummy** *n.* any withered or shrunken body, living or dead, that resembles a mummy (862)

**obsolete** *adj.* no longer in use or in fashion (907)

**old cornstalk** *n.* an ineffectual old man (Fischer, 92)

**old-fashioned** *adj.* of a style or method formerly in vogue; outdated; antiquated; attached to or favoring methods, ideas or customs of an earlier time (915)

**old fuck** *n.* old man (vulgar slang)

**old guard** *n.* reactionary, corrupt and aged politician (Fischer, 91)

**oldster** *n.* an old or elderly person (informal) (915)

**old-timer** *n.* one who has been a resident, member, or employee for a long time. Something that is very old or antiquated (915)

**old wives' tale** *n.* a bit of superstitious folklore (915)

**outmoded** *adj.* not in fashion. No longer usable or practical; obsolete (933)

**overage** *adj.* beyond the proper or required age (935)

**over the hill** *adj.* no longer useful or functional

**peevish** *adj.* querulous; discontented; fretful; ill-tempered; contrary; fractious (967)

**pop** *n.* an older man (derisive)

**rambling** *adj.* lengthy and desultory (1097)

**reprobate** *n.* morally unprincipled, profligate (1104)

**rickety** *adj.* feeble with age; infirm (1116)

**second childhood** *n.* a period of foolish, childlike behavior allegedly experienced by the elderly

**senile** *adj.* pertaining to, characteristic of, or proceeding from old age; exhibiting senility (1180)

**senile dementia** *n.* progressive, abnormally accelerated deterioration of mental faculties and emotional stability in old age (1180)

**senility** *n.* the state of being senile; mental and physical deterioration with old age (1180)

**senior citizen** *n.* a person of or over the age of retirement (1180)

**show one's age** *v.* to have the physical appearance of an elder person; to act the way society expects a person to act at a given age

**silly** *adj*. showing lack of good sense; unreasoning; stupid (1206)

**spinster** *n*. a woman who has remained single behind the conventional age for marrying (1245)

**superannuated** *adj*. retired or discharged because of age or infirmity; persisting ineffectively despite advanced age (1290)

**toothless** *adj*. lacking teeth; lacking force; ineffectual (1354)

**trot** *n*. an old woman (archaic) (1376)

**twilight years** *n*. old age (euphemism)

**witch** *n*. an ugly, vicious old woman; hag (1470)

**withered** *adj*. dried up or shriveled up as if from loss of moisture; lacking in freshness; faded; droopy

**wizen** *adj*. shriveled or dried up (1471)

**wizened** *adj*. shriveled, wizen (1471)

**wrinkled** *adj*. drawn up; puckered (1477)

**THE FAR SIDE**

"Hey! . . . Six-eyes!"

# TAXONOMIC PORNITHOLOGY
## RULES FOR THE NAMING OF
## EGREGIOUS AND OBSCENE BIRDS

## Douglas Lindsey

Synthetic pornithology is the development of avian labels to describe varieties of human appearance and behavior. The obligate brevity of ornithologic nomenclature suggests relationship with both the one-liner and the pun, but these mechanisms do not adequately explain the range of possibilities of synthetic ornithology as a form of humor.

Labeling a person as a bird is not new. All academicians are familiar with the pejorative labeling of a visiting lecturer as a **turkey**, and more than a few of us have, on occasion, legitimately earned the designation. Tucson, by virtue of its far southern location in the Great American Desert, is the destination in winter of great flocks of migrating **snowbirds**, for which more precise speciation is possible. The **greater greenbacked snowbird** is enthusiastically welcomed as a "winter guest." The **lesser sooty snowbird**, on the other hand, is regarded as a pest. Euphemistically labeled as a "transient" (we try, with scant success, to encourage it to move north to Phoenix or west to Los Angeles), it befouls the shrubbery in Armory Park, clutters the lobby of the main post office with its queues before the General Delivery window, and roost at night around campfires along the tracks of the Southern Pacific Railroad. The **lesser sooty snowbird** is accompanied by the **common stench**, always the **lesser stench**, and sometimes the **greater stench** as well.

The serious and systematic recording of collections of synthetic ornithologic species is a hobby of regrettably few devotees, and I see little prospect for a boom in the field. Perhaps the potential for proliferation of enthusiasts is greater in the field of taxonomic pornithology, a subset within synthetic ornithology which permits the venting of a pornithologic bent while offering immunity against accusation of public flatus in polite company. Provided, of course, that such verbal farting is accomplished in accordance with the recognized rules of a creative scholarly endeavor.

I will outline for you the rules of legitimate taxonomic pornithology in order to protect you from irresponsible criticism, even though I realize that taxonomic pornithology can, indeed, be practiced as a solitary vice for your own amusement, with no need for public utterance whatsoever; or it can be practiced in privy, compatible groups, where the interpersonal stimulation and instigation can be expected to lead to mutual satisfaction.

The first basic rule of taxonomic pornithology is: *it's got to sound like a bird.* You can give it a bird's name, literally, or a bird's name which is twisted slightly or punned. You can make it a bird by using avian-specific anatomy, or avian-specific functional nomenclature. You can get away with many designations which are bird-related, but not avian-specific. And when you get rolling, you can make derivations which are ornithologic only by association and context. Which brings up the second basic rule of taxonomic pornithology: *if it passes for a bird, it is.* The risk of overstretching the immunity from obscenity is your own. If you provided an adequate context, and it flies, it's a bird. If it doesn't fly, you are stuck with mouthing dirty words.

An example of the use of legitimate bird names is the **perpetual grouse**. A takeoff from the **prothonotary warbler**, which figured heavily in the Alger Hiss/Whitaker

Chambers affair, is the **penitentiary warbler**, also known as the **stool pigeon**. A medical example is the **intertriginous thrush**. But the archetypical example of the technique is the **extramarital lark**.

Tweaking the bird name just a little offers more possibilities. The **ruffled spouse** is often found in association with the **extramarital lark**. The **great American craven** proliferated enormously during the war in Viet Nam — to such numbers that large flocks migrated to Canada. The **California condom**, once thought to be near extinction as the result of advances in steroid chemistry, is now making a comeback as result of the threats induced by herpes and Acquired Immune Deficiency Syndrome (AIDS).

The door is open. If there is a *junco*, there is a **junkie**. If there is *cardinal*, there is **venial**. If there is a *phoebe*, there is a **feelie** and a **freebie**. If there is a *curlew*, there is a **curfew**. If there is a *barred avocet*, there must be a **disbarred advocate**. There are *buzzards* and *bustards*: surely there must be **bastards**, and the **yellow-bellied bastard** is one of my earliest and most faithfully recurring species.

In terms of avian-specific anatomy, my base type is the **buff-tinted due-bill**. Pornithologic? Of course. Bad enough that the scoundrel is dunning me for his ill-gotten gains; he is doing it on *off-color, laid* paper! More innocuous is **Durante's grossbeak**, from which we can develop **de Bergerac's proboscis**. But my favorite is the **right-winged sanctimoner**, or **Falwell's phallusy**. A **phallusy** is the public claim to potency and prowess which does not exist. A prime example is the man who stuffs two Kotex into the crotch of his bathing trunks to draw incredulous stares from the babes at the beach.

Anatomical terms which are not avian-specific require a little more caution. After all, there are non-avian species which can be described in their own right as full-breasted, sharp-clawed, and twitchy-tailed. But the **pearl-throated**

**dowager** will pass (there is a bird known as the *dowitcher*), as will the **mink-breasted Yentl**, the **bald gay**, and the **red-nosed lush**. The **three-toed American chicken** is synonymous with the **great American craven**, but so named for the footprint which he displayed in justification of his cry of conscientious aversion to wading through the jungles of Viet Nam and getting shot at.

Many legitimate avian species are labeled by particular function or behavior. If there is a *gnatcatcher*, there is surely a **nitpicker**. If there is a *roadrunner*, there must be a **streetwalker**. A good example of functional identification with birds is the **accidental flycatcher**, also known as the **impaled prepuce** or the **zippered thatch**.

There is a bird known as the *wandering tattler* which gives rise to the **village gossipmonger** and the **suburban fink**. The **all-night bed-thrasher** warms many hearts, two at a time. If there is a *white wagtail*, there must be a **black wagtail** and a **yellow wagtail**. The last implies oriental origin, so it may be called the **transverse snatch**. There is, indeed, a bird known as the *white-collared seedeater*, which translates to the **executive gay**. There is a *greater frigate bird*: why not a **lesser upyurass**?

Incidentally, the adjectives that ornithologists use are amusing in their own right. There are birds which are *fulvous, ferruginous*, and *flammulated*. Another legitimate ornithologic adjective is *frugiverous*, meaning "fruit-eating," which leads to the **frugiverous reciprocating gay**, implying an all-male 69.

Let us note some examples of how far out we can stretch and distort a few common and uncommon birds.

There is a Mexican bird, little known to most of you, named the *copper trogon*, from which we can deduce the **pink-ribbed Trojan** and the **rubber Ramses**. For those of you who are not from the western side of the Atlantic, I might explain that *Trojan* and *Ramses* are popular brands of condoms in the United States.

The *robin* is a common bird, but I have been able to make little of it.* The **hooded robin** comes to mind. Probably extinct now, but occasionally sighted of yore in Nottingham Forest. Hardly pornithologic, though there were some delightfully salacious obliquities in the lines of the pilot of an abortive television series. But **cradle robin** offers some opportunities: **Nabakov's Lolita** and **Polanski's nemesis**. **Cradle robin** is a species of global distribution — I remember from my youth some most exciting specimens of what was called **San Quentin quail** — but it seems to have dropped from view in Sweden since the age of consent was lowered to twelve.

The *swallow* provides much food for thought. Physicians and many patients are quite familiar with the **barium swallow**. Californians get very excited each year when the **Cappuccino swallow** returns to the mission of San Juan Cappuccino. Since this swallow always returns, we could call it the **regurgitant swallow**, but that would unnecessarily offend aficionados of Cappuccino. There is a real bird known as the *violet green swallow*, certainly a nauseating combination, perhaps to be labeled the **imminent barf**. There is a little hummingbird which is also purple and green; surely it can be labeled the **regurgitant sip**.

And then, or course, there is the **deep-throated swallow**, known also as the **plum-headed gag** or **common puke**. For the ladies who perhaps feel put upon in such matters, I offer the **avid busheater**, the **long-billed muff-diver**, the **cunning lingus**, and for those whose tastes in the matter are utterly feminine, the **Lapland gull**. But my favorite in this group is the **limber-tongued gash hawk**.

Of course, if one is serious about ornithology or pornithology one needs a "field guide" — how to identify the species if you don't have it in your grubby little hand, or in your bush. Let me tell you how to spot the **limber-**

---

*Editor's Note*: The robin is Wisconsin's State Bird. Its Latin name is *Turdus migratorius*.

**tongued gash hawk**. He hangs out in the singles bar. He comes early, but never stays late. He comes alone, but never leaves alone. He sits at the little table in the corner, where he can look out over the whole room. He orders a huge pitcher of beer, from which he drinks, in single gulps, spaced at long intervals. Most of the time he just sits there, licking the foam from his eyebrows. His favorite beer? *Slits*.

Another bird familiar to, and beloved by almost all of you, is the *cock*. Male homosexuals think there is absolutely nothing finer than the **cock**. Virtually all admitted and practicing heterosexuals think highly of the **cock**, too. And in certain forms, the **cock** is esteemed by the lesbian. Take the **many-splintered woodcock**. Few would take it, willingly, even though it featured heavily in the romantic novel *Love is a Many-splintered Thing*. But how about the **burnished woodcock**, also known as the **mahogany dildo**?

A minor variety, but worth some discussion, is the **matutinal peecock**, also known as the **early-morning hard** or **uriniferous cock**. Morphologically it is identical with the familiar **erogenate cock**; in fact, in museum specimens — skinned and dried — the two are indistinguishable. Behaviorally they are quite different. The **erogenate cock** struts proudly during the pre-mating ritual. The **matutinal peecock** is shy, almost secretive, sometimes recognizable only by the tenting of its cover. You seldom get to examine one closely unless you have a domesticated specimen. It often runs away when it is uncovered; you might even say that it disappears when it is flushed. This accounts for an alternate nomenclature, the **fugacious phallus**. *Fugacious* means "fleeting." I would not know that, except that as a physician, I am sometimes called upon to manage cases of *proctalgia fugax*, literally translated as "a fleeting pain in the ass," which is precisely and entirely all that we know about the condition.

Of course there are a few of the species of **cock** which,

like myself, work night shifts and sleep in the daytime. This
is the **vespertine peecock** which, on occasion, can be confused with the **great horny owl**.

Also familiar to you are *tits* and *boobs*. I read an article
once, in that prestigious scientific journal *Nature*, on the
feeding habits of *great tits* — nutritional requirements and
food intake. This has confused me; I had always thought
it was the other way round. Incidentally, I have never quite
understood the alleged erogenous importance of size in
**great tits**. It seems that simply quoting the numbers
*38-27-35* is supposed to be an instant turn-on. More important, I think, is form, feel and flavor. There are **silicone
tits**; their flavor is poor.

**Boobies** are closely related to **tits**. The corollary to the
*great tits* is the **saddle-bag booby**, usually observed in the
**shrouded** variety. The **lesser shrouded booby** is also
known as the **cross-your-heart bra**, and the **least shrouded
booby** is also known as **Frederick's pastie**.

Finally, there is a group of birds known as the *ani*. If
you will permit me the presumption that the singular of
*ani* is *anus*, this opens up other avenues for exploration.
There is the **patulous anus**, and the **petulant anus**. There
is the **pendulous anus**, also known as the **prolapsed pile**.
And, of course, there is the **fiery-red anus**, known also
as the **tabasco twat**, **el ano salsado**, or simply the **Mexican heartburn**.

Let me encourage you to take up the hobby of taxonomic
pornithology. If you think I have exhausted the possibilities,
think again. Get hold of a copy of *Mrs. Byrne's Dictionary
of Unusual, Obscure, and Preposterous Words.* Find an unusual
adjective, and then hang it on a bird. For example, the
**obvallate fink** is synonymous with the **penitentiary
warbler**. Find an unusual noun, and use it. The word
*rantallion* is British slang for a man whose balls hang lower
than his pecker. Obviously, then, there are *two* avian

species: the **short-dinked rantallion**, and the **big-knockered rantallion**. Find both noun and adjective. The **jubate merkin** is a female pudendum with hair like a horse's mane. The **irrumant agomphyx** is the nice little old lady — the *cute* nice little old lady — who takes her teeth out before she goes down on you. When you return the favor, you can identify the **poliotic pubis**, also known as the **mottled muff**, the **bespotted beaver**, or the **salt-and-pepper snatch**. And how about the **preprandial pallion**, literally translated as "a little piece before lunch," also known as the **quickie**?

What is the meaning of all this pornithology? One of the Justices of the Supreme Court of the United States once commented that if pornography had any redeeming virtue at all, he would give it the protection of freedom of the press. Taxonomic pornithology does have a redeeming virtue. Sit in the middle seat of an Aer Lingus wide-bodied jet. Stare up at the ceiling, and stare all around you, looking for pornithologic species. Move your lips slowly while naming species, without uttering a sound. Then smile, giggle, and occasionally break out in hearty laughter. Soon the flight attendant will find other seats for the passengers on your right and left, and you can stretch out and sleep, or continue to amuse yourself without abusing yourself, all the way across the Atlantic.

"Mating in flight during a *hurricane*?
Gee, that's *really* throwing
coition to the wind!"

# ETHIOPIAN JOKES

## Richard Christopher*

No serious student of American folk humor can fail to observe that the genre of "current event jokes" has become embedded with increasing depth and tenacity in the annals of verbal aggression. For more than two decades now, going back to the assassinations and watery embarrassment of the Brothers Kennedy, I have been collecting and recording such jokes; and, during the past five years, I have noted an astonishing increase in their range and sheer numbers.

Let a big story break—like those involving Billie Jean King, Karen Ann Quinlan, Renée Richards, Rosie Ruiz, Richard Pryor, Michael Jackson, Grace Kelly, Gerry Studds, Geraldine Ferraro, Jesse Jackson, Karen Carpenter, Natalie Wood, and Baby Fae, or the incidents at Big Dan's Pool Hall and the San Ysidro McDonald's—and within a week my far-reaching network of correspondents will have supplied me with one to ten quips about the event.

Reinhold Aman has added over two dozen new riddles to this collection, gathered from *Maledicta* readers and Henry Birdseye's computer bulletin board.

The story that most dominates our consciousness and consciences in 1985 has been the holocaust of famine and death that has devastated Ethiopia. As a member of the human race, I am staggered by the enormousness—and the enormity—of this vast tragedy. As a collector and recorder of verbal aggression, I note that this ultimate distillation of our most ghastly nightmares has spawned the greatest number of "current event jokes" that I have ever encountered.

What is an amateur scholar like me and a professional

journal like *Maledicta* to do with such information? First, we may speculate on the reasons why such a horror of an event would produce such a spate of jokes. Could the reason be the vastness of problem? The helplessness of the victims? The length of time the story has dominated the news? The sense of our own vulnerability in the face of the nuclear threat and the ecological fragility of the planet we all ride? Or could the reason be that black people are the ones who are doing the starving and dying?

Second, *Maledicta* and I can print the jokes. While we echo Kurtz's hollow cry in Joseph Conrad's *Heart of Darkness*—"The horror! The horror!"—we must also record the deeply human response to that horror in the form of the many Ethiopian jokes that have become a significant part of our current oral folklore. Here they are—all brief, all centering on starvation. Make of them what you will.

The earliest of the Ethiopian jokes was:

What's the fastest-moving flightless bird?
— *A chicken running through Ethiopia.* (Or *The Ethiopian chicken.*)

Why did the chicken cross the road?
— *He saw an Ethiopian coming after him.*

What's the lowest-selling product in Ethiopia?
— *After-dinner mints.* (Or *Maalox, laxatives, dental floss, table cloths, napkins, silverware, Tums,* etc.)

How many Ethiopians can you stuff into a phone booth?
— *All of them.*

How many Ethiopians can you fit into a shopping cart?
— *None. They fall through the holes.*

How many Ethiopians can you fit in a bathtub?
— *None. They keep sliding down the drain.*

What's black, round and covered with cobwebs?
— *An Ethiopian's asshole.*

What do you call an Ethiopian walking his dog?
— *A vegetarian.*

What do you call an Ethiopian walking two dogs?
— *A caterer.*

What do you call an Ethiopian walking ten dogs?
— *A rancher.*

What do you call an Ethiopian with long, stringy hair?
— *A mop.*

What do you call an Ethiopian wearing a turban (*or* Afro)?
— *A Q-Tip.*

What do you call an Ethiopian wearing a fur coat?
— *A pipe cleaner.*

What do you call an Ethiopian with a dime on his head?
— *A nail.*

What do you call an Ethiopian with a big toe?
— *A golf club.*

What do you call an Ethiopian with a swollen foot?
— *A three wood.*

What do you call an Ethiopian with a blue spot on his head?
— *A pool stick.*

What do you call an Ethiopian with a feather sticking out of his ass?
— *A dart.*

What do you call an Ethiopian with buck teeth?
— *A rake.*

What do you call an Ethiopian around a guy's neck?
— *Ty.*

What do you call an Ethiopian with a sesame seed bun on his head?
— *A quarter-pounder.*

What do you call a forty-pound Ethiopian?
— *"Bubba" or "Fatty."*

What's new about the McDonald's restaurant in Ethiopia?
— *It features a crawl-up window.*

What has millions of legs and weighs a thousand pounds?
— *The entire population of Ethiopia.*

Why don't Ethiopians go to movie theaters?
— *Because they can't keep the seats down.*

Who has body measurements of 18–38–18 (*or* 10–10–10)?
— *Miss Liberated Free People's Democratic Republic of Ethiopia.*

What do you call 125 Ethiopians in a Mercedes?
— *Brown corduroy slipcovers.*

What's a definition of "optimist"?
— *An Ethiopian wearing a dinner jacket.*

What is the Ethiopian national anthem?
— *"Aren't you hungry for a Burger King now?"*

What did Poland send to Ethiopia for famine relief?
— *4,000 pounds of after-dinner mints.*

What do Yoko Ono and Ethiopians have in common?
— *They both live off dead beetles.*

What does an Ethiopian use for a belt?
— *A rubber band.*

What do Ethiopians use key rings for?
— *Belts.*

How can you tell the Jewish Ethiopian?
— *He's the one wearing the fancy gold watch around his waist.*

Who's the patron saint of Ethiopia?
— *Karen Carpenter.*

What's the difference between an Ethiopian baby and an NFL football?
— *The football weighs at least 14 ounces.*

What's the difference between an Ethiopian and Levi's?
— *Levi's have only one fly.*

What does an Ethiopian do with a bag of potato chips?
— *He opens a restaurant.*

What's the nicest thing to say to an Ethiopian?
— *"My, you've gained weight lately."*

What's the meanest thing to say to an Ethiopian?
— *"What's for dinner?"*

How do you start a fire?
— *Rub two Ethiopians together.*

What does an Ethiopian feel after breakfast?
— *Guilt.*

What's the main cause of child disappearance in Ethiopia?
— *Breeze.*

What did the Ethiopian do when he fell into the alligator pit?
— *That sucker ate two before they could pull him out.*

How can you tell the sex of an unborn Ethiopian baby?
— *Hold the pregnant woman up to the light.*

What's the best thing about an Ethiopian blowjob?
— *You* know *she's going to swallow it.*

   There are also visual jokes:

What's this? [With your index finger trace the fluttering path of a falling leaf.]
— *An Ethiopian jumping out of a tree.*

What's this? [Hold a fine-tooth comb vertically.]
— *Ethiopian bunk beds.*

What's this? [Hold a fine-tooth comb with the teeth facing up.]
— *Fifty Ethiopians in a canoe.*

What's this? [Pinch your neck on both sides of your Adam's apple and pull out.]
— *An Ethiopian with a grain of rice stuck in his throat.*

What is this? [Make a circle with your forefinger and thumb.]
— *An Ethiopian stranglehold.*

# WIMP

## Reinhold Aman

### I

We do not know the origin of *wimp*, that overabundant insult found everywhere these days. *Webster's Ninth* dates it around 1963, and *Barnhart* has a 1959 citation. But in Eric Partridge's *A Dictionary of Slang and Unconventional English* (7th edition, 1970), we find **wimp** "a (young) woman, a girl: from ca. 1920. Obsolescent. Perhaps ex *whimper*." The supplement adds, "Current among Cambridge undergraduates as early as 1909," as reported by a reader in 1939. If the word has been current as early as 1909, there ought to be printed documentation earlier than *Webster's* 1963 date. The "obsolescent" death-knell was sounded too early: *wimp* is very much alive, but it may soon be killed by overuse.

After a seventy-five-year hibernation period, this relatively mild term of abuse suddenly pops up everywhere in America, especially in 1984 and 1985. It appears in essays, columns, reports, cartoons, articles. Everywhere. Why? My guess is that the popularity of the 1978 movie (and its reruns) *National Lampoon's Animal House* greatly spread its use: two freshmen — main characters in the movie — are referred to as "a wimp and a blimp" (one is a shy, mousy type; the other an obese slob). John Leo's use of *wimp* in his Ralph & Wanda discussion (see *Time*, below) probably also helped its spread among the intelligentsia. It is a good word — short, sounding like the person it describes, and reminiscent of "to whimper." Even though it is not a nasty or nasty-sounding insult, some people are devastated being called a wimp — especially wimps (see letter to Ann Landers, 1985, below). It is used mainly as the noun, **wimp**, but also in the adjectival forms **wimpy** (common) and **wimpish**, the verb phrase **to wimp out**, and in the derivative **wimpification**.

Following below, in chronological order, are all of the uses of *wimp* and its derivatives I have come across.

## II

United Press International presented a short "Glossary of College Jargon" (*MJ*, Green Sheet, 25 Nov. 1980, pp. 1-2), where *wimps* are defined as "persons who are extremely studious."

William Addams Reitwiesner of the Library of Congress informed me that in July 1981 Rep. John LeBoutillier had called Sen. Charles Percy a "wimp" (see *Maledicta* 5:324).

In the same volume, p. 323, we reported that Mike Royko had characterized the Duke of Windsor as

> that weak-faced wimp who gave up the throne of England 'for the woman he loved,' a nasty, thin-lipped woman who led him around by his nose (*WF*, 29 July 1981, p. 6).

From John Leo's essay "Of Real Men and Quiche Eaters" (*Time*, 23 Aug. 1982, p. 57):

> Quiche eaters, on the other hand, *never* see women as sex objects. They adore arugola salads, wear bikini underpants, gold chains and designer clothes, and in general are trendy, warm, sensitive wimps.

In *Benedicta!* 1 (Fall 1982, p. 3), I quoted Scott Beach's letter to me:

> Could you manage to produce a periodic newsletter without over-taxing your wimp of a heart?

to which I replied that "my wimp and I will try, period-ically."

In a *MJ* editorial (20 Oct. 1982, p. 14) entitled "Only a wimp wouldn't object," we read:

> In two major political races (one next door in Illinois) the word "wimp" has become a notorious epithet. Illinois Gov. James Thompson apparently used the word in a context interpreted as applying to his Democratic opponent, former US Sen. Adlai Stevenson. There was no pussyfooting in Maryland, where Republican Larry Hogan, a former US representative, flatly pinned the word on the man he is trying to unseat, Sen. Paul Sarbanes.

The editorial writer continues about the word's origin and wonders whether it is not an acronym with which "a candidate for a village board once lambasted his opponent, say, as a 'weak-kneed, impudent, moronic palooka', — shortening the scathing description later for the convenience of reporters to 'WIMP'." It is this kind of moronic palooka journalist who (introduces and) keeps alive the alleged acronymic origins of *wog, wop, fuck*, etc.

Lambasting some of my meaner readers in *Benedicta!* 3 (Fall 1983, p. 2), I wrote about "the henpecked whimp (whose wifey, Bertha Bullie, would slam him into the ground if he dared to open his mouth) who has no empathy and thinks he can continue using me for a scapegoat."

My favorite Canadian librarian, Bob Buckie, sent a long column by Lew Gloin, the Word Man of the *Toronto Star* (6 Nov. 1983, p. F-8), who wrote two columns about *wimp*, citing its meanings and etymology from three standard slang dictionaries, and presenting Canadian examples:

> That most unfortunate of Conservative leaders, Joe Clark, was tagged early in his career a wimp, a pejorative he didn't deserve. Since his downfall, at least one columnist referred to "the wimpification of Joe Clark" and John Edward Slinger...wrote about the "whiniest little wimp that was ever on TV." (He didn't mean Joe, though.) And Earl McRae in a guest column about singing the

national anthem at sports events said flatly, "Canadians are the most god-awful wimpy people in the world." Earl said that because he doesn't like 'O Canada' and/or the singing of it. Even Northrop Frye...referred to a letter...in which it [the name Northrop] was described as wimpy.

As reported in the *Chicago Tribune* (30 March 1984, p. 2), eight GI's referred to critics of television violence shown on the [U.S.] Armed Forces Network in West Germany as

WIMPS: Whining Idiots, Mama's boys, Pretending to be Soldiers.

*Daily Camera* reported on 1 May 1984 that the 26-year-old Willie Stokes of Chicago, shot to death in an alleged drug deal, was buried in a coffin looking like a Cadillac Seville, with flashing head and tail lights, a steering wheel, a chrome grill, and the license plates **WIMP**.

Dick Polman, Knight-Ridder Newspapers, reported on the National Conference on Men and Masculinity at Washington, D.C. (*WF*, 9 July 1984, p. 6):

How many wimps does it take to screw in a lightbulb? Two. One holds the ladder, the other finds a woman to climb it... [San Rafael] California therapist Jed Diamond...was waxing eloquent on the subject of wimps. He should know; he used to be a self-professed "tiger at work and wimp at home." ... "Scratch a wimp," said Diamond, "and you'll often find a lover of Dirty Harry, because Dirty Harry is decisive, knows what he wants and he takes charge. None of this 'Gee, honey, I don't know, should we do this, or should we do that?'" ... The culture's dominant male images, like the super-soldier, are negative. Hence, the advent of the wimp, known also as the "worm-boy," a passive shell of a man who cannot make a commitment.

From a mother's complaint to Ann Landers, about her henpecked son (*WF*, 28 July 1984, p. 5):

Our daughter-in-law forbids smoking in their home... When our son comes to visit she will not let him bring the baby. He brings pictures and says, "What can I do, I have to keep peace at home." ... I can't believe my son is such a wimp. He just hangs his head and says, "I'm sorry."

As reported in the *WF* (4 Aug. 1984, p. 2), it was speculated that Mick Jagger was to join Michael Jackson at Madison Square Garden, but

> When he heard all the predictions about mobs storming the Olympics, he wimped out and decided to stay home [in London].

The *MJ* (7 Aug. 1984, p. 2) carried the news that

> Russell Foster is a wimp and he's proud of it. Foster, 20, stripped to his underpants...in Sheffield, England, to reveal all his 126 pounds and the 32-inch chest, and that was good enough to earn him the title Mr. Wimp of 1984.

Israeli militant Rabbi Meir Kahane described Walter Mondale as a "gutless wimp" for not denouncing the Rev. Louis Farrakhan, head of the black Nation of Islam, who had made anti-Semitic remarks. (*MJ*, 1 Sept. 1984, p. 2.)

In a six-panel Feiffer cartoon (*Village Voice*, 11 Sept. 1984, p. 35, sent by L. Tanner), two men discuss the qualifications of Reagan and Mondale for the presidency: "Mondale's soft... awkward... uninspiring... wants to talk to the Russians... won't kill us all" and decide to go with Mondale: "Two votes for the wimp."

It's getting so one can't tell a kind, gentle, sensitive human being from a wimp.

In a "Bloom County" cartoon (14 Oct. 1984), featuring a sign **NO WIMPS**, two characters, the chairman of the National Organization of Liberated Men and Ralph, are talking:

"Ralphie...we're all sensitive, caring beings here...let your emotions flow!" — "Well it's my wife...she caught me reading a *Ladies Home Journal* yesterday [...] and then she called me a...a...WIMP!!"

*Chicago Tribune* columnist Mike Royko, advocating frank insults by politicians (*WF*, 18 Oct. 1984, p. 3), suggests:

Then Reagan could come right out and say what he thinks, which is probably that Mondale is a wimpy weakling.

In the *WF* (21 Nov. 1984, p. 7-B), David B. Mellor, a poultry expert at College Station, Texas, discussed the domesticated male farm turkeys that weigh as much as 60 pounds and now have so much meat in their breast, genetically added, that they are unable to form a natural union with the female. Breeders thus must remove the turkeys' sperm and artificially fertilize eggs. Mellor added that "the domesticated turkey is a bloated wimp compared to his wild cousin..."

A reader asked Ann Landers (*WF*, 29 Nov. 1984, p. 4): "What word is there to describe a female wimp?" Suggestions by readers include *wamp, wimpette, simp, mouse, doormat, buckpasser, G.W.'s = Gutless Wonders, long-suffering martyrs, Nebishess, Spineless Suzies, lightweights,* and *weakling* (*WF*, 29 Jan. 1985, p. 7). Landers closed this topic after another reader objected (*WF*, 19 Feb. 1985, p. 7):

Can you stand one more response to the query about a name for a female wimp? Oh, how I detest that word! I've seen so many men humiliated by it, and most of them were nice guys—a little bit shy, quieter than most, lacking in confidence and self-esteem.

Dr. Tim Healey, Barnsley, sent three British newspapers of 14 Feb. 1985, with St. Valentine's greetings. Neither the 3,500-plus greetings in the London *Times* nor the few in the *Daily Telegraph* contained *wimp* as a lover's name, but among the 2,500-odd greetings in the *Guardian* I spotted five (pp. 20-21):

Leaf, Kinkin, Bongo, Imp, Finger, Lion, Doggie and Ball needs and loves Rain, Wimp, Dusty Punk and Yellow Chicken. Kvetch.

Hugs and kisses to the most wonderful wimp at IPCS HQ. The idealist X.

Chomper, I just called to say I love you — and your peanut machine. All my love. — The Wimp.

Born Leader, you are still my sunshine on a cloudy day. Love Wimp. xxxxx

Dear Moldbag. Wally Wimp loves you forever.

As reported by AP's Susana Hayward (*WF*, 19 Feb. 1985, p. 9)

> Joe Bob Briggs [pseudonym of John Bloom, a *Dallas Times Herald* columnist] is the most sexist, most bigoted syndicated drive-in movie critic in America… In a typical blast, these were the tamest words Joe Bob had for Bo Derek in the movie *Bolero*: "We knew it was only a matter of time before the bimbo ripped all her clothes off and ran around acting like a goose that's been wired up for brain research." …If a woman is insulted when he calls her a *bimbo*, a Hispanic offended by the word *Meskin* or a black by the term *Negro*, Joe Bob figures they're just wimps. "There ain't no sensitive subject. Just sensitive people," says Joe Bob…

Soon after, the newspaper cancelled Joe Bob Briggs's column, after he had upset the local black community with his spoof of the song "We Are the World," calling his satire "We Are the Weird." The income from this song was to benefit "minority groups in Africa and the United Negro College Fund in the United States, 'cause I think we should be sending as many Negroes to college as we can, 'specially the stupid Negroes." (*MJ*, 17 April 1985, p. 2). Meanwhile, because of all the controversy, the writer has resigned from the newspaper and now publishes his column in a Dallas "underground" paper.

John Raymond, 53, a San Francisco free-lance writer, sent letters to hundreds of celebrities with unusual names, pretending to be a 9-year-old boy ashamed of his strange name (*MJ*, Green Sheet, 4 March 1985, p. 1). He told them that he hates his name because the kids at school joke about it. Northrop Frye (see above) seems to have been one of the victims of this hoax. Norman Mailer responded to the "boy", writing, "Tell the wise guys who think Norman is a wimpy name that 'Norman Snead was a great quarterback'."

Clifford Irving, perpetrator of the Howard Hughes hoax, ironically also was duped. He wrote to the "youngster": "I don't think Clifford is a wimpy name."

On 4 March 1985, in a speech before a conservative group, Republican Robert Dornan, 51, called "baby-faced" New York Democrat Thomas Downey, 36, "a draft-dodging wimp." For two years, a feud had been brewing between Dornan, a former Air Force jet pilot, and Downey, who received a 1-Y medical draft deferral during the Viet Nam War because of a pierced eardrum. As reported in *Time* (18 March 1985, p. 24),

> Asked to define wimp, Dornan says, "Someone who attacks someone behind his back and doesn't say it to his face." The word was bandied about during the 1984 presidential campaign, when both Walter Mondale and George Bush found themselves in the uncomfortable position of having to show that they were not wimps. ... Downey has demanded an apology. "For what?" Dornan asked a *Washington Post* reporter. "For calling him a wimp? I am willing to concede that perhaps he just walks, talks and acts like a little arrogant wimp. But maybe it's disinformation." In the end, though, Dornan wimped out [about having grabbed Downey's tie]. What was he doing with Tom's collar in his fist? "I was just straightening his tie."

The *Time* reporters Amy Wilentz and Neil MacNeil are a bit confused: only Mondale was called a *wimp*; Bush was called a *preppy*.

In a story about the International Organization of Nerds (*MJ*, Green Sheet, 7 March 1985, pp. 1-2), self-proclaimed Supreme Archnerd B.L. Chapman, Cincinnati, differentiates between a *nerd* and a *wimp*:

I used to think of a nerd as a wimpy type of guy. But then I started watching Jerry Lewis…he's really a nerd. He's a very successful, professional, respected individual. But when he wants to, you know how he dances around and walks and quacks.

Mike Royko, writing in the *WF*, (29 March 1985, p. 5) on the types of programs one sees on Public Television (PBS):

Some skinny, bearded, squeaky-voiced, wimpy guy from Seattle does a cooking show. I have never seen a grown man get so excited about sauteing a Chinese pea pod. He even jiggles the pan so that the pea pod flips in the air. I guess he does that to prove that he's macho.

*New York Times* columnist Sydney Shanberg (30 March 1985, p. 15, Midwest edition) reporting on the lack of humanity by the I.R.S., quotes a couple from Manhasset who had received a computer threat and bill of $2,108:

Being wimps and cowards and elderly, we instinctively paid, and asked for a refund.

A "Bloom County" cartoon, 5 April 1985, shows Opus taking an ad from a Playboy-Bunny-type female who wants a certain male: "Big and dumb?" asks Opus. "Right. No Alan Alda–Donahue wimps."

In Jules Loh's Associated Press story (13-15 March, 1985), on my proposed "National No-Cuss Day," one day a year when we avoid badmouthing everyone and everything, he wondered whether I had turned sissy.

"No, no, not at all,' [Aman] said. "I don't want to turn everyone into mealy-mouthed wimps. But we ought to realize how negative we are, day in, day out. One day of reflection and controlling our mouths wouldn't hurt."

In a "Bloom County" comic strip (1 May 1985), Opus (the penguin) has a date and wants to buy "an odor" at a men's cologne counter:

> I want an odor that sez I can spit tobacco juice into Walter 'Wimp' Mondale's breast pocket from fifty feet while cursing the Sandinistas and manhandling 'Madonna' *all at the same time!!*

From the Associated Press report "Wimpy Dogs Need Not Apply" (*WF*, 2 May 1985, p. 11) on German shepherd dogs that turn out to be unqualified at the Air Force Dog Training Center at Lackland Air Force Base and then are sold for $5.00, quoting spokeswoman Hildegarde Brown:

> Each canine training class starts with 400 recruits and the real wimps are weeded out early. "First, we fire a round of 35-millimeter over its head, and if the dog doesn't run away or wet itself it's OK," Brown said.

(I'd like to fire a round of 35-millimeter over *her* head — and watch her piss all the way to El Paso!)

A *Wizard of Id* comic strip shows the wizard experimenting with a non-alcoholic whiskey, which he calls *whimpskey*. (*MJ*, 7 May 1985, Green Sheet, p. 4)

As reported by Robert Reno in the *MJ* (8 May 1985, p. 15), during Reagan's European Summit Conference in Bonn,

> French President François Mitterand either shot himself in the foot by vetoing Reagan's trade talks and isolating France's position, or, as his admirers suggest, he stood alone among his wimpish colleagues to prevent a Reagan putsch at the summit.

According to Frank Aukofer, *MJ* Washington Bureau reporter (16 June 1985, "Life/Style," p. 5), you can be dour, obnoxious, brash, tyrannical, imperious or opportunistic, but wimps need not apply at the United States Naval Academy:

> "Introverted, shy, retiring people won't do," says Capt. J.W. Flight. "This is an aggressive, competitive environment. We don't want any wimps here."

Barbara Germiat of Appleton, Wis., was offended by Capt. Flight, writing to the *MJ* (1 July 1985, p. 12):

Calling introverted, shy, retiring people "wimps"…is an insult to introverts. I doubt that introverts are, by definition, incapable of being aggressive and competitive. The Navy, and US military in general, would probably be better off with some bookish, introverted people among its leaders. These are people who will think first…before shooting off their mouths or their weapons…

*Chicago Tribune* columnist Mike Royko has written four columns on *war wimp*, a phrase coined by U.S.. Rep. Andrew Jacobs of Indiana, a combat Marine veteran in Korea, who defines it as follows: "One who is all too willing to send others to war, but who never gets around to going to war himself." (*WF,* 11 July 1985, p. 3). Royko mentions *Village Voice* writer Jack Newfield, who has compiled a list of war wimps, those tough-talking conservative hawks who are in favor of big military buildups but who — when a war was actually being fought while he was a young man — found it convenient to be someplace safe, thanks to college deferments or minor ailments (*WF*, 18 June 1985, p. 3).

Among the war wimps singled out by Royko are Sylvester Stallone, the fearsome movie Vietnam vet "Rambo," who during the war taught physical education to wealthy American girls at the American College in Switzerland, then switched to the University of Miami as a drama major (*WF*, 6 July 1985, p. 3).

Ronald Reagan is a war wimp, too, who during World War II made training and propaganda films in Hollywood. Fellow Republican Robert Dornan, "a former right-wing talk show host" and "one of the most tough-talking, chest-thumping, liberal-baiting congressmen in all the land," who referred to some colleagues as "jelly-kneed, draft-dodging wimps," did not appreciate Royko's disclosure of the inaccuracies in Dornan's official biographies and "war wimp" label. Dornan claims that he was an Air Force pilot during the Korean War and that he flew combat missions in Southeast Asia (*WF*, 29 June 1985, p. 3). Royko discovered that "ace war wimp" Dornan didn't join the Air Force until a few months before the Korean War ended, and that he did fly combat missions in Vietnam...but as a TV journalist. Royko recanted his "war wimp" label because Dornan did not have a college deferment, but now calls him a "tosser of the old bull, braggart and blowhard" for inflating his military accomplishments (*WF,* 11 July 1985, p. 3).

Movie producer Steven Spielberg, recalling his youth (*Time*, 15 July 1985, p. 63):

> At school I felt like a real nerd, the skinny, acne-faced wimp who gets picked on by big football jocks all the way home from school.

In a "Bloom County" comic strip (16 July 1985), a sign in front of a house says:

THE BLOOM BOARDING HOUSE

NO WINOS, NO WIMPS, NO WALRUSES

In a television commercial for Kellogg's *Fruitful Bran* (NBC, 17 July 1985), a woman exclaims, "I don't want any wimpy-tasting cereal!"

Michael Kilian, *Chicago Tribune* (*WF*, 25 July 1985, p. 6), reflecting on various television commercials:

> Let's bring back the Marlboro men [cigarets] and get rid of all these wimps selling men's cologne who have taken over the airwaves...

From the article "How to Gossip Like a Man" (*Playboy*, Sept. 1985, p. 23):

> Don't apologize [for gossiping]. Only a wimp prefaces a remark with "I really shouldn't say this" or "It's probably not my place to ask."

The final citation for this documentation on *wimp* comes from another "Bloom County" comic strip (*MJ*, 15 Aug. 1985). Opus, suffering from amnesia, thinks he's human. A youngster tries to explain to him that he is a penguin: "Listen...we need to talk. You're simply not...a man." Opus replies, "Are you calling me a wimp?"

### III

But what is the origin of *wimp*? Fred Chambers submitted these thoughts:

> If the word comes from J. Wellington Wimpy, a character in Elzie Segar's cartoon serial "Thimble Theater" starring Popeye, the spelling would be without an *h*. Another popular character, Wallace Wimple of the "Fibber Magee and Molly" radio program, was a comical, laugh-at-himself type henpecked husband, also a possible source for *wimp*.

Both suggested sources are too old to have caused the present wimp-explosion, but they may have helped its current popularity among broad segments of society who remember these characters. The suggested source, Wimpy, the Popeye sidekick, bothers me for two reasons: time and semantics. If it were from this old character (1929 + ), why would it take until the mid-1960s to be used often enough by teenagers and students to be recorded in Flexner's *Supplement* in the *Dictionary of American Slang*? And why did it then take until the early 1980s to be used widely by all age groups? The shift of semantic fields, if from Wimpy, also is not explained. The original meaning, a gluttonous fatso, "a fat character forever eating" (**Barnhart**), is totally different from today's semantic field: "an ineffectual, insipid, weak, spineless, whimpering, passive, introverted, boring person," most often applied to males. (The British trademark Wimpy for a fried hamburger may well be from the forever-eating cartoon character.)

Until convinced by a better explanation, I'll stick to my theory that *wimp* is derived from *to whimper*, similar to *wimp* in spelling/sound and especially in meaning. Theoretically—if derived from this verb—the word should have become *whimperer*, by adding the *nomen agentis* suffix *-er* to the verb; yet the trend towards short words is common, and we got *whimp* instead. The *wimp* versus *whimp* spelling does not bother me. Many people pronounce *what, when,* *why, whimper* not /hwat/, /hwen/, /hwy/, /hwimper/ but /wat/, /wen/, /wy/, /wimper/. As it used to be a word not seen in print but only heard, e.g., /wat a wimp!/, the *h*-less spelling became common.

Popular word guru William Safire, in his "On Language" column in *The New York Times Magazine* (28 July 1985, sect. 6, p. 12) also mentions this word:

> All the sting has gone out of *wimp* (derived from *whimper*, influenced by the cartoon character Wimpy)...

The sting is still there (see above citations), and Safire offers no explanations for his assumption that Wimpy influenced the meaning or the present popularity of *wimp*.

For more information on this word, see my "Offensive Words in Dictionaries" in this volume.

As a psychiatrist, I can tell you that Mr. Hinckley's problems stem from an abnormally small brain.

# THE WHITE HOUSE
## WASHINGTON

### June 17, 1984

Mr. John Hinckley
St. Elizabeth's Hospital
Washington, D.C. 20069

Dear John:

Nancy and I hope you are making good progress in your recovery from the mental problems that made you try to assassinate me. The staff of St. Elizabeth's tell me you are doing just fine and will be released soon.

I have decided to seek a second term in office and I hope I can count on your support and the support of your fine parents in my re-election campaign.

I hold no grudge against you, John, and I do hope that if there is anything you need there at the hospital, you will let Nancy and me know.

By the way, did you know that Walter Mondale, Gary Hart and Jesse Jackson have been fucking Jodie Foster?

Sincerely,

*Ronald Reagan*

Ronald Reagan

RR/sdj

We have received five variants of this letter between July and November, 1984, from California, Illinois, Kentucky, Nevada, and Ohio.

The creator of the above work of art, here reduced, is Michele Trudu, a 30-year-old Sardinian now living in San Francisco. We printed 150 copies, on 80-pound ivory Bristol stock. Ready for framing, 11 by 14 inches. Each of the 150 copies is numbered and signed by Mr. Trudu. Price is $10 plus $2.50 for first-class postage.

We have also 80 numbered and signed copies of the Uncle Mal caricature (see MAL 5, p. 123) on 8½ by 11 stock: $5.00, including postage.

# DIALECTICS OF BRAZILIAN NEGRO PROVERBS

## Hannes Stubbe

In Brazil, the following myth is told about the origin of the different races:

> After God had created the world, He was completely exhausted but also very pleased. The birds, the flowers, the trees, the seas, the butterflies, the breeze, the sunset, all these things had turned out very well indeed. But who would be able to admire all these beauties of the earth? Someone was needed to listen to the songs of the birds, to smell the scent of the flowers, to admire the colorful flight of the butterflies, to feel the breath of the wind and to witness the sunset. God thought and thought — and then He made a man out of loam. And when He realized that the man was all alone, He also created a woman, which led to the earth becoming populated. Only there was something peculiar — all men and women were black, like the loam from which they had been made. And because they did not like being black, they all went to God and asked for help. God listened to the complaints and told them to wash themselves in a well. Those who found clean water washed themselves and became white. Those who followed washed themselves in already murky water and became mulattos. When the last of them arrived, they found hardly any water left — and it had now turned completely black. There was just enough to wash the palms of their hands and the soles of their feet, the only parts which became almost completely white. This way, the whites, mulattos and Negroes came into being since the creation of the earth. (Quoted from Souto Maior, n.d.).

The Brazilian Negro, who has replaced the Indian as work-slave in the sugar plantations and the mines since the last third of the 16th century, has played not only an important role (one should remember Portinari's famous painting "O Café") in all cycles of the Brazilian economic history (sugar, coffee, cocoa, gold, rubber), but his cultural inheritance has also left a significant mark upon Brazil. In

the gentleness of the facial expressions and gestures, which
to us appear somewhat exaggerated (see Cascudo, 1976),
in Catholicism, in which our senses take a great delight,
in the Afro-Brazilian syncretism (Bastide, 1961; Cacciatore,
1977; Elbein dos Santos, 1976; Carneiro, 1978), which
fascinates any demythologized European, in the hot and
passionate music, the samba (Carneiro, 1961), in the
*capoeira*, the African fighting sport (Caribé, 1955; Carneiro,
1968), in the swaying way of walking, in the voice, in the
lullaby — in all that which represents an unaffected expression of life, Freyre (1969) discovers almost all the signs of
the Negro's influence. In the course of the "triangular
trading" between Europe, Africa and America, the Negroes
came mainly from the Bantu area but also from Dahomey,
Angola, Mozambique and the Sudan (see Ramos, 1979).
They not only brought with them their religions, their cooking, art and smelting techniques but also enriched the
Brazilian-Portuguese language with many foreign words.
Renato Mendonça alone collected over 400. Here are just
a few examples: *acarajé, batuque, cachaça, cafuné, Exu, inhame,
jiló, maracatu, Oxum, Orixá, papagaio, quiabo, samba, senzala,
tanga, vatapá, Xangô, zebra*. Today, Brazil represents a classic
example of a cultural combination (Bitterli, 1974), i.e., a
successful acculturation development. Within the American
continent, Brazilian society — from the very beginning inclined towards interbreeding — is the one that has developed
the most harmonious attitude towards the races; according
to official statistical figures, approximately 65 mio. whites,
45 mio. mulattos (*pardos*), 7 mio. Negroes and 800,000
Asians lived in Brazil in 1980 (IBGE, 1981). Nash (1963)
once described this attitude of mind in a beautiful formula
by saying that the Brazilians were the most color-blind of
all people. They were so blind that they could look a Negro
in the face and only see the human being in him. Stefan
Zweig, a personal victim of racial hatred, once admiringly
called Brazil "a land of the future" (1981).

The racial problem in Brazil, as far as it is at all noticeable, is a social problem. Since the Negro slaves were freed from slavery by the imperial decree of Princess Dona Isabel on 13 May 1888, their belated social start in Brazilian society was mainly noted by their marginality.

Social tensions between whites and Negroes can clearly be seen in the dialectics of the "Negro proverbs," i.e., the proverbs of whites about the Negroes, and vice versa. As to the content, the proverbs of whites especially follow the general rules of prejudice and minority psychology: ingroup/outgroup thinking, belittling characterization mainly relating to looks, color of the skin (black = evil, bad), smell, cleanliness, mental capabilities, thirst for action, as well as sexual rivalry between white and black women (especially mulattos).

The following comparison of Negro proverbs, taken from Souto Maior (n.d.), Magalhães Júnior (1974), Mota (1978) and my own collection (especially from Bahia), shows how the Brazilian Negroes defend themselves against this white proverbial aggression and also at the level at which this takes place. The "white" proverb is followed by a "black" proverb, if an appropriate one exists, indicated by *N:*

**Branca para casar, preta para trabalhar, mulatta para amar.** "The white woman for marriage, the black woman for work, the mulatto woman for love."
*N:* **Negra é a pimenta e todos comem dela.** "The Negress is pepper and all eat from her."

**Do branco o salão, do negro o fogão.** "The drawing-room is for the white man, the kitchen for the Negro."
*N:* **Negro no salão; no bolso patacão.** "Negro in a drawing-room; many silver coins in his pocket."

**Onde falta branco sobra negro.** "The Negro remains where the white man is missing."

**Filho de branco é menino; filho de negro é moleque.**
"A white man's son is a boy; a Negro's son is a street urchin."

**Negro só tem de branco os dentes.** "The Negro has only the teeth of the white man."

*N:* **Sangue de negro é vermelho como o de branco.** "The Negro's blood is just as red as that of the white man."

**Negro só tem de gente os olhos.** "The Negro has only the eyes of human beings."

*N:* **Branco vem de Adão e o negro não?** "The white man comes from Adam but not the Negro?"

**Se negro fosse coisa de se gostar, todo mundo andava com um urubu debaixo do braço.** "If the Negro were something one could love, the whole world would walk around with an Urubu vulture under its arm." [The *urubu* is said to bring bad luck.]

*N:* **Café é preto e todo mundo gosta.** "Coffee is black and the whole world loves it."

*N:* **Roupa preta é roupa de gala.** "Black clothing is formal clothing."

**Abelha preta é arapuá; tempero de negro é manguá.** "The black bee is the Arapuá; the tranquilizer for the Negro is the flail." [The sting of this bee is very painful.]

*N:* **Urubu novo também é branco.** "A young Urubu is white, too."

*N:* **É branco o jasmin de cachorro.** "The dog-jasmine is white."

**Negro que não conhece seu lugar acaba no pau.** "The Negro who does not know his place ends up in the wooden yoke."

*N:* **No escuro, tanto vale a rainha como a negra na cozinha.** "In the dark, the queen is worth as much as the Negress from the kitchen."

**Em negocio de branco negro não se mete.** "The Negro should not interfere with the white man's business."

*N:* **Trabalha o negro para o branco comedor.** "The Negro works so that the white man can lead a glutton's (parasite's) life."

*N:* **Sou negro mas não sou seu escravo.** "I am a Negro but not your slave."

*N:* **Branco dançando, negro suando.** "The white man dances while the Negro sweats at work."

*N:* **Negro só trabalha para o branco carregar.** "The Negro works only to burden the white man."

*N:* **O trabalho é do negro e a fama é do branco.** "The Negro does the work and the white man gets the glory."

*N:* **Negro é o carvoeiro e branco o seu dinheiro.** "The Negro is a coal dealer and his money is white."

*N:* **Preto na cor e branco nas ações.** "Black of skin and white in deeds."

*N:* **Papel é branco mas aceita tudo que se escreve nele.** "Paper is white but it accepts everything one writes on it."

*N:* **Galinha preta só bota ovo branco.** "Even a black hen lays only white eggs."

*N:* **Branco se enterra em caixão todo preto.** "The white man is buried in a completely black coffin."

*N:* **Falta de educação no branco é nervoso.** "If the white man lacks education, he is nervous."

**Negro não come; engole.** "The Negro does not eat; he devours."

*N:* **Negro que come com o branco, o branco come e o negro paga.** "If the Negro dines with the white man, the white man eats and the Negro pays."

**Prato de negro é gamela.** "The Negro's plate is the wooden bowl."

**Bacalhau é comer de negro e negro é comer de onça.** "The cod is the Negro's food, and the Negro is the food of the jaguar."

**Negro em festa de branco é o primeiro que apanha e o último que come.** "At a white man's party, the Negro is the first to help himself to food and the last to stop eating."
*N:* **Branco não faz festa sem negro.** "The white man never has a party without Negroes."

**Bebida de negro é cachaça.** "The Negro's drink is rum."

**Negro não sorri; mostra dentes.** "The Negro does not smile; he just shows his teeth."

**Negro não se penteia; alisa o pixaim.** "The Negro does not comb his hair; he just smoothes his frizzy (kinky) hair."
*N:* **Quando o cabelo do branco fica branco pela idade, ele tinge de preto.** "When a white man's hair turns white with age, it turns color just as the black's."

**Negro não nasce; aparece.** "The Negro is not born; he just appears."

**Negro não tem cabeça; tem é quengo.** "The Negro does not have a head; he has a hollow container."

**Negro não tem nariz; tem focinho.** "The Negro does not have a nose; he has a snout."
*N:* **Branco rico nunca é feio.** "A rich white man is never ugly."

**Negro não tem estômago; tem é bucho.** "The Negro does not have a stomach; he has a belly."

**Negro não mastiga; remoi.** "The Negro does not chew; he ruminates."

**Quando se dá o pé negro quer a mão.** "If you give a Negro the foot, he wants the hand."

**Negro só dá o que tem.** "The Negro only gives what he has."

**Negro não fuma; pita.** "The Negro does not smoke; he puffs."

**Negro em pé é um toco; deitado é um porco.** "Standing upright, the Negro is a stump; lying down, he is a pig."

**Negro não dorme; se deita.** "The Negro does not sleep; he stretches out."

**Negro não aniversaria; inteira tempo.** "The Negro does not celebrate his birthday; he completes the lifetime."

**Negro não namora; embirra.** "The Negro does not love; he forces himself upon someone."

**Negro não casa; se junta.** "The Negro does not marry; he mates."

**Branca que casa com negro é preto por dentro.** "The white woman who marries a Negro is black inside."

**Negro de luva é sinal de chuva.** "A Negro with gloves is a sign of rain."

**Negro chorando, negro mangando.** "The Negro cries, the Negro jokes."

**Negro inteligente nasce morto.** "An intelligent Negro is a stillbirth."

**Negro quando anda na linha o trem atropela.** "If the Negro walks on the railroad tracks, he will be hit by a train."

**Negro quando não é rico é diodo.** "If the Negro is not rich, he is crazy."

**Juízo de negro é na sola dos pés.** "The Negro's mind is on the soles of his feet."

**Negro não é inteligente: é espevitado.** "The Negro is not intelligent: he is impertinent."

**Negro quando não suja, tisna.** "If a Negro does not make you dirty, he blackens (stains) you."
*N:* **Na seda branca é que a mancha pega.** "The stain remains particularly on white silk."

**Negro quando não caga na entrada, caga na saida.** "If a Negro does not shit at the entrance, he shits at the exit."
*N:* **Carne de branco também fede.** "The white man's flesh stinks, too."
*N:* **Carne de negro sustenta a fazenda.** "The Negro's flesh maintains the plantation (country estate)."

**Negro ensaboado, tempo perdido, sabão esperdiçado.** "Lathering (soaping) a Negro is a waste of time and a waste of soap."
*N:* **Suor de negro dá dinheiro.** "The Negro's sweat provides money."
*N:* **Suor de branco também fede.** "The white man's sweat stinks, too."

**Negro não defeca; dá de corpo.** "The Negro has no bowel movement; he gives of his body."

*N:* **A sujeira do branco sai no dinheiro.** "The white man's dirt turns into money."

*N:* **Sovaco de branco também catinga.** "The white man's armpit stinks, too."

**Negro só é gente quando está no banheiro. Quando batem na porta, ele diz: 'Tem gente.'** "The Negro is only a person (human being) when he is in the toilet. When someone knocks at the door, he says, 'There is a person inside.'

*N:* **Papel higiênico também é branco.** "Toilet paper is also white."

*N:* **Papel é branco e limpa-se tudo com ele.** "Paper is white and one cleans everything with it."

*N:* **Penico também é branco.** "The chamber pot is also white."

**Negro quando não gosta de mel é ladrão de cortiço.** "If the Negro does not like honey, he steals the beehive."

*N:* **Negro furtou é ladrão; branco furtou é barão.** "A Negro who steals is a thief; a white man who steals is a baron."

**Negro só acha o que ninguém perdeu.** "The Negro finds only what nobody has lost."

*N:* **Negro furta e branco acha.** "The Negro steals and the white man finds."

**Nem branco mente; nem negro sustenta o que diz.** "The white man does not lie; the Negro does not keep what he promises."

*N:* **A má ação do branco também pesa.** "The bad deed of the white man also counts."

*N:* **Judas era branco e vendeu a Cristo.** "Judas was white and he sold Christ."

*N:* **Preguiça não faz casa de sobrado.** "Laziness does not build a mansion."

*N:* **Branco é quem bem procede.** "White is he who acts well."

**Negro não entra na igreja: espia do patamar.** "The Negro does not enter the Church: he watches from the forecourt."

**Negro só entra no ceu por descuido do São Pedro.** "The Negro enters heaven only through St. Peter's negligence."

## BIBLIOGRAPHY

Bastide, Roger. *O candomblé da Bahia (rito nágô).* São Paulo, 1961.

Bitterli, Urs. "Berührung, Durchdringung und Vermischung von Kulturen," *Zeitschrift für Kulturaustausch* 24 (1974), 113-17.

Cacciatore, Gudolle. *Dicionário de cultos afro-brasileiros.* Rio de Janeiro, 1977.

Câmara Cascudo, Luis da. *Historia dos nossos gestos.* São Paulo, 1976.

Carybé. *O jogo da capoeira.* Salvador, 1955.

Carneiro, Edison. *Samba de Umbigada.* Rio de Janeiro, 1961.

——.*A sabedoria popular do Brasil.* Rio de Janeiro, 1968.

——.*Candomblés da Bahia.* Rio de Janeiro, 1978.

Elbein dos Santos, Juana. *Os nágô e a morte.* Petropolis, 1976.

Freyre, Gilberto. *Casa grande e senzala.* Rio de Janeiro, 1969.

IBGE. *Tabulações avançadas do censo demográfico. IX. Recensamento geral do Brasil* – 1980. Instituto Brasileiro de Geografia e Estatistica. Rio de Janeiro, 1981.

Magalhães Júnior, Roberto. *Dicionário brasileiro de provérbios, locuções e ditos curiosos.* Rio de Janeiro, 1974.

Mota, Mario. *Os bichos na fala da gente.* Brasilia, 1978.

Nash, Roy. Quoted in M. Niedergang: *Brasilien.* Lausanne, 1963.

Ramos, Artur. *As culturas negras no Novo Mundo.* São Paulo, 1979.

Souto Maior, Mário. "O folclore do negro," *Folclore* 5, 2nd ed., Recife. n.d.

Zweig, Stefan. *Brasilien, ein Land der Zukunft.* Frankfurt, 1981.

# AIDS JOKES

## OR, *SCHADENFREUDE* AROUND AN EPIDEMIC

## Casper G. Schmidt

While collecting material on the Acquired Immune Deficiency Syndrome (AIDS), I came across several jokes and near-jokes. As with all humor, the purpose of these jokes is "to absorb and control, even slough off, by means of jocular presentation and laughter, the great anxiety that both teller and listener feel in conection with certain culturally determined themes."[1]

These jokes revealed, with amazing lucidness, the underlying group dynamics of this epidemic. My hypothesis is that AIDS is an epidemic of depression, brought about by a conservative swing in American group-fantasy since the middle-Seventies. The core sign of AIDS — the reduced competence of the cell-mediated immunity — is one facet of that depression. The full exposition is published elsewhere,[2] and in this brief note I would like to report the jokes and give a brief interpretation of each within the context of this epidemic.

The first joke was told to me by a patient whose boyfriend was at that time dying from AIDS (June 2, 1983):

**How does Anita Bryant spell "relief"?**
**— A-I-D-S.** (pun on a TV commercial for Rolaids)

In one fell swoop this goes straight to the heart of the matter. It accurately highlights the dynamics of the epidemic: a scapegoating ritual in which the Moral Majority and other conservative groups were delegated the task of "declaring war"[3] on symbolic representatives of our search for pleasure during the 60s and 70s, and specifically homosexuals (with their legendary promiscuity) and drug addicts. This joke was followed over a period of two weeks by a spate of riddles and puns, all built on the same principle, and told to me by the same patient (June, 1983):

> **What do you call homosexuals camping out at the North Pole?**
> — **Koolaids.**
>
> **What do you call homosexuals on roller skates?**
> — **Rolaids.**

Legman, in his monumental tome on the dirty joke, correctly observes that puns and riddles are the simplest forms of joke. It is understandable that in a series of jokes precipitated by a particular—and recent—event such as AIDS, this should be the first and most frequent type of joke to be encountered (as attested to by the collections published previously in *Maledicta*[4] and elsewhere.[5] See also the newest riddles in "Kakologia" in this volume).

In both England and America the AIDS hysteria had hit the presses by early 1983. I found three cartoons dealing with AIDS, two in England in May and one in the U.S. in June. The first British cartoon was another pun showing a men's toilet with a "First AIDS" box, in the satirical magazine *Private Eye*.[6] Another was published in the *Daily Mail*, turning on the "blood issue," with the punchline, "Now remember, only accept blood from those who make a pass at you!"[7] In June, the *Washington Times* placed an editorial cartoon[8] depicting

> [A] member of Democratic presidential candidate Walter Mondale's campaign staff telling another, "With the AIDS scare, we'll have to treat the Gay issue with kid gloves." Responded the other worker, "Rubber gloves would be more like it, sir."

This introduces the fantasy of pestilential contagion—of

poison contained in the homosexuals, which can be spread by the touch. This found widespread resonance at that time, with dentists refusing to treat AIDS patients, morticians refusing to touch their corpses, prison inmates refusing to eat food prepared by homosexual inmates, etc. The culmination of this fantasy was to be found in the handing out of thousands of anti-AIDS kits to the followers of the Swami Bhagwan Shree Rajneesh, each kit containing a washcloth, instructions on safe sex, condoms and surgical-quality gloves (the latter to be used during foreplay).[9]

A little earlier in 1983 two near-jokes had been floated. I call them that since they lack the secondary elaboration (or defensive rationalization) which is usually interposed between the unconscious fantasy-wish and the listener. In Patrick Buchanan's syndicated column in the *New York Post* he said, apropos the AIDS epidemic,[10] that

> they [the poor homosexuals] have declared war on nature, and now nature is exacting an awful retribution.

This shows an identification with the sadistic superego, and says, in unconscious syntax: "We are exacting a retribution" (projection of sadism into nature). In a similar vein, Dr. Epstein (co-discoverer of the Epstein-Barr virus) said at a press conference in New York City: "Perhaps AIDS is Africa taking revenge for the slave trade."[11]

This is an identification with the oppressed (blacks as traditional poison containers), into whom revenge fantasies have been projected. In both of these there was an element of gloating, as was also found in

**What does GAY stand for?**
**— Got AIDS Yet?**

In the soft-porn magazine *Oui*, apart from sensationalist projections of how AIDS "slow motion death" will be killing 262,144,000 people by the winter of 1987, another joke came to light:[12]

[A] note sent to the White House informing the president that there was a plague killing off homosexuals, junkies, Haitians and criminals, came back with the handwritten notation: "Fine, but will it kill Communists?"

This joke, however grim, is one of great psychohistorical significance. Groups attempt to deal with unresolved tensions first by sacrifice of group members (internal sacrifice), and when this is not enough, they turn their hatred outwards, to kill the enemy into whom they have projected disavowed parts of themselves (external sacrifice). This joke shows how these two positions are equivalent and interchangeable.[13] For example, after the invasion of Grenada (external sacrifice) there was the general, though faulty, perception that the AIDS epidemic was "over," and it disappeared from the media. Note also the (faulty) insertion of criminals as an at-risk group.[14]

The next joke was told to me by an employee at the Metropolitan Museum of Art, New York City (March 30, 1984):

**What does AIDS stand for?**
**— Anally Inserted Death Sentence.**

This is related to the pun defining AIDS a "Toxic Cock Syndrome," and has two psychological roots: (a) the extreme *fear of passive sodomy* in the normal male (based on fears of being turned into a woman and thus homosexual submission to the father — see the fearful jokes in Legman's section on pedicatory rape and its inverse, the Ganymede revenge[15]) and (b) the *fantasy of poison sperm* which is one of the three main delusions shared by everyone concerning AIDS (and for which, in Legman's series, the prototype is the joke about poison enemas[16]).

Another AIDS joke was brought to my attention by a medical student in the Bronx (April 14, 1984):

**What's the most difficult thing about getting AIDS?**
**— Convincing your mother that you're Haitian.**

This contains two ethnophaulisms (by implication) plus an ironic twist — a flight into the lesser of two evils (i.e., that it is less shameful to be black than homosexual). All of which is made twice tragic by the fact that both groups are actually dying out there from real prejudice and scapegoating.

The final AIDS joke I collected is so subtle that, unless one unravels several symbolic transformations and all the allusions, it does not seem to be one at all. On the "Tonight Show" of August 21, 1984, Johnny Carson responded to the "mistake" of Reagan one week earlier. Reagan, while testing his microphone, had said that he had passed legislation which outlawed the Russians, and that "the bombing starts in five minutes." Carson told of a sex researcher who had strapped a tiny microphone onto a grasshopper while studying its sex habits, when

> suddenly a little voice came over the microphone and said, "I have just outlawed all fruit flies. The spraying starts in five minutes."

The audience laughed at two points: once after the phrase "he tested the microphone" (said about Reagan), and again after the punchline. There are two possible roots for the laughter after "he tested the microphone": the more realistic one refers to the Reagan incident itself, and the considerable anxiety which it had stirred up in the people (apart from the obvious relish in Reagan's warlike attitude), while the deeper one refers to a complex around the equation: voice = phallus. (See Legman's section on "The Voice as Phallus."[17]) "Testing his microphone" thus becomes the equivalent of "testing the potency of his non-erect ("micro"-) phallus." But the brunt of the joke lies elsewhere. The key is "fruit fly," which is generally-understood slang for homosexual, *fruit*, placed within the context of the 1981 infestation of Mediterranean fruit flies in California. (In unconscious fantasy, insects often represent sperm, as in

Renaissance paintings where one finds bees crawling up the legs of madonnas.) In this case there is the fantasy of wiping out all fruit flies (read: homosexuals), which is the closest to consciousness that the whole scapegoating ritual of AIDS has yet come: an image of mass extermination of a sub-human species.

## REFERENCES

1. Gershon Legman (1968), *Rationale of the Dirty Joke: An Analysis of Sexual Humor.* Castle Books, pp. 13-14.

2. Casper G. Schmidt, "The Group-Fantasy Origins of AIDS." *Journal of Psychohistory* 12 (1) (Summer 1984), 37-78.

3. This declaration of war was issued as an actual certificate and is reprinted in: Perry Deane Young (1982), *God's Bullies: Power Politics and Religious Tyranny.* (New York: Holt, Rinehart & Winston), p. 308.

4. See comments on AIDS riddles (p. 280) and 18 examples (pp. 290-291, 293) in *Maledicta* 7 (1983).

5. See Maude Thickett (1984), *Outrageously Offensive Jokes II*, New York: Pocket Books, p. 116. Julius Alvin (1984), *Utterly Gross Jokes Volume III*, New York: Zebra Books/Kensington Publishing, pp. 72-74. Blanch Knott (1983), *Truly Tasteless Jokes III*, New York: Ballantine, pp. 81, 85.

6. *Private Eye*, May 20, 1983.

7. *Daily Mail*, May 2, 1983.

8. Quoted in *Bay Area Reporter* (San Francisco), May 10, 1984, p. 5.

9. *Bhagwan*, May 1984 (Number 5), p. 15.

10. *New York Post*, May 24, 1983, p. 31.

11. Ann Guidici Fettner and William A. Check (1984), *The Truth About AIDS: Evolution of an Epidemic*, New York: Holt, Rinehart & Winston, p. 244. This was also quoted, in slightly different form, in *New York Native*, December 5-18, 1983, p. 21.

12. *Oui*, October 1983, p. 84.

13. See Lloyd deMause (1984), *Reagan's America*, New York: Creative Roots, pp. 51-67, 104-105.

14. Property-related offense (robbery, burglary, larceny over $50.00) follow the same curve as that of heroin addiction and may be an indirect association: Mark H. Greene, "The Dynamics of a Heroin Addiction Epidemic," *Science* 181 (1973), p. 716-22.

15. Gershon Legman (1975), *No Laughing Matter: Rationale of the Dirty Joke*, Second Series, New York: Dell, pp. 153-64, and 174-83.

16. Ibid., p. 157.

17. Gershon Legman (1968), ibid., pp. 336-40.

## NOTE

I would also be most interested in receiving any other jokes on AIDS from readers, which they should please send to me at: P.O. Box 314, New York, NY 10024.

"We thank Thee for the gifts of Thy bountiful herpes
and Thine blessed AIDS, O Lord...
Now send us something for all the other weirdos."

### *THE REALIST* LIVES!

Paul Krassner, who published *The Realist* from 1958 to 1974 (98 numbers), decided to reincarnate his irreverent magazine. The premier issue is No. 99, Sept./Oct. 1985, 8 pages, with the usual hardhitting stuff. It's starting out as a bi-monthly and will later change to a monthly. $23 will get you 12 issues, sent by First-Class mail. Sample copy: $2.00. Write to *The Realist*, Box 14757, San Francisco, CA 94114.

# CATULLUS *XVI*

### Joseph Salemi
(Translation and Notes)

Pedicabo ego uos et irrumabo,
Aureli pathice et cinaede Furi,
Qui me ex uersiculis meis putastis,
Quod sunt molliculi, parum pudicum.
Nam castum esse decet pium poetam
Ipsum, uersiculos nihil necesse est,
Qui tum denique habent salem ac leporem,
Si sunt molliculi ac parum pudici
Et quod pruriat incitare possunt,
Non dico pueris, sed his pilosis,
Qui duros nequeunt mouere lumbos.
Vos quod milia multa basiorum
Legistis, male me marem putatis?
Pedicabo ego uos et irrumabo.

*How would you like a double shafting,*
*First in the ass, and then the mouth?*
*Furius and Aurelius, pansies,*
*I'll ream it to you north and south!*
*You think the writer of my verses*
*Must be wanton, vicious, lewd:*
*It's not so — an upright poet*
*Often calculates his "crude."*
*Verses should be hot and salty*
*Breaking all the censor's rules:*
*Hairy relicts need such tonic*
*To resurrect their sluggish tools.*
*Just because you read of kisses*
*By the thousand, you have laughed:*
*Think that I'm a crypto-faggot?*
*How'd you like a double shaft?*

# NOTES

**Pedicabo...irrumabo**: "I'll fuck you up your ass and down your throat." *Pedicare* means "to bugger"; *irrumare* means "to penetrate orally from a superior position." Both are the acts of a dominant and aggressive sexual agent upon a more passive partner. The two words therefore carry connotations of both threat and degradation.

**pathice**: vocative form of *pathicus*, a sexually passive person who would submit to the acts mentioned above. The Romans, who did not share our romantic notions of equality and mutual respect between lovers, preferred the giving to the receiving end of sex.

**cinaede**: vocative form of *cinaedus*, a sodomite. Originally a Greek term (κίναιδος), the word was very common in Roman malediction, and is a favorite Catullan insult (see poems XXV, XXXIII, and LVII).

**quod pruriat...possunt**: "they can stir up an itch." As far as I know, Catullus is the only Latin poet who freely admits that some of his poetry is *prurient* in the strict sense; that it aims at the sexual arousal of readers.

**his pilosis**: "these hairy ones" (i.e., shaggy with age).

**duros...lumbos**: "their hard (i.e., sclerotic) loins."

**male...putatis?**: "Do you think me less than a male?" (i.e., Do you imagine that I am submissive like you?) Catullus follows up this rhetorical question by once again threatening those quintessentially masculine sexual acts which will prove both his dominance over and superiority to Furius and Aurelius.

---

## GAY FOOTBALL

A Dallas Cowboy, trying to drown his defeat by the "49ers," walked into a bar in San Francisco, not realizing that it was a full-blown gay Castro area bar. He went in as a Straight Blocker. A few drinks later, he became a very Offensive Lineman. A few more and he was a Tight End. Before the night was over, he had become a Split End and a fabulous Wide Receiver!

# FOLK-ETYMOLOGY
## LA BELLE ET LA BÊTE

## G. Legman

Naturally we are grateful when contributors to *Maledicta* only circle close, but do not dive bellyfloppers into the current ethnographico-etymological fads and eccentricities of "The Cooked and the Eaten," also Se*b*eiotic Signalfunk, *usw.* It is nevertheless painful to observe, at this late date, such feckless klang-etymologies attempted as those placed first and prominent in Profs. Whaley & Antonelli's contribution on "The Birds and the Beasts: Woman as Animal" (vol. 7:219-229). Their gallant, if soft-focus feminist approach is admirable, to be sure, but their facts are wrong.

It is acceptable in what is, after all, a linguistic journal, to begin with four such howling errors as *chippie* as a presumed animal or bird; the pejorative *pig* (for a woman!) merely as 'cattle'; *foxy* as merely vulpine; and *bitch* simply as equivalent to *shrew*, itself implied to be an animal term: again in error. In fact, even the Editor couldn't swallow that *chippie* 'animal,' as we shall see. In calling a woman a *pig*, the American male is referring to her presumed dirtiness or sluttishness, in a specifically sexual sense (sex = dirt), as one might call a man a *swine*; in calling her *foxy*, to her specific ODOR when in heat or rut (cf. *fausty, feisty, frowsty*); in calling her a *bitch*, to her presumed immorality, again as with the related vixen in heat; whereas the *shrew* is no animal-reference at all but derived from the participle

78

*shrewd* or *be-shrewed*, meaning touched by witchcraft and therefore evil and dangerous.

It is also certain that in calling someone a *son-of-a-bitch*, the insult does not refer to the doggishness of the bitch but to his mother's presumed immorality; thus, the *whoreson* victim is being called a *bastard* (sometimes a *son-of-a-bitch-bastard*), as is even more clear in the Hispanic-Arabic *hijo de mil chingadas*, or 'son of a thousand fucks' — politely 'of a thousand fathers.' (An insult sometimes made even more lethally clear by the symbolic seminal drooling of saliva from the mouth to earth.) In any case, it is only quite recently that an aggressively doggish or houndish animalism has become characteristic of *bitchiness*, on the male-supremacist equation: sexual-woman equals aggressive-woman, equals therefore social or sexual castratory danger. (See further, if you will, G. Legman, "Avatars of the Bitch Heroine," in *Love & Death*, Breaking Point, 1949.)

Finally, one observes the Editor's cautious Note, recoiling from the absurd onomatopoetics of *chippie* purportedly derived from the chipping of birds (or chirping of boids?) not to mention chipmunks; and the hopeful substitution of a 'local etymology' from one of those "Have-Fun-With-Funny-Word-Books" that bulk up the $1.98 remainder tables in the bookshops, for word-oriented serendipitists. And we are edified with the claim that a *chippy* is a 'whore in a Mexican whorehouse' who is paid with chips in *chippy-houses*; where in fact such chips were called *brass checks*, and a woman working for them in Mexico a *fichera*. Yet amid all this titillating detail, it is false that a *chippy* is a chip-bearing Mexican trollop or *doxsy* (also spelled *ducksy* and abbreviated to *duck*; again NOT an animal insult but an erotic one.

Every French slang dictionary for two centuries back to Joseph-Philibert Leroux's *Dictionnaire burlesque*, and every French-speaking person today, is aware of the common

French word *chippie* for an evil-tempered (formerly immoral) woman. So please, fellas, how the Texan customers of Mexican *ficheras* may have decided to call them *chippies* (as in the Franco-American brothels of New Orleans) might pose no problem; but would anyone care to explain how the 18th-century population BACK IN FRANCE decided to use this Texas-English equivalent of a Mexican term, a hundred years before there were any 'brass-check' brothels in Texas, and in fact a hundred years before there was any Texas?

### EDITOR'S NOTE

According to the 1984 *Harrap's Slang Dictionary English-French / French-English*, a **chipie** (pronounced "shipi") is an ill-natured / disagreeable woman; sourpuss / bitch; **vieille chipie** means "old bat / old faggot"; **une petite chipie** means "a spiteful little minx."

---

### BLACKS AND INDIANS

Two black whores—or *hos*, as they call themselves—got tired of the winters in Detroit and Chicago and moved to Arizona. There they ran into a couple of Native American women. "Hey, you be Indians?" asked one. — "Why, yes. I'm a Navajo and my friend, Gray Dove, is an Arapaho." — "Well, sheee-it! If dat don't beat all. I be a Détroit ho, and Maizie Lou here be a Chicago ho!"

Three black ladies decided to hit the big time as a singing group. They tried to come up with a name for their group. "Lennon Sister," suggested one. The other thought of "Andrews Sisters." But big momma said that they couldn't use these names, as there already were singing groups with these names. "I know. We'll call ourselves 'The Three Niggers,' 'cause that's what they're gonna call us anyway."

Black lady patient to physician: "What's the best type of sanitary napkin to use?" — "What's your flow?" — "Linoleum."

An Indian is having a drink at the bar. Suddenly he points to the floor and says to the bartender, "Big black bug!" — "Well," says the bartender, "squash it!" - "No, not squaw shit. Big black bug!"

# GIMP, PIMP, SIMP & WIMP

## POLITICAL PEJORATION
## PAST AND PRESENT

**Reinhold Aman**

### I. THE 1984 PRESIDENTIAL CAMPAIGN

Compared with earlier presidential campaign invective, the 1984 campaign was as boring and unimaginative as the two finalist, Ronald Reagan (the Simp) and Walter Mondale (the Wimp). An earlier contender, Gary Hart (the Gimp), lamely dropped out of the race when his John F. Kennedy mimicry was justly pilloried. To many whites not familiar with the black orator style, the Rev. Jesse Jackson (the Pimp) came across as a slit-selling pimp turned soul-selling preacher.

The official, public utterances by the candidates were the usual hypocritically polite, non-offensive pablum fed to the people who react negatively to so-called "name-calling" by the elite, even if the term is an objective description of the opponent. A prime example of this dichotomy of language was Richard Nixon. His public language was that of Mr. Clean, but in private — as revealed by the Watergate Tapes — he used vulgarities and racial slurs.

Carefully dividing their utterances into non-offensive ones when speaking in public and offensive ones when talking in private, today's politicians follow the standard practice of most middle- and upper-class folks, be they corporation presidents, family newspaper editors, professors, lawyers, physicians, or clergy. This practice bothers me greatly, especially when those publicly oh-so-clean people attack others for using offensive language in private which, through some blabbermouth's indiscretion, becomes public.

Most of these indiscretions leaked to the public cause damage to the person whose confidentiality was betrayed. Texas Governor Bill Clements who, in what he considered a "privileged discussion" with the editorial board of the *Texarkana Gazette*, characterized President Jimmy Carter as "a goddamn liar." (*Dallas Morning News*, 25 Oct. 1980, p. 1-A. Sent by Len Frazier). The press published Clements's confidential remarks and embarrassed him. He refused to apologize, and that was the end of it.

***EARL BUTZ.*** However, the better-known cases reported below resulted in more than simple embarrassment. Well-publicized victims of indiscretion include former Secretary of Agriculture Earl Butz who was forced to resign when tattletale John Dean told of Butz's private joke that "Colored want only three things: first, a tight pussy; second, loose shoes; and third, a warm place to shit." The media had a field-day with this indiscretion but found it difficult to report. *The Capital Times* (Madison, Wis., 4 Oct. 1976, p. 1) was one of the few newspapers that printed the quotation in full. *Time* magazine (18 Oct. 1976, p. 23) euphemized *pussy* to *p—* and *shit* to *s—*. Even the liberal *Die Zeit* (Hamburg, 15 Oct. 1976) weaseled out by "translating" *pussy* as "...", explaining that it referred to female genitalia, and euphemized *Scheißen* to *Sch...* Almost everyone who expressed shock at the joke Butz told in private has told nastier jokes in his or her private life.

***REAGAN.*** During the last campaign, there were several such instances of private language made public by unethical, blabbering reporters and other vultures who violated the trust put in them. Reagan's "Let's-bomb-Russia" joke made while testing the recording equipment was blown way out of proportion, causing a lot of ruffled feathers among the peace-loving Commies. This was Reagan's second time: in 1982, while testing his sound equipment, Reagan said, "My fellow Americans, yesterday the Polish government, a military dictatorship, a bunch of no-good lousy bums..." (*Time*, 25 Oct. 1982, p. 40).

*JACKSON'S "HYMIE"*. The black *Washington Post* reporter Milton Coleman who publicized Jesse Jackson's private comments about *hymies* (Jews) and *Hymietown* (New York City) was a traitor but, hey, anything for a flashy news story (*Playboy*, June 1984, p. 188). Trouble was, nobody had ever heard of these so-called anti-Semitic slurs before, and no record of them exists in any of the dozens of standard and slang dictionaries I consulted. I received telephone calls from the Library of Congress and the Los Angeles Public Library asking me to shed some light on the meaning of *hymie*. Let's be honest: *hymie*, from the first name *Hyman*, is not a nasty slur. It is as *relatively* harmless as *Leroy* for a black, *Hans* for a German, or *Giovanni* for an Italian. It is not on the same low level of nastiness as *kike*, *nigger*, *hun* or *wop*. *Hymie* and *Hymietown* are about as offensive as *Sam* and *Samtown* — big deal. But everyone is so easily offended these days, and the media went into a frenzy over these unknown terms made public by a blabbermouth. Jackson, who said he heard and used the term *hymie* growing up in Greenville, S.C., did not consider the terms derogatory, characterizing them as "noninsulting colloquial language." (*Newsweek*, 23 April 1984, p. 7) He probably lost more credibility for denying that he had used the terms, and later being forced to admit it, than for using them (*MJ*, 20 Feb. 1984, p. 4, and 27 Feb. 1984, p. 3).

Even though *hymie* has become a household word, only *National Lampoon* has been using this term fairly often. In its January 1985 issue, in a comic strip, Mr. T shouts to a yarmulke-wearing elderly man, "Yo! Hymie!" (p. 28). And on page 69 (actually, p. 43), there is a reference to the Jewish sex expert Ruth Westheimer: "You featured a brilliant piece by Dr. Ruth Wursthymie..." Also, *Hymietown* appeared in the same magazine (February 1985, p. 12), in a bogus letter from the Rev. Jesse Jackson:

> Ah nevah, to the best of my relocation, referred to the great city of New York as "Hymietown." What I did call it was a Jew-jammed, synagogue-stuffed, knish-clogged matzoh ball of a shiny sheeny Big Appleberg...

In its May 1985 issue, there are two further uses: Mr. T, on his way to hock a gold medal at Rosenblat's Pawn Shop, says, "Ah might as well see what Uncle Hymie goan' cough up." (p. 22) On page 16, Muhammad Ali, refusing to fight "The Kosher Butcher," chants, "He floats like a butterfly, / He stings like a bee. / I'd rather fight Parkinson's / Than that ugly Hymie."

***THE BUSHES.*** Vice President George Bush and his wife Barbara also were victims of indiscreet reporters who made public their private comments. When George Bush said that he "tried to kick a little ass," Ferraro-wise, waves of indignation spilled all over the media and caused shocks of disbelief that "Mr. Preppy" would use such language. Mr. Bush was talking privately to a longshoreman in Elizabeth, New Jersey, and he adjusted his language to his partner. The boom microphone of WNEW television picked up their private conversation and indiscreetly reported it, despite a Bush aide's request that the remark be off the record. John Sasso, Ms. Ferraro's campaign manager, dutifully called Bush's remark a very insulting "locker-room vulgarity." Mayor Ed Koch, practitioner of verbal aggression that he is, was the only public figure who was "not offended by that language." (*New York Times*, 14 Oct. 1984, p. 28) It was most shocking to me that the pristine *Times* — the last bastion of artificial civility — actually printed the word *ass*; a few years ago, it refused to print it, when Jimmy Carter said he could whip Ted Kennedy's ass.

Columnist Russel Baker expressed disbelief that Mr. Bush would shrug off his "kick ass" remark as a common "Texas football expression."

> Does anybody think he's a namby-pamby afraid to talk vulgar? Around the Bush house, he says, you're apt to hear regular-guy, locker-room talk any time... I have the impression he is trying to persuade us to visualize the Bush family sitting around the dinner table cussing up a storm...[but] all I can hear is, "Golly!" and "Gee whiz!" (*MJ*, 24 Oct. 1984, p. 15)

That's where Baker is wrong. Even preppies, in private or when sufficiently angered, use "locker-room vulgarities." Believe it or not.

While privately bantering with reporters, Mrs. Bush characterized Ms. Ferraro as a "four million dollar — I can't say it, but it rhymes with rich." This private remark also was indiscreetly made public by some weasel-faced reporter. Later, Barbara Bush apologized to Ms. Ferraro, saying that she would "never call her a witch for anything."

(Associated Press, 9 Oct. 1984) This still leaves the possibility that she would call her a *bitch*, a more appropriate designation for Ms. Ferraro than *witch*. Vice presidential spokesman Peter Teeley added to the *bitch* interpretation by saying that Ms. Ferraro is "too bitchy. She's very arrogant" and later repeated to the *Wall Street Journal* that "on television, she appears bitchy." (AP, 12 Oct 1984)

*Chicago Tribune* columnist Mike Royko was the only journalist who tried to infuse some reality into this artificially decent campaign:

> A little name-calling by both sides wouldn't hurt this campaign. If anything, it might simplify issues, eliminate a lot of windy rhetoric and get more people interested in the political process.
>
> Wouldn't it be much more honest if Mondale bluntly accused Reagan of being **an addled, confused old coot?** I'm sure he believes it, as do many Democrats... So why not just get it out in the open?
>
> Then Reagan could come right out and say what he thinks, which is probably that Mondale is a **wimpy weakling.** (*WF*, 18 Oct. 1984, p. 3)

### II. EARLIER POLITICAL MUDSLINGING

*Preppy*, *wimpy weakling*, *old coot*, and *Teflon President* (sleaze and dirt don't stick; *Time*, 18 June 1984, p. 20) are harmless when compared with the nastiness of earlier campaign epithets. Those were the good old days, before television and overly sensitive hypocrites, when politicians still flung dung at their opponents. The personal attacks ranged from one-word terms to elaborate comparisons and chains of insults, and from amusing stabs to vicious vulgarities. Below is a sampling of political pejoration, by and against politicians, mainly from earlier campaigns. My main source of the insults quoted below is Donald Hook and Lothar Kahn's *Book of Insults & Irreverent Quotations* (Jonathan David, 1980). I would also like to thank Professor Emeritus Paul Boller, who sent me his *Presidential Campaigns* (Oxford University Press, 1984) after the New York Oxford amoeba-brains refused to send a copy.

Politicians are among the most despised professions worldwide. And rightly so, for they have brought more misery upon mankind than all natural disasters and diseases combined. Today's politicians have become very civil-tongued, at least in their public utterances and published records. If they do slip up, they censor the *Congressional Record* before allowing it to be printed, to avoid disillusioning their constituents with profanities and vulgarities. Here, however, are many examples of political pejoration recorded in the two books mentioned above. The targets, in boldface, are in alphabetical order, and the source to whom the insult is ascribed is listed in parentheses. I restricted the examples mainly to adjectives, nouns, and adjective-noun combinations.

## U.S. PRESIDENTS AND OTHER POLITICIANS

**John Adams**: "Petty, mean, egotistic, erratic, eccentric, jealous-natured, and hot-tempered" (Alexander Hamilton). "A fool, hypocrite, criminal and tyrant" (Republicans).

**John Quincy Adams**: "The Massachusetts Madman" (anonymous). "A short, stout, bald, brilliant and puritanical twig of a short, stout, bald, brilliant and puritanical tree" (Alfred Steinberg, author).

**Chester Arthur**: "A non-entity with side whiskers" (Woodrow Wilson).

**William Jennings Bryan**: "His mind was like a soup dish: wide and shallow" (Irving Stone, author). "A disgusting, dishonest fakir" (Elihu Root, politician). "A money-grabbing, selfish, office-seeking, favor-hunting, publicity-loving marplot from Nebraska" (unknown). "A half-baked, glib little briefless jack-leg lawyer" (John Milton Hay, U.S. Secretary of State). "Loony, a degenerate" (*New York Times*).

**Jimmy Carter**: "A chicken-fried McGovern" (Sen. Robert Dole).

**Lewis Cass**: "A mutton-headed cucumber" (unknown).

**Henry Clay**: "A drunkard, gambler" (contemporary newspapers). "An ingrate, brawler" (Jacksonians).

**Grover Cleveland**: "Cruel, dogmatic, obtuse, and insensitive" (Richard Hofstadter, author). "A rake, libertine, moral leper, father of a bastard, gross and licentious," "worse in moral quality than a pickpocket, a sneak thief or a Cherry Street debauchee," "a wretch unworthy of respect or confidence" (*New York Tribune, New York Sun*).

**John Connally**: "The worst, most reactionary and vicious governor in Texas history...just nasty and vindictive" (Sen. Ralph Yarborough).

**Calvin Coolidge**: "This runty, aloof, little man, who quacks through his nose when he speaks" (William Allen White, author).

**Jefferson Davis**: "As ambitious as Lucifer, cold as a snake" (Sam Houston).

**Everett Dirksen**: "The Wizard of Ooze" (John F. Kennedy).

**Dwight Eisenhower**: "The extremely General Eisenhower" (unknown). "A lying son-of-a-bitch" (John F. Kennedy).

**Millard Fillmore**: "A Vain and Handsome Mediocrity" (Glyndon Van Deusen, author).

**Gerald Ford**: "Poor, dull Jerry" (Betty Ford). "A dumb-dumb" (Rev. Duncan Littlfair).

**Benjamin Franklin**: "A crafty and lecherous old hypocrite" (William Cobbett, English journalist).

**John Garner**: "A labor-baiting, poker-playing, whiskey-drinking evil old man" (John L. Lewis, Labor leader).

**John Glenn**: "This joker" (Fritz Hollings, presidential aspirant).

**Ulysses Grant**: "A drunkard, swindler, fool" and "an utterly depraved horse jockey" (various opponents).

**Ella Grasso**: "A fat, sort of a sweaty thing" (Lillian Carter).

**Alexander Hamilton**: "The bastard brat of a Scotch pedlar" (John Adams).

**Warren Harding**: "A he-harlot" (William White, author). "A slob" (Alice Roosevelt Longworth, socialite).

**Benjamin Harrison**: "A cold-blooded, narrow-minded, prejudiced, obstinate, timid old psalm-singing Indianapolis politician" (Teddy Roosevelt).

**Rutherford Hayes**: "His Fraudulency" (anonymous).

**Thomas Jefferson**: "A mean-spirited, low-lived fellow, the son of a half-breed Indian squaw, sired by a Virginia mulatto father" (Federalists).

**Lyndon Johnson**: "A riverboat gambler" (John F. Kennedy).

**Henry Kissinger**: "An eel icier than ice" (Oriana Fallaci, journalist).

**Abraham Lincoln**: "A huckster" and "a first-rate second-rate man" (Wendell Phillips, abolitionist). "A filthy story-teller, despot, liar, thief, braggart, buffoon, usurper, monster, ignoramus, old scoundrel, perjurer, robber, swindler, tyrant, field-butcher, and land-pirate" (*Harper's Weekly*). "A horrid-looking wretch" (*Charleston* [S.C.] *Mercury*).

**William McKinley**: "An irresponsible, unregulated, ignorant, prejudiced, pathetically honest and enthusiastic crank" (*New York Times*). "A socialist, anarchist, communist, revolutionary, lunatic, madman, rabble-rouser, thief, traitor and murderer" (various opponents).

**Fritz Mondale**: "Vice President Malaise" (Ronald Reagan).

**Richard Nixon**: "A shifty-eyed goddamn liar" and "a no-good, lying son-of-a-bitch" (Harry Truman). "Tricky Dick," "Slippery Dick," and "a human Edsel" (various). "A cheap bastard" (John F. Kennedy).

**Thomas "Tip" O'Neill**: "Big, fat, and out of control—just like the federal government" (Repr. John LeBoutillier).

**William Peffer**: "A well-meaning, pinheaded, anarchistic crank" (Teddy Roosevelt).

**Ronald Reagan**: "Herbert Hoover with a smile" (Tip O'Neill, speaker).

**Franklin D. Roosevelt**: "Two-thirds mush and one-third Eleanor" (Alice Roosevelt Longworth, socialite).

**William Taft**: "A fat-head with the brains of a guinea pig" (Teddy Roosevelt).

**Zachary Taylor**: "A cruel, semi-literate slavemaster" (Democrats).

**Harry Truman**: "A two-bit president of a five-star general" (unknown). "Son-of-a-bitch" (Joseph McCarthy).

**George Washington**: "That dark, designing, sordid, ambitious, vain, proud, arrogant and vindictive knave" (General Charles Lee, Revolutionary Army).

**Woodrow Wilson**: "An utterly selfish and cold-blooded politician" (Teddy Roosevelt)

Finally, a small sample of insults used against politicians in other countries. These do not include the many terms of abuse formerly hurled freely by members of parliaments in several countries but now forbidden, about which I'll report some other time.

**Earl Clement Attlee**: "A sheep in sheep's clothing" (Winston Churchill). "A modest little man with much to be modest about" (Aneurin Bevan).

**Menachim Begin**: "A little Polish lawyer from Warsaw" (Bruno Kreisky).

**Anthony Eden**: "An overripe banana, yellow on the outside, squishy on the inside" (Reginald Paget).

**Moammar Kkadafy**: "An infantile lunatic" (Anwar Sadat).

**Nikita Khrushchev**: "A pig-eyed bag of wind" (Frank L. Howley).

**Helmut Kohl**: "Asshole" (member of the opposition party of the Greens).

**Pierre Trudeau**: "A political leader worthy of assassination" (Irving Layton, author).

# A NOTE ON SEXISM AND INSULTING
# WITH EXAMPLES FROM POLISH

## Adam Jaworski

Gregersen (1977) claims that *fuck you* "has usually been hurled at men, for whom being a vagina-substitute had traditionally constituted the most degrading possible role" (p. 262). In the same article one finds references to other sources saying that it is also most degrading in other cultures for a man to be relegated to a passive role in sexual intercourse. The reason why it is not insulting to accuse of woman of sexual passivity (at least in the Western, male-dominated tradition) is that women are considered to be passive participants in sexual intercourse, anyway.

Spender (1980) shows how language reflects the traditional sexist asymmetry in the treatment of male and female roles in the area of sexual behavior. To mention just a few of the issues of this sort raised by Spender, there are no comparable feminine equivalents of the terms *virile* and *potent* and the terms *emasculate* and *effeminate*, and *impotence* and *frigidity* carry different respective attitudes and connotations; all these differences favor men's sexual superior status.

Similar asymmetry exists in the way males and females are insulted in Polish, at least when some of the most obscene, sex-related terms are employed by the speaker.

A man may be insulted by being called a male or female sexual organ, e.g., **Ty huju!** ('You prick!') or **Ty pizdo!** ('You cunt!'), but a woman can only be insulted with the

91

latter. This implies that if insulting is connected with downgrading one's status a man can be downgraded by two means: first, he (his ego) may be equated with his sex organ, and secondly, he can be leveled to the status of the female sex organ. Because women's status is lower than men's, their downgrading (in the way of using obscene insults) can be achieved by identifying them with the female organ.

A common Polish (male) saying, very insulting to all women, states that every woman "thinks with her ass" (**myśli dupą**). This implies that women are very stupid and/or they only seek an opportunity to find a man and stay with him. This in fact corresponds with one of the stereotypes of women's sexuality noted by Scully and Bart (1973:286) as quoted in Spender (1980:175): "...in the woman acquiescence to the masterful takes a high place."

The most approximate phrase to the one above, directed at males is **Ty (chyba) myślisz hujem** ("[It seems that] you think with your prick") and it is not so much an insult as a reaction to a man's excessive reporting of his erotic experiences, and thus it is an expression of the speaker's belief that the addressee is sexually hyperactive (or at least pretends to be so).

An actual insult that can be used with men and women (although informants disagree on whether it can be aimed at females) is **Ty masz pizdę w głowie** ("You have a cunt in your head") and means that the addressee is acting quite stupidly. The sexist asymmetry here is created by the fact that no counterpart of the above with the word **huj** ("prick") is used as an insult. Again, degrading a person is done by leveling his (her?) brain with the female, and not the "superior status" male sex organ.

Calling a person a homosexual is an effective insult only when directed at a man. Saying to someone **Ty pedale!** ("You faggot!") is a way of denying his masculinity and attributing to him the female, passive and subordinate sexual position. Since, in the male-dominated language, women are sexually passive and subordinate, no matter if they are hetero- or homosexual, calling a woman a lesbian is not an equivalent insult. (Likewise, there is no corresponding term to the English *dyke*.)

One of the commonest and strongest ways of insulting a woman is to say to her **Ty kurwo!** ("You whore!"). This insult is not used with men, and typically the closest phrases toward men differ in their connotations. **Ty kurwiarzu!** ("You whore-fucker!") implies a man's high prowess and rather "indecent" but broad sexual experience (a quality that some admire in men). **Ty kurwo męska!** ("You male whore!") is an insult only because it implies homosexual relations of the addressee (cf. above).

Spender (1980) says that Scully and Bart (1973) "found medical statements that most women [unlike men — A.J.] were frigid" (p. 175). This stereotype is also reflected in many Polish insults. While it is insulting to call a man **Ty impotencie!** ("You impotent (one)!") (cf. also **Ty huju złamany!**["You broken prick!"]), the feminine counterpart is not used because the stereotype of women's common frigidity is so strong that insulting a woman by attributing to her something that is believed to be true of her anyway is not conceived to be an effective insult. (Note a relation of this statement with the rules for ritual insults among black adolescents in Harlem formulated by Labov (1972).)

The above has been an informal analysis of some of the most obscene, sex-related insults directed at men and women in Polish. One can also see that, in this area of verbal behavior, language reflects sexist patterns of social organization. It might be worthwhile examining whether other Indo-European languages other than Polish reveal similar sexist patterns of abuse, and how these insults operate with respect to men and women in other cultures.

# REFERENCES

Gregersen, Edgar A. 1977. "A Note on English Sexual Cursing." *Maledicta* 1, pp. 261-68.

Labov, William. 1972. "Rules for Ritual Insults." In Thomas Kochman (ed.). *Rappin' and Stylin' Out: Communication in Urban Black America.* Urbana: University of Illinois Press, pp. 256-314.

Scully, Diana and Pauline Bart. 1973. "A Funny Thing Happened on the Way to the Office: Women in Gynecology Text Books." In Joan Huber (ed.). *Changing Women in a Changing Society.* Chicago: University of Chicago Press, pp. 283-88.

Spender, Dale. 1980. *Man Made Language.* London: Routlege & Kegan Paul.

## CONSTRUCTION LINGO

Little Jimmy, four years old, was bugging his mother. So she told him to go across the street to watch the construction workers and learn something. After two hours he came back inside, and mother asked him what he had learned.

"Well, first you take a goddamn door and you try to fit it into the fucking doorway. But if the son-of-a-bitch doesn't fit, you have to take the cocksucker down again. Then you take a cunt-hair off on both sides and put the motherfucker back up again."

Jimmy's mother was shocked by his language. "You just wait till your father comes home! I want you to repeat that for your father!"

When Jimmy's dad came home, mother told him to ask Jimmy what he had learned across the street.

Jimmy told dad the whole story. His dad was furious and told him, "Son, go outside and get me a switch!"

"Fuck you!" replied Jimmy. "That's the fucking electrician's job!"

*(This joke was first reported to us by John M., Labrador, in June 1984. A cleaned-up version (dingbat-euphemized) appeared in* Reader's Digest, *Sept. 1984, pp. 59-60)*

# A RUNNING COMMENTARY ON DIARRHEA

## Mac E. Barrick

That diarrhea is an affliction unfit for man or beast is made evident by the story of a boy whose father died of an excessive dose of the disease:

> One day an Irish boy's father died, and after the funeral, the boy was walking home with his friend, Pat.
> "Mike," said Pat, "what did your father die of?"
> "He died of gonorrhea."
> "That's not what I heard," Pat said. "Somebody told me he died of diarrhea."
> "Now listen," said Mike, "my father was a fuckin' man, not a shit-ass."[1]

The boy's filial pride was hurt by the real cause of his father's demise; diarrhea was not a noble way to go.

The ignominy of the subject, its suddenness, unavoidability and occasional embarrassment, make it an unfit topic for polite conversation. The many slang and colloquial expressions for the affliction suggest that it ranks with drunkenness, death and venereal disease as an unmentionable item. Ironically, the most common substitute term for the ailment is the equally unacceptable pluralization, **the shits. To have the shits**[2] is appropriately clear, though it is sometimes felt necessary to amplify the meaning by augmenting the grammatical structure with colorful but superfluous adjectives: "One of the previous day's customers had diarrhea or the 'screaming shits' as it was known locally"

(James Montague, *The Sheriff's Daughter* [San Diego, 1971], p. 26). The development of the linguistic concept behind **the shits** is suggested by the spooneristic conundrum, "What's the difference between an epileptic oyster shucker and a prostitute with diarrhea? — The epileptic oyster shucker shucks between fits, and the prostitute fucks be-tween shits."[3] In the conundrum **shits** represents a plurality of action or a multiplicity of individual occurences. The same concept is implied by **the shits** "diarrhea," though the definite article has transformed the count noun into a mass noun, which one would expect to have a singular grammatical function.

The most effective slang terms for diarrhea are onomato-poetic, suggesting both the action and its sound. Farmer and Henley[4] list both **squirt** (VII, 339, dating from 1551; cf. the modern student slang, **Hershey squirts**, which is phonetically and visually vivid) and **squitters** (VII, 340, from 1678). Eric Partridge dates **squitters** from "mid-C. 17-20: S.E. till C. 19, then dial.; in late C. 19-20, also schoolboys' s[lang]."[5] The modern American pronunciation (and spelling) is usually **skitters**.

Not unexpectedly, considering their Freudian interest in such matters, the Germans use many colorful, often onomatopoetic euphemisms. **Scheiße** itself derives from a Middle High German word for diarrhea, *schîze* "Durchfall."[6] **Dünnschiß**, lit. "thin-shit," is logical, but perhaps only the Germans would conceive of the running drizzles as **Dünnpfiff**, "thin-whistle." On other occasions the word **Pfiff** is a polite substitute for **Schiß**.[7] Other words in German for the ailment are based on the prefix *Durch-*, "through-": **Durchlauf** (through-run), **Durchgang** (through-going), and **Durchmarsch** (through-march). The Pennsylvania Dutch used a wide variety of colloquialisms, some of them facetious, others recognizable variants of stan-dard German: **darrichlâf, darrichfall, leibweh, dapper-**

**schpring, schpringdapper, flutter**, and **ruhr**. "*Darrichlâf* (through-run) is a general term for all sorts of diarrhea, exclusive of the 'red' or bloody dysentery which was usually spoken of as *rotruhr* or merely as *rotlâf. Ruhr* was quick painful diarrhea; it was also sometimes applied to colic pains in the abdomen."[8]  **Die Scheiss'** is now the most common Pennsylvania Dutch name for the affliction, however.

Second only to **the shits** in popularity in English slang is **the trots**, a term that Partridge dates from about 1910.[9] It has been common in print, however, only since the 1930s: "Give me the trots, them things do" (John Dos Passos, *1919* [New York: Harcourt Brace, 1932], p. 471); "I got the trots. Been on the run all morning" (James Gould Cozzens, *The Last Adam* [New York: Harcourt, Brace, 1933], p. 180); "'What'd you have, anyway?' 'Trots,' Carmody said" (George V. Higgins, *The Judgment of Deke Hunter* [Boston: Little, Brown, 1976], p. 219). In central Pennsylvania, where rural sanitation is still outstanding in its field, the term is usually **the back-door trots**.[10] There is a Philadelphia variant, **back-way trots**.

Many of the less common euphemisms relate the malady to its cause or place of origin. A particularly colorful example is the **green-apple quickstep**, suggesting the speed of both the reaction and the counterreaction. Green apples are in the folk mind synonymous with their effect:

The teacher was talking to the class and said, "What's the fastest thing in the world?"

One little girl held up her hand and said, "Lightning."

Then a little boy held up his hand and said, "Thoughts's faster'n lightning. I saw the lightning and thought it would come down, and it did."

Another little boy held up his hand, and the teacher said, "Johnnie, surely you don't know anything faster than thought or lightning."

"Yes, teacher, green apples. I ate two or three a' them the other day and shit before I thought."[11]

Several European terms suggest the rapidity of movement associated with **trots**. The British **thorough-go-nimble** dates from at least 1694 and a modern variant, **jerry-go-nimble**, from the 19th century (Partridge, pp. 437, 877). In French slang, the common term for diarrhea is **la courante**.[12] The somewhat archaic **flux** suggests by its initial phoneme the quality of *flowing* (cf. German *Fluß*), though the single phoneme *f-* also has a strong anal association (cf. *flatus, fart,* and German *furzen* and *Pfiff,* already mentioned). Compare also the American slang word, **flutters**: "Flutter is a mix fart and liquid shit! Which comes at times when least expected! Damp and stinks like hell!"[13]

The popular comparison **loose as a goose** sometimes refers to diarrhea (see Randolph and Wilson, p. 178), because it suggests the frequency and abundance of goose goings. In folk belief the goose has a "straight gut," i.e., everything it eats goes straight through it. Frank Wilstach did not include the phrase in his *Dictionary of Similes* in 1916, apparently recognizing its vulgar reference. Like most proverbial phrases, "loose as a goose" is rarely used in the literal sense (cf. *Sex-to-Sexty,* No. 37 [1972], p. 36) but currently refers to a lack of tenseness in public actions or behavior: "He's loose as a goose" (oral usage, Carlisle, Pa., October 1968); "He simply comes on 'loose as a goose'" (Albert Govoni, *A Boy Named Cash* [New York: Lancer, 1970], p. 22). "They're loose as a goose, Howard" (Alex Karras, "Monday Night Football," ABC-TV, December, 8, 1975); "Southern Cal's loose as a goose" (Frank Broyles, ABC-TV, December 6, 1980). The phrase occasionally has other meanings; a central Pennsylvania auctioneer uses it to describe rickety furniture, and Frances Barbour notes that it is "said of a tongue which wags too loosely."[14]

Because diarrhea, or its counterpart dysentery, is frequently contracted while traveling, many slang terms for it involve ethnic or geographic slurs. There is a certain irony in the fact that the Mexican term is **las turistas** (adopted into English as **the touristas**; see Wentworth and Flexner, p. 750), since travelers to that country are warned with what has become a catch phrase, "Don't drink the water," the implied result of failing to heed this being one of the "dances" listed by Sterling Eisiminger in his recent collection,[15] **Aztec hop, Mexican fox-trot, Mexican two-step**, or **Mexican toothache** (but isn't that V.D.?). All of these appear in an earlier listing by Ed Cray, together with the more commonly recorded **curse of Montezuma** and **Montezuma's revenge.**[16] The latter phrase is so familiar that it figures frequently in television humor, e.g., "McMillan and Wife," NBC-TV, April 1, 1973; "Sanford and Son," NBC-TV, January 18, 1974; and "Taxi," ABC-TV, February 12, 1981, where it was made into a malapropism: "Mrs. Mackenzie's revenge...I picked up a touch of that in Mexico once."

The student slang term, **Chinese creeping crud** (Ohio, 1970s), with its alluringly allusive alliteration, suggests the treacherously unexpected nature of the onset of diarrhea. The reference may derive from military usage in Korea[17] or Viet Nam, since soldiers, like other travelers, are particularly susceptible to digestive disorders. **New Delhi belly** also relates intestinal infirmity with oriental travel. Leitner and Lanen list **G.I.s** as synonymous with **the trots**. Wentworth and Flexner see this as a shortening of **G.I. shits** and suggest that it is an abbreviation of "gastrointestinal" (*Dictionary of Slang*, pp. 216, 704). Thus "G.I." apparently has no military connection in this usage except for a possible subconscious association with the abbreviation's full form, "government *issue*."

The German **Durchmarsch** does have a military origin, suggesting that it is an army affliction in general (and in privates). Ernest Hemingway has one of his characters, after examining the spoor of a German military unit, identify "Eight that could execremenate [!] and three of these with the bubbleshits" (*Islands in the Stream* [New York: Scribner's, 1970], p. 380). Of course, the military malaise may be the result of bad food. Contaminated food, particularly that spoiled by bad refrigeration, was the cause of **summer complaint**, a polite euphemism dating from Victorian days.[18]

In some instances, the slang term for diarrhea is applied backward to its cause. **Thorough-go-nimble**, Partridge informs us, was such a term, referring originally to the ailment, and later ("ca. 1820-60") to "inferior beer." **Squirt** and **squitters** were also slang terms for "the cheapest (and worst) beer...from ca. 1920" (Partridge, p. 820). Beer, cheap or otherwise, is still a recognized cause of diarrhea, as bemoaned by a Shippensburg State College student in the following graffito (May 1980): "I hate having the shits when I didn't get drunk the night before. There's no justification! I don't deserve this punishment!"

Intestinal laxity is often logically attributed to an excessive dose of cathartics. Folk jokes on the subject include one of a woman whose doctor prescribes a heavy laxative as a cure for cough: "Take this, and you won't *dare* cough." A similar joke tells of a woman who is on her deathbed, suffering from constipation. She calls her minister, who recommends that she take a large swallow of croton oil. She does and exclaims, "Oh preacher, I'm goin' to heaven." He says, "Yes, and you'll shit too."[19] The humor of his retort lies in the literalization of a figurative sarcastic rejoinder commonly meaning, "The hell (shit) you will!" One final joke relating an Exlax excess to a resultant excrementitious excess involves the taking of salts:

> A guy was in a bar, and he'd been drinking for a while, when he had to go to the bathroom. He said he was going home to go to the bathroom, and of course the bartender didn't want him to leave, so he said, "Why don't you use the bathroom here?" The fellow said,

"Oh, I don't want to mess up your bathroom. You see, I take salts."
The bartender said, "That doesn't matter. Go ahead and use it."
So when he came out, he was covered all over and the bartender
looked in the bathroom, and it was covered all over the walls and
ceiling, and he said, "Say, what kind of salts to you take?" "Somer-
saults."[20]

Shittiness is also associated with nervous disorders. One
who is frightened "shits himself," "has the shit scared out
of him," or by reverse logic is "scared shitless.[21] Compare
also the euphemistic "scared witless." It is even possible that
the "yellow streak" down a coward's back may be the result
of sphincteral failure,[22] although the related phrase "to be
yellow" probably refers to the ashen complexion produced
by extreme fear. German has several such scatological
phrases: **Er hat sich in die Hosen gemacht** ("He went in
his pants") and **Er hat Schiß** ("He has  shit").

Another cause of diarrhea is strong emotional distur-
bance. American slang commonly uses the phrase "to give
someone the shits" to imply deliberate or unintentional pro-
vocation. "To have a shit hemorrhage" indicates similar
annoyance at improper social behavior. The following joke
is illustrative:

A nun goes into a State [liquor] Store and wants whiskey, but the
clerk won't sell her any. She says it's for Mother Superior's bowels,
so he finally sells her a bottle. Later he sees her drunk and says,
"I thought you said that was for Mother Superior's bowels." She
says, "It is. She's gonna shit when she sees me."[23]

One of the curious results of the proliferation of substitute
terms for the less respectable word **diarrhea** has been that
many of them, improper nouns that they are, are less
acceptable than the word they replaced. Diarrhea is not
yet a suitable topic for dinner table conversation but it is
sufficiently acceptable to be used in everyday activities.
Sports announcers, for example, are sometimes described
as suffering from "diarrhea of the mouth,"[24] from which

one could establish a logical extension, that it is better to die of gonorrhea than to be a sports announcer, but perhaps that is going too far.

What was originally intended as a brief note listing colorful slang words, euphemisms and colloquialisms for diarrhea has run a bit long. With diarrhea, once you start, it is difficult to stop.

## NOTES

1. Told by a high school student, Carlisle, Pa., ca. 1951. A variant appears in Victor Dodson (pseud. for John Newbern and Peggy Rodebaugh), *The World's Dirtiest Jokes* (Los Angeles: Medco Books, 1969), p. 69, and in *Jackpot* 10, No. 6 (October, 1975), p. 69. Cf. Gershon Legman, *Rationale of the Dirty Joke* (New York: Grove, 1968), p. 655.

2. See Margaret Fleming, "Analysis of a Four-Letter Word," *Maledicta* 1 (1977), p. 176; cf. Martin Laba, "Urban Folklore," *Western Folklore* 38 (1979), p. 167: "I start getting diarrhea and the shits." Legman includes "drizzling shits" in the Second Series of his *Rationale of the Dirty Joke* (New York: Breaking Point, 1975), p. 682.

3. Told by an employee of the Carlisle [Pa.] Tire and *Rubber* Co., December 22, 1980. See also Richard Christopher, "Poonerisms," *Maledicta* 7 (1983), p. 32. Cf., for the genre, Alan Dundes and Robert Georges, "Some Minor Genres of Obscene Folklore," *Journal of American Folklore* 75 (1962), p. 222.

4. J.S. Farmer and W.E. Henley, *Slang and Its Analogues* (1890-1904; New York: Arno Press, 1970).

5. *A Dictionary of Slang and Unconventional English*, 7th ed. (New York: Macmillan, 1970), p. 821.

6. Lutz Mackensen, *Reclams Etymologisches Wörterbuch* (Stuttgart: Philipp Reclam Jun., 1966), s.v. *Scheiße*.

7. I am indebted for information on German slang to my colleague, Prof. Hans Meuer.

8. Thomas R. Brendle and Claude W. Unger, *Folk Medicine of the Pennsylvania Germans* (Norristown: Penna. German Soc., 1935), pp. 168-169. Another Pennsylvania Dutch phrase, "Ich den Schitler gehatt," is noted by William T. Parsons, "Shuler Family Correspondence," *Pennsylvania Folklife* 29 (1980), p. 100.

9. *A Dictionary of Slang*, pp. 1481-82. Cf. M.J. Leitner and J.R. Lanen, *Dictionary of French and American Slang* (New York: Crown, 1965), p. 135; also *the runs*, p. 110.

10. Listed in Farmer and Henley, *I*, p. 87; L.W. Payne, "A Word-List from East Alabama," *Dialect Notes* 3 (1908), p. 288; Vance Randolph and George P. Wilson, *Down in the Holler: A Gallery of Ozark Folk Speech* (Norman: Univ. of Oklahoma Press, 1953), p. 119. Cf. Bruce Cassiday, *Operation Goldkill* (New York: Universal, 1967), p. 27: "The turkey trots, the runs, the G.I.s."

11. From oral circulation, central Pa., between 1942 and 1963. Variants appear in Legman, *I*, p. 68; Joseph Fleisler, *Anecdota Americana*, Series 2 (1934; North Hollywood: Brandon House, 1968), no. 319; and Richard Rodman (pseud. for John Newbern), *Sex-to-Sexty Stag Treasury* (Fort Worth: SRI Publishing Co., 1967), p. 461.

12. Etienne and Simone Deak, *A Dictionary of Colorful French Slanguage and Colloquialisms* (Paris: Robert Laffont, 1959), p. 54. Cf. Leitner and Laner, p. 181, who also list *la foirade* and *avoir la foire* (p. 202).

13. *Little "Dirty" Comics*, ed. R.G. Holt (San Diego: Socio Library, 1971), p. 148. Cf. the Pennsylvania Dutch *flutter*, above.

14. *Proverbs and Proverbial Phrases of Illinois* (Carbondale: Southern Illinois Univ. Press, 1965), p. 78.

15. "A Glossary of Ethnic Slurs in American English," *Maledicta* 3 (1979), pp. 165-66.

16. "Ethnic and Place Names as Derisive Adjectives," *Western Folklore* 21 (1962), p. 28. Harold Wentworth and Stuart Flexner, *Dictionary of American Slang* (New York: Crowell, 1975), pp. 673, 724, list *Aztec two-step* and *Montezuma's revenge*. Ed McBain (pseud. for Evan Hunter, *Beauty and the Beast* [New York: Holt, Rinehart and Winston, 1982], p. 86) suggests a "drug named Lomotil, to be taken only if and when Montezuma's Revenge struck anyone." Cf. Joseph Wambaugh, *The Black Marble* (New York: Delacorte, 1978), p. 99: "Aztec revenge."

17. Cf. the joke collected by Legman in 1953: "A Negro soldier refuses to go and fight in Korea...'I had the gonorrhea and diarrhea both, and if this *Korea* is anything like it — go ahead and shoot.'" (*Rationale, I*, p. 655).

18. Farmer and Henley, *VI*, p. 26; Deak, p. 54. *Collywobbles* (see Partridge, s.v.; Legman, *II*, p. 682) apparently derives from indigestion's egestion.

19. Both from oral circulation, central Pa., 1973. Legman discusses this type of joke in *Rationale, II*, pp. 898-900.

20. Told by a female computer operator, Carlisle, Pa., March 1971. Cf. Legman, *II*, p. 978.

21. Cf. "*Avoir la chiasse* to be scared shitless" (Leitner and Lanin, p. 174), and "*Foirer* to have diarrhea; to be scared" (ibid., p. 202).

22. Cf. Legman, *II*, p. 898.

23. Oral tradition, Carlisle, Pa., July 1967. Also in Jim Boycan, *Time to Laugh* (n.p., 1965), p. 29; George Carey, *A Faraway Time and Place* (Washington: Robert B. Luce, 1971), pp. 119-20; cf. Dodson, *World's Dirtiest Jokes*, p. 191.

24. Cf. Ira Levin's definition of *logorrhea*: "Diarrhea of the mouth. Words keep running" (*A Kiss Before Dying* [New York: Simon and Schuster, 1953], p. 133.

## EDITOR'S NOTE

The author's location may have caused his excursion to Pennsylvania Dutch and German terms for "diarrhea," but he took only a few careful steps where a long march would have been better.

The German compounds formed with *Durch-* ("through-") are easily explained as partial translations; after all, Greek-derived *diarrhea* literally means "through-flow." The euphemism *Dünnpfiff* is not as weird as the author believes: while suffering from "thin-whistle," one expulses *thin*, watery fecal matter, often accompanied by *whistling* farts.

As to other German terms for "diarrhea," see Ernest Borneman's *Sex im Volksmund*, which lists nearly fifty in section 72.6, and Heinz Küpper's *Wörterbuch der deutschen Umgangssprache, III*, listing about twenty. *Harrap's Slang Dictionary* lists six French terms (*chiasse, cliche, courante, foirade, foire, riquette*), and Richard Spears's *Slang and Euphemism* shows over fifty varieties from the English-speaking world, gathered under *quickstep*. — Regarding *to be scared shitless*, I do not believe that this phrase is associated "by reverse logic" with *to have the shit scared out of someone*. The former expression is a logical and physiologically correct intensification of the latter: when one is quite scared, one defecates; when *extremely* scared, one defecates and defecates until all fecal matter is expulsed, to the point that one cannot defecate any more. One is literally "shitless," as there is no more *caca* in the colon. Medical research showed that passengers trapped in a doomed airplane, for instance, go through the entire range of physiological reactions to the fear stimulus, including involuntary bowel movements and urination, according to Kenneth Miller, a Chicago personal injury lawyer commenting on the September 6, 1985, airplane crash in Milwaukee (*MJ*, 8 Sept. 1985, pt. 1, p. 8).

# OFFENSIVE LANGUAGE VIA COMPUTER

## Reinhold Aman

Computer networks can be used to gather information from throughout the world. Unlike in traditional fieldwork, one does not have to interview informants personally but simply posts a query, or an entire questionnaire, on the electronic *bulletin board* (BB), and the users respond. BB's make this novel way of collecting data and responding easy: one calls the BB's number and leaves one's response. The quality and range of the responses depend on the precision of the questions asked, as well as on the type of user. Naturally, one can ask only those who have a computer and modem, which severely restricts the field of informants. However, these informants can gather information locally from those lacking such equipment and send it to the BB.

Henry Birdseye's "The Unknown BBS" (see MAL 7:276-77) is such a system for collecting information. It runs at 300 and 1200 baud and contains about one-quarter million characters' worth of kakological riddles, jokes, and other offensive language. It can be reached 24 hours a day by calling (303) 988-8155.

To test the usefulness of his system, Mr. Birdseye asked his BB users about terms for masturbation, urination, and vomiting. He did not request other essential information from the informants, such as their sex, age, geographic location, education, profession, etc., but the simple data below prove that such a BB system can be used successfully. To transmit the information gathered to others, one can either call up the BB and download it (have it sent by telephone to one's own computer), or ask for a printout, which I did.

Following below are the terms, after organizing and alpha-betizing the raw data.

**to masturbate** (of females): beat the beaver, buttonhole, clap your clit, cook cucumbers, grease the gash, hide the hotdog, hit the slit, hose your hole, juice your sluice, make waves [from "the (little) man in the boat" = clitoris?], pet the poodle, slam the clam, stump-jump.

**to masturbate** (of males): beat the bishop, beat your little brother, beat the meat, burp the worm, butter your corn, choke the chicken, clean your rifle, consult Dr. Jerkoff, crank your shank, dink your slinky, feel in your pocket for your big hairy rocket, file your fun-rod, fist your mister, flex your sex, flog the dolphin, flog your dog, grease your pipe, hack your mack, hump your hose, jerkin' the gherkin, milk the chicken, Onan's Olympics (n.), one-stick drum improvisation (n.), pack your palm, paint your ceiling, play a flute solo on your meat whistle, play the male organ, please your pisser, point your social finger, polish your sword, pound the pud, pound your flounder, prompt your porpoise, prune the fifth limb, pull the pope, pull your taffy, run your hand up the flagpole, shine your pole, shoot the tadpoles, slakin' the bacon, slam your hammer, slam your Spam, slap your wapper, spank the monkey, spank the salami, strike the pink match, stroke the dog, stroke your poker, talk with Rosy Palm and her five little sisters, tickle your pickle, thump your pumper, tweak your twinkie, unclog the pipes, varnish your pole, walk the dog, watch the eyelid movies, wax your dolphin, whip your dripper, whizzin' jizzum, wonk your conker, yang your wang, yank the yam, yank your crank.

**to urinate**: bleed the liver, drain the dragon, drain the (main) vein, get rid of the bladder matter, siphon the python, visit Miss Murphy.

**to vomit**: drive the big white bus, hug the porcelain, kneel before the porcelain throne, pray to the porcelain gods, school lunch rerun (n.), technicolor rerun (n.), upchuck.

# VERBAL AGGRESSION
# IN DINGA

## Mukumar Mpang

**Translated from the French
by Joseph G. Foster**

Our people live along the banks of the river Kamtsha, a tributary of the Kasia, in the Republic of Zaïre (19° longitude East and 4° South of the equator). We belong to the Badinga or Dzing tribe which numbers some forty thousand natives.

## I. LEXICOLOGY OF DINGA INSULTS

In Dinga, several expressions are used in the context of insults:

### 1. NOUNS

(a) **bitswa** (always plural): It signifies an insult to the male or female sex.

(b) **naal** (invariable): "insult." To insult someone from the toe to the hair [i.e., from head to foot].

(c) **uzul mur ndaa**: "manner of speaking." One repeats the utterance of a person whom one wants to insult. For example, a man asks his wife for something to eat: "Ngansongo, bring me something to eat, I am very hungry!" And Ngansongo replies: "Bring me something to eat, I am very hungry!" or she may reply with "Fofofo!"

(d) Insult gestures: one makes mocking gestures with the eyes, the mouth and the nose. There are three categories:

107

1. **ognan kinkieng**: "mimicry with the eyes." One looks slightly sideways in lowering the chin a little toward the left shoulder without blinking the eyes.

2. **musweng**: "mimicry with the mouth." Example: A mother orders her child to go draw water, and the boy thinks she has deprived him of his freedom by making him go to the well, instead of letting him play with his friends. To show that he finds her order ridiculous, the boy clenches his teeth and exhales while whispering: **Tswen!** This noise coming from between his teeth is called **musweng**.

3. **ofotola**: "mimicry with the nose." Example: Ngolomingi boasts to Mbokolo, wanting to measure his strength against him. Ngolomingi says to Mbokolo: "Say 'Foo!' and you will smell me!" Then Mbokolo will say it, and they start scuffling. **Foo!** is an insult coming from the nose and is quite serious. Breathing thus through the nose means that the aggressor is as foolish as ever and very cowardly and stupid.

### 2. VERBS

(a) **otswa bitswa**: to insult the sex of the aggressor.

(b) **osan**: to insult a person because of a noticeable physical defect (such as a mutilated eye) when quarreling with him.

(c) **onaal**: to insult or offend a person 'from the toes to the hair.'

(d) **ozul mur ndaa**: to imitate someone's speech mockingly and with mimicry of the mouth.

### 3. VERBAL EXPRESSIONS

**magpa e bitswa**: "to die from insults." That is, a person who has been greatly insulted by a large crowd for a harmful reason.

**mapara e bitswa**: "to go crazy from insults." Refers to a person of bad reputation because of bad acts; the public has insulted him very much and he loses his identity or, as it is said, his value, his weight, and becomes light.

**mazwab e bitswa**: "to wash with insults." A person who has been much insulted for his bad conduct in the community. This is insulting a person 'from toes to hair.'

**maser bitswa**: "to rub with insults." That is, a person who has been much insulted by the people. The metaphor suggests that the insults hurled at this person were "oily" and that the people who insult him rub him with insults instead of oil.

**mabuila e bitswa**: "to grow thin from insults." A person much insulted by the crowd from all sides becomes very thin because of these insults which wound his feelings.

**manway e bitswa ba**: "to grow thin because of insults." One loses weight because of insults. Example: Two women who bicker from morning to night. After their quarrel, one of the rivals becomes thin because of serious and sharp insults that she has received from her aggressive adversary. She then becomes unhappy and full of trouble.

**matoba e bitswa**: "to burst from insults." That is, the insults offered by the other person are so serious that the insulted one is close to bursting.

**mapasa e bitswa**: "to tear oneself because of insults." A person mistreated with serious insults is seen to tear himself like a worn garment.

**mabara-mabara e bitswa**: "to tear oneself because of insults." If one casts serious insults at a person, the victim will crack and be torn like the sweet potato boiled in the pot.

**masianga e bitswa**: "to become light from insults." A person who loses weight and becomes as light as the leaf falling from a tree into the water, without value, without weight, and following whatever direction the wind may impose on him.

**maluna e bitswa ba**: "to be pierced by insults." A person is pierced by insults, greatly shamed in public, if from morning to night he is forever insulted by an evil, aggressive, wicked woman.

**manema-nema e bitswa**: "to turn to dust because of insults." A much-insulted person is seen as tiny bits, dust.

**maliana e bitswa**: "to be weary from insults." A person threatened by serious insults feels weariness. He lacks the strength to work, to speak or simply to move about.

**matiar e bitswa, ngakier ba**: "to tremble because of serious insults." A person trembles because of biting and serious insults and not feeling any relief or ease from serious insults received.

**mapwan e bitswa, ngakier ba**: "to rot from insults." After being greatly insulted, one feels rotten, withdraws from the public, isolates oneself. One is filled with shame as if one's body were rotten and stinking, and flies were pursuing him.

**mabwala e bitswa**: "to become mealy like a cooked potato because of insults." A person becomes soft and fatigued when he has received very serious insults. He will subsequently lack courage, the strength to stand upright and work.

**mazeya e bitswa, ngakier mutwi bo ba**: "to hide because of serious insults received." An honest person hides when he receives serious insults in public.

**matwiy mweana e bitswa**: "to break out in sweat from insults." A person breaks out in sweat if he has been much insulted.

**maliel e bitswa**: "to weep because of insults." A person who cries as a result of serious insults received in public.

**matsien e bitswa, ngakier ba**: "to flee because of insults." A person of quality may escape because of harsh insults thrown at him before a surrounding public.

**mabam mude e bitswa**: "to hang oneself because of insults received." A person who has no courage hangs himself because of serious insults hurled at him in front of his friends or subordinates.

**maka-lung-lung e bitswa**: "to undress because of insults." A girl or woman may take off her clothes because of insults received. Example: If one insults her for having an itch on the buttocks, she disrobes to show her buttocks to the people who heard the insult.

**mazur e bitswa**: "to gorge oneself with insults." This expression is addressed to a person who has been much insulted but makes no reply whatever to his aggressor. By his action, the others say that he is surfeited with insults.

**masia e bitswa**: "to laugh in consequence of insults received." A person may laugh at the insults to which he is subjected when he sees that these insults mean nothing, that they are amusing and do not affect him.

**makaam e bitswa**: "to squeeze with insults." As one squeezes the palm nuts to extract the oil, insults (like an oil press) drain a substance from the victim.

**maza e bitswa**: "to be cooked because of insults." To become dry like a food substance which no longer contains any liquid.

**matame bitswa**: "to play with insults." A person who insults vaguely, who considers his insults to be no more than a child's toys, without value, amusing to the ear.

**matwal e bitswa**: "to gather or harvest insults." To have many insults heaped upon oneself. Example: A man insults a woman thus: "Your hair is shaved, your teeth are rotten, your vagina is like that of a bitch, your belly is swollen like that of a toad, your toes are eaten by chiggers." The woman has gathered insults as one gathers caterpillars from the leaves of a tree.

## II. VERBAL ATTACKS ABOUT THE BREASTS

**Mabial atea-teal mabial me nsiem!** "(You have) breast as long as an eel!" Boys throw this insult at proud girl-mothers who do not want to dance with them. This insult means that the female has very long breasts which may reach to the level of the navel.

**Mabial liele-liele ke mabial me mvha!** "Breast as pendulous as those of a bitch!" Boys habitually use this insult to shock the girls who wear no brassières; when a girl without a bra runs, her breasts swing from side to side like the pendulum of a clock.

**Mabial ke mabial me ngul!** "These breasts resemble the teats of a sow!" This insult is thrown at a girl or woman whose breasts hang down and have pointed nipples.

**Mabial agpi-agpi ke mabial nganswang!** "Very short breasts like the breasts of a porcupine!" Said to a woman who is sterile and whose breasts are very thin.

**Mabial tsu-tsu ke makwal!** "Very short and blackened breasts!" Said about the breasts of girls approximately 14 years old.

**Mabial inear-inear!** "Emaciated breasts!" Insult used against old women (aged 50 to 70 years). Especially the young ones insult the older women thus.

**Mabial nkemvha-vha!** "Fallen breasts!" Said to a woman who nurses her baby. Boys throw this insult at girls who refuse to marry, even though their breasts are already fallen. According to Dinga custom, a female with fallen breasts is no longer counted as a girl but is rather considered a mother. She no longer has the value of a girl.

**Mabial isim-isim!** "Breasts full of muscles!" Said to women with big breasts. One day when I was passing through Mbembey to go fishing, a woman named Gertrid insulted the wife of Lesiy thus: *Feete mabial mengia ma isim-isim e bidem bingia adzwa ngia mwan me!* "Félicité, you have breasts full of muscles, big, you have eaten my child

through a fetish!" There was a fight about having be-
witched her child and caused its death. Among the
Dinga, sorcerers have no comrades.

**Mabial ke mabial menom!** "Breasts that resemble those
of the civet-cat!" Used to insult a woman with a very
black skin, so that her breasts resemble those of this
animal.

**Mabial mimbum-mimbum!** "Big swollen breasts!" A
woman who has small breasts insults the other thus.

**Mabial bear-bear!** "Flattened breasts!" Boys insult women
who have this kind of breasts. These breasts do not have
a good appearance.

**Mabial sui-swi kembweal!** "Breasts reddened like a red
fruit!" This insult is thrown at a woman who habitually
wears a brassière, so that the skin of her breasts is brown.

**Mabial nkelum ongbe obule osan!** "Breasts so long that
one could throw them over her shoulder!" To insult a
woman whose long breasts hang down to her waist.

**Mabial ke mabial me ntab!** "Breasts like a nanny-goat's!"
This insult is addressed to a woman whose breasts are
thin, lengthened, and pointed at the nipples.

### III. VERBAL ATTACKS ABOUT THE BELLY

**Dem ngazam!** "Swollen belly!" This insult is habitually used
to insult a person afflicted with the belly sickness commonly called *kidzia* in Dinga.

**Dem inear-inear!** "Greatly lined and wrinkled belly!" Used
to insult old women. One also finds this type of belly
among women who have borne many children.

**Dem ke dem lengom!** "A belly that resembles a cow's belly!"
To insult persons whose big bellies stick out to the left
or to the right.

**Idem kwid!** "The belly swollen at a single spot!" (Or
"...only on one side!"). The young often address this insult to the old ones who eat ears of corn, called *masang*
or *ndwaa* in Dinga.

**Idem ke idem kentab mpiangpa!** "The belly similar to the belly of a goat!" Said to a person who grows only in the belly or to a dwarf who has a large belly.

**Dem ke tswel leli-lianga!** "Belly like those of young swallows!" This insult is addressed to small children afflicted with the belly sickness. Also used to insult greedy youngsters.

**Dem ke dem le tswer!** "A belly like the belly of a wild rabbit!"

**Dem akwaka-akwaka!** "A belly full of balls!" [?] The person's belly is compared with the branches of a failed [?] tree. Used to insult a person who has a very large navel, and when he becomes old, his belly will become thus.

**Idem ke kidem ke ngan!** "The belly that is identical to the belly of a crocodile!" Said to a person who has a belly that is flattened, big and distended on each side.

**Dem mpwear-mpwear!** "A belly covered with scabies almost everywhere!" This insult is thrown at a person who sleeps badly, because his bed has bedbugs. Such a person may have scabies almost everywhere. This insult also refers to uncleanliness: the insulted person is very dirty.

**Dem mika-mika!** "A belly covered with hair almost everywhere!" Women throw this insult at people whom they consider to be wretched. One also says:! "It's a gorilla!" The tradition in Dinga says: "A man who has hairs on his belly will be the father of children."

**Idem ke kidem ke mpuu!** "The belly is like that of a big wild rat!" This insult is hurled at a person who has a big short belly.

### IV. VERBAL ATTACKS ABOUT THE NAVEL

**Mukwom umpwal!** "Swollen navel!" This kind of navel resembles a newly-sprouted mushroom. This insult is addressed to a person who has this kind of navel. The people who have this navel are gluttons.

**Mukwom bwil!** "Navel swollen to look like an orange!" This insult is addressed to a person who has a protruding and rounded navel. One often finds this kind of navel among men; among women this navel is not common.

**Mukwom ntsweang!** "Pointed navel!" Used against a person whose navel is slightly protruding, but pointed.

**Mukwom ntsweang-ntsweang!** "Very pointed navel!" For a person who has a navel that is long and pointed at the end.

**Mukwom nkemena bu!** "Buried navel!" To insult a person whose navel disappears in the belly; one notices a small hole.

**Mukwom ngabela bu!** "Submerged navel!" Used against a person whose navel is concealed in the belly.

**Mukwom kibal-kibal!** "Flattened navel!" This insult is thrown at a person who has a slightly protruding belly.

**Mukwom bear-bear!** "Flattened navel!" Used to insult a person whose navel protrudes very slightly.

**Mukwom moninin!** "Large navel!" An insult thrown at a person who has a very large navel.

**Mukwom bwal!** "Big navel!" Used against a person with an enlarged navel.

**Mukwom swi!** "Reddened navel!" This is how one insults the navel of a person who has a light skin color.

**Mukwom ngapwan!** "Rotten navel!" This insult is thrown at a person who has a navel that smells bad.

**Mukwom ke kimwa mbin!** "Navel with the face of a little calabash!" This insult is thrown at a person whose navel protrudes like a small gourd.

**Mukwom ngepula men!** "Wounded navel!" Used against a person who has a sore on the navel.

**Mukwom ngakwara!** "Navel sticking out!" To insult a person whose navel sticks out.

**Mukwom ke mukwom me ngul!** "Pig's navel!" This insult is addressed to a person whose navel sticks straight out in front and is knotted.

**Mukwom ngendzwila!** "Hanging navel!" Used to insult a person whose navel is big and hangs down toward the lower belly.

## BIBLIOGRAPHY

Mertens, J. 1935. *Les Ba-Dzing de la Kamtsha.* I.R.C.B., Brussels.

Mpang, Mukumar, and Mpang, Manzanga. 1977. *Ne me tue pas, épouse-moi!* ["Don't kill me, marry me!" Dinga myth. Dinga-French text]. CEEBA II, 39, Bandundu.

———. "Appellations de Dieu et noms théophores dinga." In *Dieu dessécha le fleuve.* CEEBA I, 7, Bandundu.

Struyf, I. 1939. *Esquisse de grammaire du kidinga de Mukene Mbel, d'après trois fables codifiées en écriture phonétique.* I.R.C.B. (IV, 3:97-119), Brussels.

van Bulck, G. 1934. "Les Ba-Dzing et nos sources de littérature ethnographique." *Congo* II, 3:297-331.

### THE HARVARD SNOB

A freshman at Harvard University asked an upperclassman, "Can you tell me where the library is at?" — "At Harvard, we never end a sentence with a preposition. Try again." — "All right. Can you tell me where the library is at, you asshole?"

### GRAFFITO

When I was young and had no sense
I pissed on an electric fence.
It shocked my dick and shocked my balls
And made me shit in my coveralls.

### DEAR ABBY

I just met the most terrific girl and we get along fabulously. I think she's the one for me. There's just one problem: I can't remember from our first date if she told me she had T.B. or V.D. What should I do?

—Confused

*Dear Confused: If she coughs, fuck her.*

# MILWAUKEE
# MEDICAL MALEDICTA

## Sue Ture*

Many of the derogatory terms used by physicians and nurses, as recorded by Drs. Scheiner (2:67-70), Monteiro (4:53-58), and Taller (7:38-40), also are known and used in metropolitan Milwaukee (Wisconsin) hospitals. The following terms, not recorded in the above-mentioned glossaries, or recorded with different meanings, are currently employed by some local hospital staff.

**albatross** a very sick patient with multiple problems who cannot be cured. The doctor is stuck with that patient until one of the two dies.

**bug juice** antibiotics. A local specialist in infectious diseases is known as "Bug Buster."

**camel driver** derogatory designation used by doctors for foreign (especially Middle East) physicians working here. Also called **flying-carpet salesman**

**cracked squash** skull fracture. See SQUASH

**crotch rot** a fungus infection in the pubic area caused by use of antibiotics

**expert from the big city**. See SON-OF-A-BITCH WITH SLIDES.

**F.L.K.** Funny-Looking Kid. Said of a child-patient with a strange appearance or a combination of appearance and behavior not considered normal but not fitting any particular pattern of disease.

**flying-carpet salesman**. See CAMEL DRIVER

**fruit ranch** psychiatric unit

**goose grease** KY jelly, a water-based lubricant

**jungle rot** same as CROTCH ROT

**King Richard the Turd** nickname for a pompous, self-important Milwaukee surgeon

**let sleeping sloths lie** request not to awaken a THREE-TOED SLOTH

**professional patient** one who cultivates and enjoys poor health

117

**rotten squash**   brain damage. See SQUASH

**SICU**   Surgical Intensive Care Unit; pronounced "sick-u"

**son-of-a-bitch with slides**   a guest speaker at a medical meeting. Also called **an expert from the big city**

**squash**   1. brain; 2. head

**three-toed sloth**   a slow-thinking, slow-talking, slow-acting patient, such as a degenerated alcoholic

**to fertilize one's vegetables**   to order vitamins or tube feedings. See VEGETABLE

**to have lice and fleas**   to have more than one disease

**to have a room-temperature IQ**   to be stupid, to have an IQ of about 70

**to need one more neuron**   to be very stupid; two neurons are needed for a synapse to take place, to be able to think or act.

**to water one's vegetables**   to order intravenous fluids

**vegetable**   a permanently comatose patient

**vegetable garden**   ward with comatose patients

**whiney gyne club**   patients who had gynecological surgery and always complain whiningly that they cannot urinate, that their genitals hurt, etc. Pronounced "whiney gyny."

**witch doctor**   specialist in internal medicine

**W.P.**   wounded pigeon; applied to little old lady patients (mainly of Italian descent) who rule their families by procuring sympathy.

### EDITOR'S NOTE

Two terms just received from a San Francisco hospital employee:

**Ten F**   a stereotypical gall bladder patient who is a *Fat, Fair, Fecund, Fortyish, Flatulent Female with Foul, Frothy, Floating Feces.*

**Thorazine shuffle**   the characteristically slow, foot-dragging gait seen in psychiatric patients receiving heavy, long-term doses of phenothiazines. The movements are similar to Boris Karloff's as Frankenstein's monster or the Mole People in the 1950s movie.

# "KISS'D OUR *ANOS*" IN BEN JONSON'S *THE ALCHEMIST*

## Edgar C. Knowlton, Jr.

Two lines in the fourth act of *The Alchemist*, Ben Jonson's play dating from 1610, derive humor from the meaning of the word *anos* (is it English, Latin, or Spanish?). Editors provide no comment; a recent glossary which includes the word provides partial aid for the meaning.

Surly has entered, "like a Spaniard."[1] He says to Face and Subtle: *"Sennores, beso las manos, à vuestras mercedes. "*[2] In this scene his speeches are in Spanish. Editors interpret the lines more or less as follows: "Gentlemen, I kiss your (honors' *or* worships') hands,"[3] though one edition has the English singular "hand" as rendering the Spanish plural *manos.*[4]

Subtle makes reply: "Would you had stoup'd a little, and kiss'd our *anos.*"[5] Most editors interpret "stoup'd" as "stooped." This humorous reply they do not comment on. Usually *anos* is printed in italics as Spanish (or Latin). "Our" may be used editorially but it seems more likely that the Spanish plural *vuestras mercedes*, "your worships, your graces, your honors," is being matched in "our *anos*," and that the reference is to the pair, Face and Subtle. Spanish, unlike English, prefers the distributive singular in the case of body parts, like *manos*, where a difference in meaning is possible.[6] Strictly speaking, Surly's polite greeting implies that he is kissing, perhaps figuratively, both hands of Face and Subtle; otherwise, *la mano* would be preferred. The plural *manos*, then, would lead, by attraction, to an echoing plural form, *anos*, since *manos* (and *anos*) could be singular in meaning but plural because two people are involved.

One editor prints "anos" as an English word, though the word is not in the dictionaries.[7] This may have been the view of the author of a recent glossary, who seems to imply by his gloss for *anos*, 'anus,' that it is a case of spelling variation of the English Latinism.[8] A problem immediately arises. English "anus" is first attested in the *OED*, I, 377, in 1658, almost five decades after the performance of *The Alchemist* in 1610. The form *anos* could also be an accusative plural of Latin *anus*, but in that case, too, the word were better italicized. The argument against *anos* here as representing the Latin plural largely rests on the fact that in other passages from the same scene, a Spanish word used by Surly is echoed by the other characters, *casa*, 'house,' by Subtle,[9] and *sennora*, 'lady,' by Face.[10] It is natural to interpret *anos* as Spanish; it is the plural of Spanish *ano*, 'anus,' first documented for Spanish in 1555, and characterized as a medical term.[11]

Factors of play production favor the pronunciation of *manos* and *anos* as Spanish, since otherwise, with change in vowel of the first syllable, members of the audience might not catch the wordplay.

Subtle, then, is teasingly suggesting that the "Spaniard" stoop, or humiliate himself, and kiss their anuses. To interpret the verb as "stop" rather than "stoop" is once again to lessen the joke.[12] Jonson was using, it seems certain, *anos* as a Spanish, learnèd word. The use of this word is doubly humorous, inasmuch as it suggests an unlearnèd, inelegant equivalent like "ass (-hole)," but remains learnèd, scientific in form. Jonson is freed of the charge of not knowing how to spell an English Latinism, "anus," decades before its earliest attestation in English. Steane and Henke were ill-advised to treat *anos* as an English word, though they earn praise for having understood the drift of the joke. The editors who gave no comment may have been overly prudish, or they may have not realized that the joke might need, for some readers at least, clarification. Such further possibilities in appreciating the humor as the possible implication that Subtle and Face each had as many anuses as hands or that *anos* is equally Spanish and Latin as a form might bear mention, and for the actor in performance it is a matter of some importance that the vowel of *anos* here is to rhyme with that of Spanish *manos*, and not with the first and stressed vowel of contemporary English "anus." The pompous "Spaniard" is amusingly deflated in this use of an inoffensive, learnèd, exotic term.

## NOTES

1. C.H. Herford and Percy Simpson, eds., *Ben Jonson*, V (Oxford: Clarendon Press, 1937), p. 368.

2. Herford and Simpson, *loc. cit.*

3. C.H. Herford, Percy and Evelyn Simpson, eds., *Ben Jonson*, X (Oxford: Clarendon Press, 1950), p. 102; G.E. Bentley, ed., Ben Jonson, *The Alchemist* (New York: Appleton-Century Crofts, 1947), p. 76; Robert Ornstein and Hazelton Spencer, eds., *Elizabethan and Jacobean Comedy: An Anthology* (Boston: D.C. Heath and Co., 1964), p. 184; Douglas Brown, ed., Ben Jonson, *The Alchemist* (New York: Hill and Wang, 1965), p. 98; F.H. Mares, ed., Ben Jonson, *The Alchemist* (Cambridge, Mass.: Harvard University Press, 1967), p. 137; S. Musgrove, ed., Ben Jonson, *The Alchemist* (Berkeley, Los Angeles: University of California Press, 1968), p. 149; Alvin B. Kernan, ed., Ben Jonson, *The Alchemist* (New Haven, London: Yale University Press, 1974), p. 140; Robert M. Adams, ed., *Ben Jonson's Plays and Masques*, (New York, London: W.W. Norton and Co., 1979), p. 242 have been consulted with reference to the passage in question.

4. J.B. Steane, ed., Ben Jonson, *The Alchemist* (Cambridge: University Press, 1967), p. 111.

5. Herford and Simpson, *op. cit.*, V, p. 368.

6. Robert K. Spaulding, rev. Marathon Montrose Ramsey, *A Textbook of Modern Spanish* (New York: Holt, Rinehart and Winston, June

1967 printing, pp. 36-37, paragraph 1.26: "In speaking of a thing which is found singly in a number of individuals, it is most often placed in the singular in Spanish—contrary to the English usage, especially when dealing with a part of the body or an article of clothing... To say *todos los animales tienen cabezas* would convey the idea that each one has several heads. However, when there is no chance for equivocation, the plural is used." We have omitted the example; the Spanish phrase means 'all animals have heads.' The Spanish sentence, given as example, *Todos los animales tienen cabeza*, with the singular *cabeza*, implying one head, has—in Spaulding-Ramsey—the same English equivalent.

7. J.B. Steane, *ed. cit.*, p. 111.

8. James T. Henke: *Renaissance Dramatic Bawdy (Exclusive of Shakespeare): An Annotated Glossary and Critical Essays*, II (Salzburg: Institut für Englische Sprache und Literatur, Universität Salzburg, 1974), p. 82.

9. Herford and Simpson, *op. cit.*, V, p. 369.

10. Herford and Simpson, *op. cit.*, V, p. 369.

11. J. Corominas, *Diccionario crítico etimológico de la lengua castellana*, I (Bern: Francke, 1954), p. 218. For the characterization as a *voz de la cirugía* or medical term, see the *Diccionario de autoridades*, I (Madrid: Gredos, 1963, facsimile of 1726 edition), p. 301.

12. G.E. Bentley, *ed. cit.*, p. 76. Perhaps "stopp'd" is a misprint here.

MR. TWEEDY — By Ned Riddle

"I'm not doing very well on the instrument, but
I'm learning some great Spanish curse words."

# OFFENSIVE WORDS
# IN DICTIONARIES

II. *Arse, Arsehole, Ass, Asshole, Blabbermouth, Bullshit, Cripple, Cunt, Dildo, Meathead, Merkin, Prick, Slob, Wimp, Yente*

## Reinhold Aman

### I. INTRODUCTION

In this second installment of comparing dictionaries as to inclusion or suppression of "offensive" words, their definitions, usage labels, and etymologies (see *Maledicta* 7, p. 109), I have broadened the coverage by checking dictionaries from other English-speaking countries. In addition to the ones used in the first installment, I now also consult a Canadian, a British, and an Australian "college-size" general dictionary. While in the future only these general works will be checked, this time I also included two slang dictionaries, Flexner's and Spears's. I could have broadened this comparison by consulting Barrère & Leland, Farmer & Henley, Partridge, and many others, but that would defeat my original intention, namely, to show the information presented in *general* dictionaries, of which one or more are, or should be, in every household. Obviously, these comparisons are *not* in-depth studies of the individual words, which would involve extensive research and are a task and opportunity I leave to others.

As you will see in the following pages, there are many words with unknown or disputed origins begging for etymological investigations. Such studies demand access to many dictionaries and much research. Just as Prof. Gerald L. Cohen doggedly tracked down the suggested origins of *shyster* and through sound scholarly research disproved most of the alleged origins, you can make a name for yourself by investigating the unknown or disputed origins of *dildo, fuck, gay, gringo, kike, merkin, shmuck, wimp, wog,* and others to be discussed in this journal. Further, the first recorded dates of common words need scrutinizing: for example, it seems impossible that *asshole* is not recorded before 1951, or that the verb *bullshit* is not found in print before 1942. Likewise, the geographic and social distribution of vulgar synonyms for terms such as *smegma* (*cock-cheese, dick-cheese, prick-cheese*) are awaiting thorough research. Of course, you need the courage of Allen Walker Read or Stuart Berg Flexner to study the words and expressions shunned by the proper profs and popular word gurus who would rather die with their pristine reputation intact than be associated with "unprintable" and "unspeakable" language. (If you should decide to tackle any of these words, please let me know, so that I can inform others who might be doing research on the same word.)

I wish to thank Tim Hendrie, editor of the *Gage Canadian Dictionary*, for donating a copy, and to express my gratitude to James Bettley and Brian Taylor for purchasing and shipping the dictionaries that the publishers refused to send me, the British *Longman Dictionary of the English Language* and the Australian *Macquarie Dictionary*.

## II. REACTIONS TO *SMEGMA* (1983)

Excerpts from personal letters by Laurence Urdang, dictionary editor:

> On copying by dictionary makers, *Maledicta* 7, pp. 114 and 117: "The *Collins* did not use American sources. You may find yourself in hot water using words like *copied*. 'Based on' is less committal, and may even be correct. But you haven't gone deeply enough into the other sources (e.g., those used by *Dorland's*, etc.) to be able to make statements you do. Two sources you examine may owe a great deal to a third source that you have not seen."

On the 'ideal' definition, pp. 118-120: "If everyone wrote a nine-page exegetical essay on every definition in every dictionary, dictionaries would undoubtedly have better definitions. Similarly there is no end to the sort of criticism you have undertaken, and I am not sure that it serves any useful purpose. You have omitted information, too, e.g., What does *smegma* taste like? How does it feel when it gets in your ear? In short, I don't think your project is exactly the answer to a dictionary mayven's prayer."

One dictionary editor did not like my "petulant and testy" comments about Oxford (p. 114) and Longman (p. 116) but wrote that the Longman offices in New York and Harlow "are populated by gormless ninnyhammers, though New York is, by far, the worse." (The British term *gormless* means 'lacking understanding and intelligence; dull-witted; stupid' and *ninnyhammer* means 'simpleton; silly or foolish person; simpleton; idiot.')

From David Guralnik, Editor in Chief of *Webster's New World Dictionary*:

A mild demur to your assumption that the entry in *WNW* was "borrowed [camouflaged, yet]" from that in the Random House Unabridged, which you say was published in 1963. Actually that work first appeared in October, 1966, and it is highly unlikely that we saw a copy before 1967. The entry for our dictionary was prepared in early 1966. Moreover, as I was the one who wrote that definition, I can tell you that it was constructed without reference to any other general dictionary, but with the guidance of our special contributing editor for medical terms.

I also find it interesting that your "ideal" definition is remarkably close to the one we already have... You might also have noted that our etymology alone carried the term back (via cross-references to *smectic* and *smite*) to its Indo-European base. But I forgive you these lapses because you have introduced your readers to "the joys of lexicography."

Mr. Guralnik sent me a copy of a letter from a lady at Harvard University (21 December 1982) who complained about his dictionary's definition of *smegma*:

I would like to call your attention to an offensively inaccurate defini-

tion which deterred me from buying the second college edition of
the *Webster's New World Dictionary*.

The definition of *smegma* reads "a cheeselike, foul-smelling
sebaceous secretion..." My smegma is not foul-smelling, nor do
friends I have consulted consider theirs or their partners to have
a foul odor.

The Webster's dictionary does not pass judgment on the taste
of anchovies, nor does it indicate an opinion on the odor of feces — I
therefore see no reason for an editorial comment on the smell of
smegma.

I look forward to your comments on your rationale for such a
biased definiton.

## Mr. Guralnik replied to her:

You might have a point if we were discussing some substance such
as perspiration — or anchovies, or even feces, whose odors are
variably received in different cultures. There are some substances,
however, which are universally, or almost universally, regarded as
malodorous, such as the ejection of a skunk or the emanations from
a skunk cabbage (*Symplocarpus foetidus* — the genus name means foul-
smelling), and the odor becomes as much a part of the description
as color or size. Smegma would appear to be such a substance, judg-
ing from the literature on the subject. Perhaps you are confusing
*sebum*, the sebaceous secretion that is itself relatively odorless, with
*smegma*, the accumulation that contains scaly epithelial cells and that
acquires a cheeselike consistency and a strong (unpleasant to most
people) odor if it is not regularly removed. Or perhaps we have
here a classic case of *de gustibus...*

In either event, I regret very much that you have based your
choice of so important an aid in your studies as your dictionary
upon so trifling a point.

## Allen Walker Read submitted a three-paged article, "Notes on the Word 'Smegma'," presented here in condensed form:

Your study of the word *smegma* is very revealing of the imprecision
to be found in the current dictionaries. In my opinion, the unfavor-
able criticism that it "emits a foul smell" is not well founded. As
I remember it, smegma had no foul smell. I remember smegma
from the ages of twelve to about fifteen, because I was worried by

not knowing what it was. Your "ideal definition" is erroneous, I believe, by including the criterion "foul-smelling."

Smegma is actually a beneficial substance, developed through evolution to prevent irritation when the foreskin rubs against the corona. The notion that it is "foul-smelling" is the result of folklore of a puritan people that regards the body as evil. It is often thought that sweat smells bad, but that is not the case, for fresh sweat in a healthy young person has a delightful odor: only when it has had time to get rancid on the flesh or in the clothes does it smell bad.

The smell of urine or faeces is problematical. It may well be a tendency ingrained by evolution (in the interests of sanitation) to regard their smell as unpleasant, but in a healthy person "foul-smelling" would be too strong. Certainly one must admit that suppurating wounds, gangrene, and a decaying corpse are "foul-smelling."

I wrestled with this problem when I was defining *fart* in my study of folk epigraphy in 1935 (see *Classic American Graffiti*, p. 50), and I came up with the phraseology "usually accompanied by a whistling sound and a characteristic odor." That is as far as I would want to go — "a characteristic odor," in order to avoid any stigmatizing of the delightful, sublime, glorious human body.

Your suggestion of "prick-cheese" is a clever flourish, an attention-getter, but is utterly impractical as advice to a lexicographer, because of the sound doctrine of "levels of usage"...

Actually, I was neither trying to be clever nor get attention; I merely reported a quite common vulgarism I had heard repeatedly. There are regional variants of *prick-cheese* — naturally ignored by maledictaphobic profs and pop linguists — as shown by some responses I received: Roger P. wrote that in the Chicago area and in Iowa the term *cock-cheese* is common, while Brett B. of South Carolina reported that he had heard for years the terms *dick-cheese* and *cunt-cheese* (for my coinage *clit-cheese*), adding, "I guess you don't hang out at the same bus station that I do." These are genuine, actual terms, whereas John H. of Seattle facetiously suggested *Monterey Jock* and *Vulveta*. Another new term for *smegma clitoridis* is *clitty-litter*, circulating as a riddle.

Anna B. (Canada) sent an "Ask the Doctor" letter:

The question in my mind concerning smegma, after reading your enlightening piece on it, is this: Is this secretion of the sebaceous glands actually smegma when first secreted, or does it have to take some time to...er...ah...mature before it becomes "cheese-like & foul-smelling"? And if so, how *long* does it take? Is it possible to be smegma-free, e.g., if one bathes daily? Also, before reading your study, I understood smegma to be "left-over come that stuck in the folds of the penis."

My reply to Anna is as follows:

Dear Confused: I am neither a medical doctor nor Ann Landers, but here it comes. Some of your questions are answered on page 119, after my definition. Yes, it's always called *smegma*, whether it's the freshly excreted odor- and colorless kind or the aged *Liederkranz* variety. The time it takes to change from the former to the latter depends mainly on the temperature: in summer and in hot regions, it takes a day or less to mature; in winter and in cold zones, it takes several days. Further, warm, tight underwear speeds up the Limburgerizing of smegma, whereas boxer shorts or no undies retard the decay. And no, you can't be smegma-free, as smegma is produced continuously; but that's not a problem if you bathe before engaging in certain depraved acts. (Note, however, that Mr. Guralnik calls the first stage *sebum* and the second one *smegma*.) Last, the principal method of distinguishing between aged smegma and dried ejaculate is to smell that whitish stuff.

### REACTIONS TO *AARDVARK*

When I asked you to send me your off-the-cuff definition of *aardvark* (p. 111), I was not only curious about your attempts at defining but also about the quantity of responses I would get to future questionnaires. I received seven (out of many thousands of readers)...

- A small mammal native to Africa with a long snout and powerful front paws with which it digs for its principal food, termites. (Bob L., Baltimore)
- A four-legged mammal with a long snout used for routing out ants, its chief dietary source. (Marlene S., Chicago)
- An African marsupial with a scaly back and tail and a long snout. Also known as scaly anteater. (James F.-N., New York)

- A mammal about the size of a large dog. It has a spine that curves up, rather like a one-hump camel, and its head resembling a kangaroo's with large ears and a long/skinny snout. It's fur-covered, brown. Its feet are padded and have claws, not hooves. The tail is more an elongated tapering off of the body rather than a separate item such as a dog wags. (Anna B., Vancouver)
- From Dutch or similar language: earth-pig. A large, stout-bodied African mammal, sole member of the genus Orycteropus; ecological analog of anteaters and pangolins of American and Asian tropics, it opens ant and termite mounds and eats the inhabitants. (Chris Starr, zoologist, Philippines)
- An anteater which sounds funny. (Chris's wife)
- The name means "earth-pig." It's a kind of South African anteater. It isn't the same thing as an "aard-wolf," but I can't remember what exactly an "aard-wolf" is. (Agnes C., San Francisco)

### III. WHO CENSORS DICTIONARIES?

Some dictionary makers do censor their works, as seen in Nat Hentoff's "The Deflowering of *The American Heritage Dictionary*" (*Maledicta* 7, pp. 121-28). Thus I asked two editors about their policies, choosing the more liberal *Random House College Dictionary*, and *Webster's New World Dictionary*, whose editor is frequently questioned about the exclusion of "offensive words" in his dictionary.

Random House Editor in Chief, Stuart Berg Flexner, commented on the inclusion and labeling of offensive words in his dictionary as follows:

> Your planned comparison of the major college dictionaries and what "offensive" words they include, the labels, definitions, etymologies, etc., will be most interesting. Our general rule is to include such terms on the same basis as we do any others: if there are enough citations and other evidence, in they go. We label some of these words as *vulgar* and others as *offensive* and/or *derogatory* by which we mean that certain groups either take them to be offensive or that certain users purposely use them to be taken as derogatory (naturally, some terms are both *offensive* and *derogatory*). As you know, the problem with including such terms is that many of them are much more widely used orally than in writing, which means they

appear in citations less frequently than they otherwise should. However, we do try to collect oral citations, even though the very nature of oral citations means that they are less systematic than written ones. Another problem is that many of the offensive terms were banned from publications for so long that when one examines the written evidence it appears that they appeared much later in the language than they actually did, or it appears that they were much less popular during the earlier decades and centuries than they actually were.

The amazing thing is that our attitude towards specific "offensive" words, and specific sub-groups of them, keeps changing. For example, in the past we have labeled certain words for homosexuals, including such old ones as *pansy, fag*, etc., as *slang*; however, I am increasingly adding the label *derogatory* and/or *offensive* to such items, because for the last decade or so we have become aware just how offensive these words are to gays. In like manner, we are labeling some of the words referring to women which our previously more male-dominated society did not consider especially offensive, though perhaps women always did. Thus, we are slowly changing our labeling of such words as *broad* to show that it is more than slang, that it is considered offensive by a great many women.

Incidentally, your mention that when you first came to this country you kept hearing *fuck*, but couldn't find it in any dictionary, was interesting. The other evening I was on a train sitting next to two seemingly very well educated, very upper class Vietnamese who, according to what I could hear in my eavesdropping, seemed to have been in the United States for approximately six months. Much to my amusement, in their rather British accents and high-level vocabulary the words *shit, bull shit*, and *fuck* were heard frequently, and I had the very distinct impression that they didn't realize these English words were considered "offensive," and they probably would have been very embarrassed if told they were not perfectly acceptable standard terms.

David B. Guralnik of *Webster's New World Dictionary* (Simon & Schuster), submitted his personal explanation of why "certain words regarded, especially formerly, as taboo," are not in his dictionary:

I am unalterably opposed to any censorship imposed from above by government or by any self-appointed group seeking to effect such

governmental bans. The only form of censorship that I find acceptable is that which results from action by individuals in refusing to
purchase or patronize that which they find objectionable. If such
objections are sufficiently widespread, they will inevitably affect
commercial products to which they apply. If there were not enough
accepting readers of *Maledicta*, it would cease publication.

At the time the Second College Edition of *WNWD* was being
planned (January, 1963), the so-called obscene terms were not to
be found in any general dictionary, not even the 13-volume *Oxford
English Dictionary*. At the planning conference, attended by staff and
consultants from various college faculties, there was much discussion
about including these terms for the first time in any general dictionary. The decision concerning the inclusion or omission of those
terms was a difficult one to make. Until relatively recently they were
taboo in all publications, and the decision was made for the lexicographer by the law. It is easy to forget that not too many years
ago, Lenny Bruce went to jail for uttering just one of these words,
and in the confines of a night club at that. Even today, these terms
are still largely taboo in the major media — general newspapers,
radio, and television. And our citators have noted that in the past
few years, there has been a marked falloff in the appearance of these
words in print generally, possibly because of the influence of the
Moral Majority and other self-appointed censors. At the time that
we were confronted with our decision, the ban was even more
widespread.

The decision of the conferees, virtually unanimous, was that it
would be unwise at that juncture to invite the banning of the dictionary in many areas. It is more than possible that if the conference
had been held in 1973, rather than 1963, we would have come to
another decision. But that decision must await a total revision of
the dictionary. I have not found it necessary to sneak these terms
into our minor updatings, which focus on the inclusion of new
vocabulary.

I can assure you that no moral judgment went into our decision.
It was made on purely practical grounds, and I explain our reasons
candidly in my foreword to the dictionary. What real purpose would
have been served if the book had been banned from schools throughout the States of Texas, West Virginia, Louisiana, and elsewhere?
And I can assure you it would have been. It is not we who are
passing the moral judgments, but the society in which we circulate.
As it is, we are banned in some school systems anyhow because

we enter such "dirty words" as *slut, keister, shack up,* and the like. I must add that I have resisted all efforts to have us purge such terms from editions sold to such systems.

Having dealt with the "obscene" terms, the conference addressed itself to the inclusion of the vernacular terms used contemptuously for members of various racial and ethnic groups. Again — this time with less than unanimity but nevertheless a substantial majority — the conferees decided that we would be well within our lexicographical responsibilities in the difficult task of lexical selection to omit these terms of opprobrium that some of us view as the true obscenities. For one thing, during the period that our citation files were beginning to show increasing use of the formerly taboo terms, there was a marked decline in the occurrence in general media of the derogatory racial and ethnic terms. Perhaps our liberation from one set of taboos is resulting in the creation of another. Apparently we cannot do without some linguistic taboos. It would be an interesting development.

To sum up: *Webster's New World Dictionary* is not censored by any governmental power or by the administration of this company. The staff of the dictionary, however, arbitrarily determined not to include certain terms widely recognized as obscene. This decision was arrived at for two reasons: a) all our dictionaries are, in fact, abridged dictionaries whose word stock represents no more than a selection of vocabulary from the much larger body of English terms; b) the inclusion of these few terms in the dictionary could have resulted in the banning of the entire work in some schools, thereby negating the years of labor and scholarship that went into its preparation. The dictionary, as a record of usage, also necessarily reflects the prevailing social attitudes of the community that it serves.

Censorship of dictionaries and other books used in schools is, however, alive. This subject is too large and well-documented for us to go into; however, some comments about self-appointed censors are in order. The most notorious schoolbook smut-hunters are Norma and Mel Gabler of Longview, Texas. This shortsighted frump and her husband, a retired oil company clerk, have spent some 22 years scrutinizing dictionaries and textbooks for moral lapses and erosion of traditional values (*Time,* 23 August 1982, p. 47). Other censorship attempts are carried out by gormless school board members, and "concerned" parents and teachers. Evelyn Ching sent me some pages from *California English* (Jan.-Febr. 1980, pp. 4-5), from which the following paraphrased excerpts are taken:

> A high school teacher of business education at Palm Bay High School (Rockledge, Florida) charged that *The Random House Dictionary of the English Language* (College Edition) contains 23 "vulgarities." She filed a formal complaint with the school board...requesting that the dictionary not be used...[because it] could lead to widespread usage of these vulgarities by students... The superintendent's task force rejected her complaint: "This dictionary clearly labels the words slang or vulgar. The definitions are not sensationalized."
>
> The obscenity obliterators abhor words like **hot, horny** and **hooker.** They disapprove of **crocked, coke** and **clap. Across-the-board** leaves them aghast. Specific definitions of **deflower** and **bed** are on the list of "blatantly offensive language."
>
> In 1976, the school board removed the *American Heritage Dictionary* from classrooms in Anchorage, Alaska, after a group of parents complained about definitions of **ass, ball, bed, knocker, nut** and **tail.**
>
> In Cedar Lake, Indiana, several parents charged that "70 or 80" words in the *AHD* are obscene or otherwise inappropriate for high school students. The school board removed the dictionary. A school board member noted that "We're not a bunch of weirdo book burners out here, but we think this one [*AHD*] goes too far." The board later reconsidered and reinstated the dictionary.
>
> Twenty-four parents filed a complaint in Eldon, Missouri, that 39 words in the *AHD* are objectionable; the school board removed the dictionary from a junior high school.
>
> In 1976, Texas Education Commissioner Marlin Brockette stated that no works would be purchased that "present material which would cause embarrassing situations or interfere in the learning atmosphere in the classroom." By quoting this sub-section of the Texas textbook adaptation proclamation, he justified the removal from the purchase list in Texas of the *American Heritage Dictionary, Doubleday Dictionary, Random House Dictionary, Webster's New World Dictionary* (Student Edition), and *Webster's Seventh Collegiate Dictionary.*

The chairperson of a textbook committee of a prominent organization of women wrote this about *Webster's New World Dictionary*, which we know is among the cleanest available:

Reviewer is shocked that a supposedly reputable publisher would offer for adoption a book which is debasing the English language. Students need the basics rather than sub-standard language.

She listed the following twelve words as objectionable, giving her reasons: **across-the-board** (betting on horse racing in Texas is illegal), **attempt** (ties word into subject of murder), **banana republic** (insulting to Latins), **bawdy house** (unnecessary), **bed** (why is sexual intercourse mentioned?), **the big house** (slang—unnecessary), **brain** (definition denotes violence), **bucket** (slang: the buttocks), **clap**, sense 2 (refers to a brothel [claper] and gonorrhea: slang), **coke** (slang for cocaine), **crocked** (slang for intoxicated), **deflower** (to cause loss of virginity: slang?). Other words considered "blatantly offensive" are **bastard, easy rider, fag, fairy, gay, G-string, head** (as in *acidhead*), **john** (prostitute's customer), **lay, queer, shack, slut, tail** and **tail-end**.

Bruce Rodgers sent an article from the *San Francisco Chronicle* (26 Nov. 1981, p. 57) reporting that the Westminster (Colorado) Board of Education banned the *Dictionary of American Slang* from 21 elementary and junior high schools because of racial slurs and "gutter language," after the mother of an elementary school pupil complained that she found her son "chuckling over the dictionary." Board member Karen Scheuerman said, "It appears to me they have taken all the sexist slurs and put them in one place."

Book censorship extends into other fields as well, as reported by the Associated Press (*MJ*, 29 March 1985, Accent, p. 13). For example, the word **evolution** is a dirty word to peabrained fundamentalists. Three of 18 high school biology textbooks do not contain this word, and references to evolution and other scientific theories are watered down by publishers bowing to pressures from ultrafundamentalists.

## IV. COMPARISONS

The differences among the dictionaries quoted below are self-evident, thus need little commentary. The treatment of the same word by various dictionaries can be observed neatly in this arrangement, especially the varying number of definitions (senses) and the differences in labeling. One must bear in mind that the labels reflect changes over the years and editorial policy: the older **Dictionary of American Slang** labels *taboo* what the Australian **Macquarie** calls *colloquial*; not all *colloquial* mean the same; one dictionary's *slang* is another's *informal*; some are beginning to add *derogatory* or *offensive* to terms formerly just labeled *slang* or *colloquial*; some use *obscene* where *vulgar* would be more appropriate; **Webster's Ninth** seems inconsistent in its use of *often* vs. *usually considered obscene* and *obscene* vs. *vulgar*; some dictionaries suppress vulgar terms or ignore high-frequency non-vulgar words, e.g. *meathead*; some present terse definitions, others give examples (**Macquarie**), still others add encyclopedic information (**Slang & Euphemism**).

In most cases, additional but non-offensive definitions (senses) have been disregarded. All labels are shown in italics. Etymologies are noted only where disputed. Abbreviations used: *coll.* = colloquial, *esp.* = especially, *etym* = etymology.

The following abbreviated titles will be used throughout:

**AHD** = *The American Heritage Dictionary.* Second College Edition. Boston, 1982

**Chambers** = *Chambers 20th Century Dictionary.* New Edition. Edinburgh, 1983

**Collins** = *Collins Dictionary of the English Language.* London & Glasgow, 1982

**DAS** = *Dictionary of American Slang. With Supplement.* New York, 1967

**Gage** = *Gage Canadian Dictionary.* Toronto, 1984

**Longman** = *Longman Dictionary of the English Language.* Harlow, England, 1984

**Macquarie** = *The Macquarie Dictionary*. McMahons Point, Australia, 1982

**Oxford** = *The Concise Oxford Dictionary of Current English*. 6th ed. Oxford, England, 1980

**Random** = *The Random House College Dictionary*. Revised Edition. New York, 1982

**Slang** = *Slang and Euphemism*. Middle Village, N.Y., 1981

**WNW** = *Webster's New World Dictionary of the American Language*. Second College Edition. New York, 1982

**W9** = *Webster's Ninth New Collegiate Dictionary*. Springfield, Mass., 1983

## ARSE and ASS

Dictionaries other than American ones differentiate between the animal (*ass*) and the body part (*arse*). It is not always made clear whether the metaphorical/figurative usage applied to humans is derived from the animal or the body part. Here are listed all senses derived from the entries *arse* and *ass*.

### AHD
1: a vain, self-important, silly, or aggressively stupid person. 2: the buttocks. *Vulgar slang*. 3: the anus. *Vulgar*. 4: coitus. *Vulgar*.

### Chambers
*ass* a dull, stupid fellow.
*arse* the buttocks. *Now vulgar*.

### Collins
*ass* a foolish or ridiculously pompous person.
*ass/arse* 1: The usual U.S. word for arse. 2: sexual intercourse or a woman considered sexually (esp. in the phrase *piece of ass*). *U.S. slang, offensive*.
*arse (U.S. ass)* 1: the buttocks. *Taboo*. 2: the anus. *Taboo*. 3: a stupid person; fool. *Taboo*. 4: sexual intercourse. *Taboo. Slang*. 5: effrontery, cheek. *Taboo. Australian slang*. Also called *arsehole* (senses 2 and 3).

### DAS
1: a fool; a stupid or foolish person. *Coll*. 2: the rectum. *Taboo, coll*. 3: the buttocks. *Taboo, coll*. 4: the vagina; generally, the female function. *Taboo, coll*.

**Gage**
*ass* a silly or stupid person; fool.
*arse* 1: buttocks. *Vulgar slang.* 2: anus. *Vulgar slang.*

**Longman**
*ass* 1: a stupid, obstinate, or perverse person or thing.
*arse* 1a: the buttocks. *Vulgar.* 1b: (*arse, arsehole*) the anus. *Vulgar.*
2: (*arse, arsehole*) a foolish or stupid person. *Vulgar.*

**Macquarie**
*ass* 1: a fool; a blockhead. 2: arse. *U.S. coll.*
*arse* (all definitions *coll.*) 1: rump; bottom; buttocks; posterior.
2: a despised person. 3: impudence: *what arse!* 4: a woman considered as a sex object: *she's a nice bit of arse.*

Comments: This work also lists nine noun phrases with *arse*,
e.g., *up Cook's arse*, and others, e.g., *arse about, around*: to act like
a fool; waste time; *arse up*: to spoil; cause to fail.

**Oxford**
*ass* 1: stupid person. 2: arse. *Vulgar.* 3: fool about, around. *Slang.*
*arse* buttocks, rump. *Vulgar.*

**Random**
1: a fool; blockhead. 2a: the buttocks. *Slang.* 2b: the anus. *Slang.*
*Vulgar.* 2c: sexual intercourse. *Slang. Vulgar.*

**Slang**
1: the rectum, anus, or posteriors. 2: the female genitals; women
considered sexually. 3: a fool; an oaf.

**WNW**
1: a stupid or silly person; fool. 2: the buttocks: *A vulgar term.*
*Slang.*

**W9**
1: a stupid, obstinate, or perverse person. 2a: buttocks. *Often
considered vulgar.* 2b: anus. *Often considered vulgar.* 3: sexual intercourse. *Usually considered vulgar.* 4: used as a derogatory intensive
'fancy-ass'. Adj. or adv. combining form. *Often considered vulgar.*
5: a contemptible person 'smart-ass'. Noun combining form. *Often
considered vulgar.*

# ARSEHOLE and ASSHOLE

*No entry in* **AHD, Gage, Oxford, WNW**

### Chambers
*arsehole*, U.S *asshole* 1: the anus. *Vulgar.* 2: a worthless, contempt-ible, etc. person. *Vulgar slang.*

### Collins
*No separate entry, but listed under* arse

### DAS
a good friend (from *asshole buddy*). *Taboo.*

### Longman
*No separate entry, but listed under* arse

### Macquarie
*arsehole* (all definitions *coll.*) 1: the anus. 2a: a despised place: *this town is the arsehole of the universe.* 2b: a despised person. 3: com-pletely: *from arsehole to breakfast time.* 4: to remove a person from a place quickly and without ceremony; to throw someone out. 5: to dismiss, sack. 6: to fool around: *arsehole about.* 7: to depart quickly or unobtrusively: *arsehole off.* 8: arse holes. *Interjection* (an exclamation of disgust or disbelief).

### Random
1: the anus. *Slang, vulgar.* 2: a mean or contemptible person or thing. *Slang, vulgar.*

### Slang
1: the anus. 2: bad; rotten. 3: a contemptible person. *Slang.* 4: a very good pal or buddy (ass-hole friend, ass-hole buddy).

### W9
1: anus. *Usually considered vulgar.* 2: a stupid, incompetent, or detestable person. *Usually considered vulgar.*

    *Comments:* First recorded in 1951, according to this dictionary. But see Allen Walker Read, *Classic American Graffiti*, p. 32, dating *arce-hoole* about 1400 (MS Harl. 1002), as printed in Thomas Wright's *A Volume of Vocabularies* (1857), p. 183.

# BLABBERMOUTH

*No entry in* **Oxford, Slang**

## AHD
one who chatters indiscreetly and at length. *Slang.*

    *Comments*: Wrong. A *blabbermouth* can tell a secret without chattering at length. Definition should use *or* instead of *and*.

## Chambers
*No separate entry, but listed without definition or label under* blab: to talk much; to tell tales; to let out (a secret).

## Collins
a person who talks too much or indiscreetly. *Informal.*

## DAS
one who talks too much or reveals secrets. *Coll.*

## Gage
a person who talks too much, especially one who reveals secrets. *Informal.*

## Longman
*No separate entry, but listed under* blabber: one who talks too much or indiscreetly. *Informal.*

## Macquarie
one who talks too much or who talks indiscreetly. *Coll.*

## Random
a person who talks too much, esp. indiscreetly. (No label).

## WNW
a person who blabs. *Coll.*

## W9
one who talks too much; esp. *tattletale.* (No label).

# BULLSHIT

*No entry in* **AHD, Gage, WNW**

### Chambers
1: nonsense (all definitions labeled *slang*). 2: deceptive humbug.
3: to talk nonsense (to), often with the intention of deceiving.

### Collins
1: exaggerated or foolish talk; nonsense (all definitions labeled
*taboo slang*). 2: exaggerated zeal, esp. for ceremonial drill, cleaning, polishing, etc. Usually shortened to *bull. British Army.* 3:
to talk in an exaggerated or foolish manner.
*Comments*: This work also lists *bullshitter.*

### DAS
1: anything that is distasteful, useless, or unnecessary (all definitions labeled *taboo*). 2: insincerity, lies, exaggeration. 3: menial
tasks or jobs. 4: to speak or write insincerely or with exaggeration;
to brag; to speak idly, without thought; to pass the time by talking; to gossip. 5: an expletive showing incredulity and contempt.
*Comments*: This work also lists *bullshitter, bullshit artist.*

### Longman
1: foolish or empty talk; nonsense (all definitions labeled *slang*).
2: to talk loudly or confidently about something of which one
has no knowledge. 3: to try to deceive or impress by bullshitting.
*Comments*: In definition (3), Quain[t] Professor Randolph
Quirk's favorite dictionary violates two basic rules of defining
(according to Ladislav Zgusta): "The defined word may not be
used in its definition" and "Avoid circularity."

### Macquarie
1: the excrement of bulls. 2: nonsense. *Coll.* 3: to deceive; outwit.
*Coll.* 4: an expression of disgust, disbelief, etc. *Interjection. Coll.*
*Comments*: This work also lists *bullshit artist.* This is the only
dictionary showing the literal meaning (1) which, however, is
not labeled *colloquial.*

## Oxford
1: nonsense; bull (sense 6). *Vulgar.* 2: bull (sense 6): unnecessary routine tasks or discipline; nonsense; trivial or insincere talk or writing. *Slang.* 3: bull (sense 6): bad blunder. *Chiefly U.S., often also Canadian, Australian, etc. Slang.*

*Etym*: From (*Irish*) *bull*, expression containing contradiction in terms or implying ludicrous inconsistency.

## Random
1: nonsense, lies, or exaggeration. *Slang, vulgar.* 2: used to express disagreement, disapproval, or the like. *Interjection.*

## Slang
1: nonsense. 2: to utter nonsense; to lie or deceive.

*Comments*: This work also lists *bullshit artist, bullshitter.*

## W9
1: nonsense; esp. foolish insolent talk (all labeled *usually considered vulgar*). 2: to talk foolishly, boastfully, or idly. 3: to engage in a discursive discussion. 4: to talk nonsense to esp. with the intention of deceiving or misleading.

*Comments*: According to this work, the noun was first recorded in 1915, the verb in 1942.

## CRIPPLE

*No entry in* **DAS, Slang**

## AHD
one who is partly disabled or lame.

## Chambers
a lame person.

## Collins
1: a person who is lame. 2: a person who is or seems disabled or deficient in some way: *a mental cripple.*

## Gage
a person or animal that is partly disabled, especially one that is lame.

**Longman**
1: a lame or partly disabled person or animal. 2: a person who is deficient in a specified way 'an emotional cripple'.

**Macquarie**
one who is partially or wholly deprived of the use of one or more of his limbs; a lame person.

*Comments*: This dictionary defines a crippled animal separately; it also defines *emotional cripple*.

**Oxford**
(permanently) lame person.

**Random**
1: a lame person or animal. 2: a person who is disabled in any way: *a mental cripple*.

**WNW**
a person or animal that is lame or otherwise disabled in a way that prevents normal motion of the limbs or body.

**W9**
1: a lame or partly disabled person or animal. 2: something flawed or imperfect.

**Note**: For more information on this word, see my "James Watt's *Cripple*" in this volume.


## CUNT

Note the variety of definitions for the same thing: *female genitals, genital organs, genitalia, pudendum, pudenda*. Also note the feminists' influence in several dictionaries now featuring the modern-thinking addition, "woman considered as a sexual object." In the definitions of *prick*, however, one does not find the equivalent, "man considered as a sexual object."

*No entry in* **Gage, WNW**

## AHD
1: the female genital organs. *Obscene*. 2: a woman. *Obscene*.
*Etym*: Middle English *cunte*.

## Chambers
1: the female genitalia. *Vulgar*. 2: a term of abuse. *Vulgar*.
*Comments*: *A term of abuse* and similar "definitions" one finds in English and foreign dictionaries are useless. What does it mean?
*Etym*: Middle English *cunte*. Etymology doubtful.

## Collins
1: the female genitals. *Taboo slang*. 2: a woman considered sexually. *Taboo slang. Offensive*. 3: a mean or obnoxious person. *Taboo slang. Offensive*.
*Etym*: 13th cent. Of Germanic origin; related to Old Norse *kunta*, Middle Low German *kunte*.

## DAS
a girl or woman. [May apply to a sexually attractive girl or a mean old woman]. *Taboo*.
*Etym*: Not given.

## Longman
1: the female genitals (all definitions labeled *vulgar*). 2: a woman regarded as a sexual object; *also* sexual intercourse with a woman. 3: an offensive or unpleasant person. *British*.
*Etym*: Middle English *cunte*; akin to Middle Low German *kunte* female genitals, Middle High German *kotze* prostitute.

## Macquarie
1: the female pudendum (all definitions labeled *coll.*). 2: woman considered as a sexual object. 3: any person. *Derogatory*. 4: sexual intercourse.
*Comments*: This work also lists a related term: *cunthook*, an unpleasant or despicable man. *New Zealand, coll., derogatory*.
*Etym*: Not given.

## Oxford
1: female genitals. *Vulgar*. 2: person, esp. woman. *Vulgar. Derogatory*.
*Etym*: Old Norse *kunta*. Germanic *\*kunton*.

**Random**

1: the vagina (all definitions labeled *slang, usually vulgar*). 2: a woman, esp. as an object of sex. 3: sexual intercourse.

*Comments*: Not only the *vagina* but also the *vulva*. About this widespread confusion see Mildred Ash, "The Vulva: A Psycholinguistic Problem," *Maledicta* 4:213-19.

*Etym*: Middle English *cunte*; cognate with Old Norse *kunta*, Old Frisian *kunte*; cf. Latin *cunnus*, Greek *kusthos*.

**Slang**

1: the female genitals, specifically the vagina. 2: women considered sexually. 3: copulation [followed by encyclopedic information, here deleted]. 4: a rotten fellow; a low, slimy man. *Coll.* 5: to intromit the penis.

*Comments*: The author claims in def. (3) that *cunt* "is the most elaborately avoided word in the English language." I don't think so; *cocksucker* and *motherfucker* have a higher taboo rating and are at least as shunned as *cunt*.

*Etym*: Said to be from Latin *cunnus*.

**W9**

the female pudenda; *also*, coitus with a woman. *Usually considered obscene*.

*Etym*: Middle English *cunte*; akin to Middle Low German *kunte* female pudenda, Middle High German *kotze* prostitute; akin to Old English *cot* den. 14th cent.

**Classic American Graffiti**

1: the vagina. 2: the male genitals. 3: almost any disliked object, occasion, or person. (The author quotes Grose: "A nasty name for a nasty thing.")

## DILDO

The etymology of *dildo* remains unknown. It has been suggested that it derives from Italian *diletto*, "delight," but the sound changes bother me. Semantically, *diletto* fits well; note another word for this delightful instrument, *godemiché*, said to be derived from Latin *gaude mihi!*, a command meaning "Please me!" or "Make me happy!" [Translation from Prof. Salemi].

Merritt Clifton, editor of *Samisdat* magazine, sent a copy of *Format* (vol. 5, no. 4, 1984), where he reports on pages 11-13 about the Québec professor Suzanne X., a feminist who is "the world's foremost collector and chronicler" of dildos.

## AHD
an object used as a substitute for an erect penis.
*Etym*: Origin unknown.

## Chambers
1: an object serving as an erect penis substitute. *Slang*. 2: a weak or effeminate man. *Obsolete*.
*Comments*: This work also lists other meanings: *word used in refrains of songs; a cylindrical curl; a West Indian spiny cactus*.
*Etym*: Origin uncertain.

## Collins
an object used as a substitute for an erect penis.
*Etym*: 17th cent. Of unknown origin.

## DAS
1: an artificial device resembling an erect penis, used by female homosexuals. *Taboo. Not common*. 2: a foolish, stupid person; a prick. *Common among boys between 10 and 14 who do not know the primary meaning of the term*.
*Comments*: The limitation of use to *homosexual* women is wrong; dildos are used by all kinds of women. Also, the alleged common use of the word by boys may be disputable.
*Etym*: Not given.

## Gage
a device shaped like an erect penis, used for sexual stimulation.
*Etym*: Unknown origin. 17 cent.

## Longman
an object serving as an artificial penis for inserting into the vagina.
*Comments*: Sir Randolph Quirk's favorite dictionary slipped up again: the information "for inserting into the vagina" is

superfluous. (It is even wrong; godnose into what other orifices some lonely fellows, such as passé poets & family newspaper editors, may insert it.) *Longman* used and reworded *Webster's* definition (see **W9**, below; only these two works contain the vaginal insertion information). *Longman* used Merriam-Webster's files, and M-W holds the copyright.

*Etym*: Perhaps modification of the Italian *diletto* delight.

**Macquarie**
an artificial erect penis.
*Etym*: Not given.

**Oxford**
artificial penis used by women for sexual pleasure.
*Comments*: This edition does not list the meaning "effeminate male," as does its source, the big *Oxford English Dictionary*, which in vol. III, p. 362, has a citation: "O thou faint-hearted dildo!"
*Etym*: 17th cent. Origin unknown.

**Random**
an artificial erect penis.
*Etym*: Origin unknown.

**Slang**
1: to arouse a woman sexually by fondling her sexual parts. *British, 1600s-1700s*. 2: an artificial penis made of various substances (e.g., wax, leather, horn) and used by women to obtain sexual gratification. It can be fastened to the body of a female homosexual who then functions as a male. They have occasionally been equipped with ribs and other appendages to heighten their effectiveness. 3: the penis. 4: an oaf or jerk. 5: an effeminate male.

*Comments*: Inappropriate, excessive, encyclopedic information given in definition (2). Why not go on describing its use in the harem, the use of candles, bottles, sausages, zucchini? Or the motorized versions, the deluxe liquid-squirting models, etc? Again, women who use dildos need not be homosexuals; and dildos can also be fastened to males, chairs, washing machines, etc.

*Etym*: Not given.

**WNW**
a device of rubber, etc., shaped like an erect penis and used as a sexual stimulator.
*Etym*: Perhaps from Italian *diletto*, delight.

**W9**
an object serving as a penis substitute for vaginal insertion.
*Etym*: Origin unknown. Dated 1598.

## MEATHEAD
*No entry in* **AHD, Chambers, Collins, Gage, Longman, Oxford, W9**

**DAS**
a stupid person. [Dated 1949]

**Macquarie**
a stupid person. *Chiefly U.S.* [Spelled *meat-head*].

**Random**
blockhead; dunce; fool. *Slang.*

**Slang**
an oaf; the same as *beef-head. U.S. coll.*

**WNW**
a stupid person; blockhead. *Slang. Americanism.*

## MERKIN
In Stanley Kubrick's movie *Dr. Strangelove* (1964), Peter Sellers plays three characters: *Mandrake, Strangelove* and *Merkin Muffley*. Few viewers are aware of the bawdy meanings of these names: *mandrake* means "sodomite", "bugger" (in the legal sense; Partridge); it is also a phallic, man-shaped root formerly used to promote conception or as a love potion. Dr. Peter Metzger informed me that the real (German) name of *Dr. Strangelove*, mentioned in the movie, sounds like *Merkwürdige Liebe*, which could be an allusion

to *merkin*. A *merkin* is a pubic wig for women. *Muff* means "vulva, esp. when covered with much pubic hair" (Wentworth & Flexner); cf. *muff-diver* "cunnilinguist." And *Muffley* could be interpreted as "muff-lay," if you are so inclined.

G. Legman's *The Limerick* lists *merkin* in the index, but No. 1318 does not contain the word. In 1982, Drew Downey composed the following limerick, the only one known to me containing the word *merkin*:

> **There once was a lady named Durkin,**
> **Who wore a removable merkin.**
> **Preparing to shunt,**
> **She'd de-fur her cunt,**
> **To minimize friction from firkin'.**

Elizabeth C., New Jersey, reported *moxie* as a local term for *merkin*. Her brother-in-law described it as "a wig for a bald-headed cunt."

And who could forget President Lyndon B. Johnson, who used to begin his speeches with "Mah Fella Merkins"?

For a detailed treatise of this word, see Roger Phillips's "All About Merkins" in this volume.

*No entry in* **AHD, DAS, Gage, Longman, Macquarie, Oxford, Random, WNW, W9**

**Chambers**
a hairpiece for the pubic area.
  *Etym*: Origin unknown.

**Collins**
1: an artificial hairpiece for the pudendum; a pubic wig. 2: the pudendum itself. *Obsolete.*
  *Etym*: 16th cent. Of unknown origin.

**Slang**
1: the female genitals. *British.* 2: the female pubic hair. 3: false female pubic hair. *British.*
  *Etym*: Not given.

# PRICK

**AHD**
1: the penis. *Vulgar slang.* 2: a highly unpleasant person. *Vulgar slang.*

**Chambers**
a penis. *Vulgar.*

**Collins**
1: a taboo slang word for *penis.* 2: an obnoxious or despicable person. *Slang. Derogatory.*

**DAS**
1: the penis. *Taboo.* 2: a smug, foolish person; a knave, blackguard; a heel, a rat.

**Gage**
*Does not list any vulgar, offensive meaning.*

**Longman**
1: the penis. *Vulgar.* 2: a disagreeable or contemptible person. *Vulgar.*

**Macquarie**
1: the penis. *Coll.* 2: an unpleasant or despicable person.

**Oxford**
1: penis. *Vulgar.* 2: man. *Slang, derogatory.*

**Random**
1: the penis. *Slang, vulgar.* 2: an obnoxious man; cad. *Slang, vulgar.*

**Slang**
1: the penis; the erect penis. 2: an oaf; an offensive male. *U.S. slang.* 3: a hard taskmaster. *U.S. slang.*

**WNW**
*Does not list any vulgar, offensive meaning. See, however, the etymology of* **perique** *for* prick, *vulgar for "penis."*

**W9**
1: penis. *Usually considered vulgar.* 2: a spiteful or contemptible person often having some authority. *Usually considered vulgar.*

# SLOB

Many of us use this common term, but if the dictionaries are any indication, everyone seems to have a different idea of what exactly a **slob** is. To my mind, a **slob** is a person who is careless, sloppy as to his or her body, clothes, work, or conduct; *in addition*, he or she may be very fat. But a **slob** need not at all be fat, stupid, clumsy, obnoxious, crude, uncouth, rude, boorish, etc.

## AHD
an obnoxious, crude, or slovenly person. *Informal.*

## Chambers
1: a sloven. 2: a boor. *Slang.* 3: a person of wealth but no refinement. *Slang.*

## Collins
a stupid or coarse person. *Slang.*

## DAS
1: a fat or ungainly person, esp. one of unattractive or untidy appearance. 2: a hopelessly ineffectual person. 3: an untalented, congenitally average person; any common man whose chance of happiness or success is no better than another's.

*Comments*: Definition (1) is influenced by the standard collocation **fat slob**; a slob need not be fat. Defs. (2) and (3) are not good; they mean about the same and are influenced by the standard collocation **poor slob** (a person we pity).

*Etym*: From *sloppy*. All other dictionaries derive it from Irish Gaelic *slab*, mud.

## Gage
an untidy or boorish person.

## Longman
a slovenly or uncouth person. *Informal.*

## Macquarie
a stupid, clumsy, uncouth, or slovenly person. *Coll.*

**Oxford**
stupid or careless person.

**Random**
a clumsy, slovenly, or boorish person. *Slang.*

**Slang**
a rude, fat, and unpleasant person. *Slang and coll.*

**WNW**
a sloppy, coarse, or gross person. *Coll.*

**W9**
a slovenly or boorish person.


# WIMP

*No entry in* **Collins, Gage, Longman, Macquarie, Oxford, Random**


**AHD**
a person who is weak or ineffectual. *Slang.*
   *Etym*: Origin unknown.

**Chambers**
1: an ineffectual person. *Slang.* 2: a young girl. *Old.*
   *Etym*: Origin obscure.

**DAS**
1: an introverted, boring, overly solicitous person. 2: a meek, passive person. 3: one who is out of touch with current ideas, trends, fads, etc. 4: a "drip" or "mince." *Some teenage and student use.*
   *Comments*: Definition (3) is now wrong. See also John Leo's quotation in my "Wimp" article.
   *Etym*: Not given.

**Slang**
a spineless, whimpering, undesirable person. *U.S. slang. Mid 1900s*-present. Also *whimp.*
   *Etym*: Not given.

## WNW

a weak, ineffectual, or insipid person. *Americanism. Slang.* Adj. *wimpy.*

    *Etym*: Origin unknown.

## W9

a weak or ineffectual person. [Dated ca. 1963]

    *Etym*: Perhaps from British *wimp* girl, woman, of unknown origin.

## The Second Barnhart Dictionary of New English (1980):

an unathletic or unaggressive person, often considered a weakling or sissy.

    *Etym*: Probably short for *Wimpy*, a fat character forever eating in the comic strip "Popeye," created in 1929 by Elzie Segar. Dated 1959.

**Note**: For many citations of this word, see my "Wimp" article in this volume.


## YENTE

All dictionaries except **WNW** use the transliteration *yenta* only, which is wrong and responsible for the common mispronunciation "yentah." The final sound is a *schwa*, not an *ah*. This word must be spelled *yente*.

*No entry in* **Chambers, Collins, Gage, Longman, Macquarie, Oxford, Random**

## AHD

a gossipy woman, esp. one who pries into the affairs of others. *Slang.*

    *Etym*: Yiddish *yente*, from the name Yente.

## DAS

a talkative or gossipy woman.

    *Etym*: From the Yiddish.

## Slang

a gossip or a shrew, usually a woman.

    *Etym*: Not given.

**WNW**

*yenta, yente*: a woman gossip or busybody. *Yiddish.*
Etym: Not given.

**W9**

one that meddles; *also*, blabbermouth, gossip.
Etym: Yiddish *yente* vulgar woman, probably from the name
Yente.

*Definitions from various sources in my files:*
1: a woman of low origins or vulgar manner; a shrew; a shallow,
coarse termagant. 2: a gossipy woman; scandal-spreader; rumor
monger; one unable to keep a secret or respect confidence;
blabbermouth. 3: gossip, busybody. 4: vulgar, sentimental
woman. 5: gossip, hag, nag, "washerwoman." 6: coarse, loud-
mouthed female; female blabbermouth; gaggy, talkative woman.
Etym: Leo Rosten, *Joys of Yiddish*, was told it is derived from
a lady's name, from Italian *gentile*.

B.C.

# YOUR MOTHER HAS YAWS
## VERBAL ABUSE AT ULITHI

## Norman Cubberly

Ulithi is a coral atoll at 10° North and 140° East, the same longitude as Tokyo and about 400 miles southwest of Guam. The small population, between 500 and 1000 persons, is of the mixed ethnic stock loosely termed Micronesian. It is a so-called "native paradise" with a tropical trade-wind climate, little clothing worn, and large sailing canoes still hewn from logs and used for trading with nearby islands. In short, the basic stuff of dreams to a western culture.

Ulithi was well known in World War II as the staging area for the Okinawa campaign. The largest battle fleet ever seen was assembled in the atoll's immense 183-square-mile lagoon. This lagoon is surrounded by 43 islets, or *motus*, on a necklace of coral. They total exactly one per cent of the area of the lagoon. When I was stationed there as commanding officer of a U.S. Coast Guard Loran station in 1956-57, the island was still recovering from the vicissitudes of war.

The population had gone through many metamorphoses. The island had, in turn, been part of the Yap Empire, the Spanish, German and Japanese occupations, and was then a part of the U.S. Trust Territory of the Pacific Islands. These occupations, however mild, had made the population skeptical of western ways. Ulithians were nominally Roman Catholic and had a part-time Jesuit mission, but in general they had a casual attitude toward religion.

When a subsistence culture is packed ultimately into 1000-plus people per square mile, there seem to be only two ways to avoid self-destruction: ceremonial aggression as practiced by the Yapese, or total pacifism. Ulithi had

154

chosen extreme non-violence. A blow was never struck. Children were not spanked. The society, basically matriarchal, used extreme forms of social pressure to further its existence. Among these methods were verbal and visual aggression. These forms of combat were strictly, joyfully, and reasonably enforced.

Should a middle-aged husband start taking up with young girls, his mother, or perhaps an aunt, would secretly work up and practice a song-and-dance routine called *hamath*. She would gather as many women as possible into the performance, delightedly using as many of the "victims" as possible. At the next large social gathering, they would minutely describe his outsized sexual parts, his singed pubic hair, his worn-off tattooing, and anything else they could get on him. Firsthand, lurid, graphic accounts were preferred.

The much-embarrassed male would have to find the author of the *hamath* and stage a rebuttal at the first opportunity. If he could not track her down, he could abuse women in general. This whole sequence went on and on to the great delight of all.

The *hamath*, and other less heartrending pressures, were used to enforce the many taboos worked out over the years to prevent disasters like overpopulation. With a natural limit of about 1800 persons, Ulithi preserved the maintenance level of one child per couple every five years by abstinence alone.

It seems the average child can swim underwater at about the age of five. Success at this venture meant that the parents could take wholeheartedly to sex again. An impartial (?) aunt or uncle would signal success at the child's ability to swim by shaving its head. Since there is far more water than land to Ulithi, it is obvious that the swimming lessons are meant to save the child from disaster. Enthusiastic commentary from bystanders indicate some self-interest.

To prevent a seriously ingrown population, brothers, sisters, and near-cousins would be segregated at puberty. Here too, *hamath* was the general leavener. A good time was had by all, and the guilty suffered.

An example of visual aggression was the use of dark red, *cha*, the color of blood — but more important — the color of the vulva. Dark red flowers dropped in front of someone, or a wreath of that color tossed on the head, was a marked insult. Alternately, an individual might wear such a wreath to indicate a grudge at the world. Subtle variations were numerous.

Any wreath worn on the head was a signal, depending on the angle:

Square on the head : *I am wearing a wreath.*
Over the eyes : *Don't speak to me.*
High on the forehead : *Let's be social.*
Over the left eye : *I desire a life mate.*
Over the right eye : *I want a piece of ass.*

There were many variations, but in the case of the latter two, any smile in return by a member of the opposite sex was a contract if the wearer returned it. Naturally, if boy seeks girl, she will be the last to smile. Every old hag in the village, however, doesn't hesitate. If the wreath wearer smiles back, everyone cracks up.

To the Ulithian, variations of visual and verbal aggression are endless. They constantly invent new ones. The language, a variant of Yapese, is highly inflected and full of such traps as glottal stops and significant pauses. A slight change of pitch can change a word from actively hostile to mildly playful.

An error in pronunciation by an outsider could cause enormous glee. When people sailed across the lagoon to ask you to pronounce a word, it was wise to ask them why. Myself, the local Jesuit, and petty authority from the Trust

Territory were shown amused tolerance face-to-face. The real howlers were passed along.

In one case, the delight was so great that it lasted many years. Our poor missionary never did find out that his church on Falalop and the menstrual (blood) hut were the only two buildings parallel to the beach. Everything else faced it. In one case taboo and custom reigned; in the other, amused tolerance.

Although I heard many choice Ulithian phrases of combat, I retain most of them only as dim phonetic memories. The following short list is from *The Ethnography of Ulithi* by William A. Lessa,* who passed through a few years before I did.

**böriel silömi**   Your mother's asshole!

**buthokh hang löl mele börie**   Come eat my ass!

**bwel silöm**   Your mother's hole!

**bwosul silöm**   Your mother's pubic area!

**ei! homa waswu's**   Hey! Sisterfucker!

**fälfúlul silöm**   Your mother's pubic tattooing!

**firel silöm**   Your mother's labia minora!

**hola bocha meleue silöm**   Go eat your mother!

**hola feia mwangom**   Go fuck your sister!

**hola feia silöm**   Go fuck your mother!

**lisel silöm**   Your mother's cunt!

**lol le metal silöm**   Inside your mother's eye!

**löl lïpich**   Bastard! (Never said to a real one.)

**melewe silöm we ie maragus**   Your mother has yaws!

**melewe silöm we itefatngakh**   Your mother fucks around!

**mwasal silöm**   Rottenness from your mother!

**silöm**   Your mother!

**telekhel silöm**   Your mother's clitoris!

**túwethel silöm**   Your mother's ass!

---

*William A. Lessa. 1950. *The Ethnography of Ulithi*. University of California Press.

# GAY, GEI, HOMO, AND HOMOSEKSUAALI IN FINNISH

## Joel A. Nevis

English is not the only language in which people argue over the use of words like *gay, homosexual*, and *lesbian*. Very few languages even have a positive (or neutral) term like English *gay*. Many languages—German, French, Swedish, Finnish, and (according to John Boswell*), Dutch, Danish, Japanese, and Catalan—have borrowed this word in one form or another. Borrowings of *lesbian* and neo-Greco-Latin *homosexual* are still more common in the languages of the world.

Finnish has borrowed both **gay** and **homoseksuaali**, and although both terms are rival words in the gay community in Helsinki, the argument takes a different form from that of English. **Homo** is preferred over both **gay** and **homoseksuaali**, and the use of these terms in Finnish differs significantly from their use in English.

The word **gay** does not quite sound natural to a Finn. Linguistically it does not fit the language. First of all, there is no *g* in native Finnish words, so the use of this sound marks it as foreign. (Finns typically substitute *k* for *g* in pronunciation.) Second, the spelling of the vowel(s) *ay* is odd—the sounds *a* and *y* never appear in the same stem in Finnish as a result of vowel harmony. The pronunciation of the diphthong, however, is fine; in fact, the word is often spelled **gei** in accordance with the phonemic writing system of the language. Third, **gay** or **gei** is an awkward stem at

---

*Christianity, Social Tolerance, and Homosexuality* (Chicago: University of Chicago Press, 1980), p. 41, footnote 1.

best in Finnish—there are very few monosyllabic stems in the language, the preference being for polysyllabicity. Finally, the word **gay** fails to inflect for case and number, which is demanded of any regular noun and adjective in Finnish. Instead, the word must be used as a noun in the first part of a compound so that the last member can be inflected. For example, the phrase **iloisia gay-ruotsalaisia** 'happy gay Swedes' has an adjective *iloisia* (from *iloinen*) and a noun *ruotsalaisia* (*ruotsalainen*), both in the partitive plural. But **gay**, having no inflections, is compounded with *ruotsalainen* 'Swede.'

For these four reasons the word **gay** has an awkward ring to it. And since a native gay Finn, I assume, does not want to appear foreign in her/his own country and language, it is not favored. **Gay** is used nevertheless, because of the prestige of its English background, English being the current international language, especially among the western-oriented youth. Influence also comes from the active gay movement in the United States, standing in a way as a model for many European gay communities. Northern Europe is at least as active as the U.S., but the vocabularies of the languages in the area have yet to produce a suitable counterpart to English *gay*. It should be noted further that the semantics of Finnish **gay** and **gei** are slightly different from its English source word; it evokes an image of sex and western sexual imports (sex toys, bathes, etc.), rather than the positive image of pride found in English.

In Finnish the rival to **gay** is **homo**. As recent loanwords, the terms **homoseksuaali**, its clipping **homo**, and its derivatives (e.g. **homoseksuaalisuus** 'homosexuality,' etc.) lack the negative connotations that they have in English. The longer **homoseksuaali** does sound, as in English, rather clinical and too long for everyday use. But the shorter form **homo** sounds Finnish enough. It has native sounds and spelling; it has two syllables—typical of many Finnish stems; and it can be inflected (*homo, homot, homon, homojen, homoa, homoja, homoon, homoihin*, etc). Like **gay** and **gei**, the word **homo** is used as a noun. As an attribute to another noun it must appear in compounds rather than as an adjective (e.g. **homopappi** 'gay priest'). Indicative of the preference for **homo** over **gay** is its use in unclassified ads (often shortened to **h**): **h-poika** 'gay boy,' **h-mies** 'gay man' and **h-pari** 'gay couple.'

One native term in Finnish is **hintti** 'faggot.' This slang word has negative connotations for the general public, and even in the gay community is restricted in reference to males. Another word unfamiliar to English speakers is **setalainen**. Ostensibly it refers to anyone (or anything) having to do with the organization SETA (*Seksuaalinen tasavertaisuus ry* = The Group for Sexual Equality). But, it now has the additional meaning of someone having the opinion that gay people deserve equal rights. One SETA activist recalls an older man using the term **esisetalainen** '*pre-setalainen*' or roughly "pre-Stonewall." The Stonewall analogy is especially apt here.

In Finnish one finds also **hetero(seksuaali)** and **bi(seksuaali)**, though the latter shortening, **bi-**, is as awkward as **gay** in the minds and mouths of Finns, and is similarly restricted to compounds such as **bi-poika** 'bi(sexual) boy.' The term for *lesbian* is **lesbo** (or even **lesbolainen**), and this term, from a brief look at publications and graffiti, appears rather common.

In their concerns over the correct use of language, English speakers have it easy in comparison to speakers of a language like Finnish which also has the added dimension of foreign vs. native.

# WRESTLING WITH THE TRUTH
## WHAT NEWSPAPERS DON'T REPORT

## Reinhold Aman

Professional wrestler Kenneth Patera, on his way to his Waukesha motel on the night of 5 April 1984, wanted to get something to eat at McDonald's restaurant. As the restaurant had already been closed for the night, an employee refused to serve Patera. The world champion wrestler became angry, allegedly made an obscene gesture (finger) at the employee, and allegedly threw a 30-pound rock through the drive-through window of McDonald's. Short time later, three Waukesha police officers went to the motel to question him and his fellow wrestler, Japanese Olympic champion Masanori Saito. Saito, apparently unaware of what Patera had done, and clothed in his underpants only, was not cooperative. The police overreacted and sprayed the wrestlers with Mace and beat them with their nightsticks. Now the wrestlers got angry, threw the police officers against the walls, knocked them to the floor, used headlocks and knee-drops, smashed their faces, and broke a leg. The worst hurt was a 19-year-old, 130-pound female rookie, a "girl officer" who (while doing her thing for women's equal rights) suffered chipped teeth, a concussion, and a ruptured appendix. After ten more officers arrived, the wrestlers stopped bashing the police.

At the trial (May-June 1985), Patera claimed that he did not make an obscene gesture but merely said, "Screw it" to the employee, threw up his arm, and left. He also denied having thrown the rock, claiming that some fellow came up from behind who said, "These guys are a bunch of [assholes]," then threw the rock. *WF* reporter John Schroeder and *MJ* reporter Robert Riepenhoff confirmed that the deleted word "..." and "........" respectively, as printed in the newspapers, was *assholes*. Riepenhoff, who covered the trial, also informed me of other deletions in the newspaper stories, shown here in brackets: The McDonald's employee testified that Patera had told him, after having been refused service, "I'm going to throw a [fucking] rock through your window." Later, the wrestler, annoyed by an officer's questioning about the rock-throwing, testified: "I told him if he wanted to know anything further about it [he could shove the rock up his ass] and go get a warrant." (*WF,* 3 June 1985, pp. 1-2; *MJ,* 29 May, 3 and 4 June 1985, all pt. 2, pp. 1-2).

The wrestlers were sentenced to two years in prison and six years of probation.

*Funny footnote:* Saito had used a Japanese-English interpreter during the trial, giving the impression that he didn't know English. When the jail nurse and doctor came to his cell to perform a routine examination, the nurse — in a "You Tarzan, me Jane" style of communication — said very slowly to the Japanese wrestler, "I am nurse, nurse," while pointing repeatedly to the name tag on her uniform. Saito grunted to show that he understood. Then the doctor said, "I am doctor, doctor. Do you have any pain, pain?" and patted his chest to indicate where pain might occur. The puzzled-looking Saito responded in relatively good English, "Yes, the cartilage in my leg is sore." (*MJ,* 17 June 1985, pt. 2, p. 2).

# THE GOLD-DUST TWINS
# OF MARGINAL HUMOR
## BLACKS AND JEWS

## Joseph Dorinson

A young black, riding on the subway, looks at a Yiddish newspaper. An old Jew approaches and asks: "Du bist a Yid?" (You're a Jew?) The black replies: "Man, I have enough *tsores* (troubles) being a *shvartser.*" (black). Trouble has indeed linked the two groups, the ultimate "odd couple" in American popular culture. Deep are the roots of prejudice. Jews are demeaned, Hurwitz points out, in the Oxford dictionary. The Bible sanctions racial pejoratives. "Black-boy" vies with "Jew-boy" among children as number one on the hit parade. As a child, I remember hearing: "A Jew is a nigger turned inside out." In 1944 when I was eight, I heard this billingsgate:

> Roses are red, violets are blue,
> You court the niggers, I'll court the Jews.
> And we'll stay in the White House
> As long as we choose.

A succinct summary of FDR's New Deal coalition, this jingle echoed in another:

> Sheeny, sheeny, alley picker
> Your father was a Jew,
> And your mother was a nigger.

Jews and blacks have been baited, mated, and equated:
*What do you get when you cross a black and a Jew?*
*— You get a janitor but he owns the building.*

In his cogent analysis, Hurwitz concludes that blacks and Jews are rebuked and scorned in sacred writings, folklore, and in the humor of dominant Christian society. Behind every joke, another scholar asserts, lies infinite aggression. In our collective subconscious, blacks represent *id* while Jews reflect *super ego* imperatives. Both are perceived, ironically, as sexual threats to the dominant white Christian male animal. Put in economic terms, blacks constitute a working — Jews, a trading — minority.[1] Both frequently function in American jokelore as objects of derision or as in Emma Lazarus's infelicitous phrase, "wretched refuse."

In this paper, part of a larger work in progress, I shall focus on the humor of these two marginal people: their folklore, jokelore, and comic spirits. For example, when a Negro courier tried to deliver a message in person to the great J.P. Morgan, his loyal secretary declared: "You can't go in there, that is J.P. Morgan of J.P. Morgan and Co." "Das all right," replied the messenger as he whizzed past her, "I'm the coon of Kuhn, Loeb & Co." The latter, I hasten to add, was a Jewish firm. Speaking of Jewish entrepreneurs, a group of Christian merchants insisted that Abe Cohen show sufficient respect during Easter. Bowing to his rivals' pressure, Cohen lined his window with artificial grass, decorated eggs, and Easter bunnies. Next to a big bunny he placed a sign in bold block letters: CHRIST HAS RISEN. Below in smaller print he wrote *but Cohen's prices remain the same.*[2] This is comparable to the current adage, perhaps canard: "Jesus saves, but Moses invests."

Our subject is invested with rich ambiguities and poor delineation. Too often the masks adopted by each group were taken at face value. Clearly, both the Jew as "pariah" and the black as "nigger" were compelled to develop certain strategies of survival among which the most effective was humor. When all else failed in the eye of adversity, humor functioned as a line of defense — Howe and Greenberg insist that in the Jewish experience it is the only line of defense.[3] Both groups assumed ironic masks to cope with life's exigencies. Both created a formidable brand of protest humor which one scholar spelled out in the following way.[4]

> First and most basic is the belief that personal salvation is to be found strictly within the group and that acceptance of the customs of the majority group will lead to heavy personal loss. The second utilizes a favorite form or retaliation, the trickster motif whereby a minority member scores. Third, a parody is devised against an alleged somatic or cultural image. The fourth logically follows the majority group's thinking but twists the conclusion to allow for minority group escape. The fifth derides the majority group member...or discloses how the majority group member actually feels toward the minority. Sixth, the close relationship between the minority group and the prized majority personality is emulated but mimed. Last, the entire scene is reversed so that images appear topsy-turvy, and the minority group emerges triumphant.

A few jokes will illustrate the above paradigm.

> A Jewish man decided to convert to Christianity and entered a program of conversion. After months of religious training he was baptized into the church. On the following morning, his wife found him praying with *talis* and *tefillin* in the customary manner and a *yarmulke* on his head. "What are you doing, Harry?" his wife cried out. "You're praying in the traditional Jewish way." Harry looked up, slapped his forehead, and shouted, "Oy mein goyishen kop!" (Oh, my Gentile [stupid] head!)[5]

In another version, it is the wife who insists on conversion in order to join an exlusive — no Jews and dogs allowed — country club. One morning she plunges into the pool's chill water. She shrieks "Oy vey iz mir!" (Woe is me!) Exposed, she looks around sheepishly and declares, "Whatever that means." A black variant pits a beautiful black woman, Cindy Ella, against the magic mirror. "Who is the fairest one of all?" she implores. The mirror replies: "Snow White, you black bitch, and don't you forget it." When a Senator told reporters that he had many friends who were Negroes, that he was completely devoid of prejudice, that he was writing a book about his famous Negro friends: athletes, singers and statesmen, the reporters queried: "Senator, what is the title of your book?" He replied, "Niggers I have known."[6] He too wore a mask.

One type not fully covered in the above seven part model though peculiar to both groups is "gallows humor."[7] "What time is it, officer?" a black tourist from the north asks a southern sheriff. "Three-o'-clock!" the authority cracks the black three times with his club. The black offers a strange response: he laughs. "Why are you laughing?" "I'm sure glad, sir, that it ain't twelve." Though there are many black jokes of this genre, the Jews have cornered the market on this brand of psychic masochism or "gallows humor." Irving Kristol prematurely buried Jewish humor as an alleged consequence of the Holocaust. Actually, humor of the gallows variety experienced a resurgence during Hitler's hateful hegemony.

Deplorable conditions in 19th-century Eastern Europe spawned this form whose classic statement is found in Sholem Aleichem. One of his characters writes to a friend in America after the heinous Kishenev pogrom of 1903.[8]

> Dear Yankel: You ask me to write you at length and I'd like to oblige, but there's really nothing to write about. The rich are still rich and the poor are dying of hunger, as they always do. What's new about that? And as far as pogroms are concerned, thank God we have nothing more to fear, as we've already had ours—two of them, in fact, and a third wouldn't be worth while... Mendel did a clever thing though; he up and died. Some say of hunger, others of consumption. Personally I think he died of both. I really don't know what else there is to write about, except the cholera, which is going great guns...

Much of Jewish humor is preoccupied with death. Stephen Whitfield has argued that it is a way of keeping the *Malakh Hamoves* (Angel of Death) at bay.[9] Take the

Hitler jokes as illustrations. A German teacher describes the great benefits Hitler bestowed on the German people. "He is like a father to us. Is there anything, students, that you would ask 'father' to do for YOU?" "Yes," said a little Jewish boy, "to make me an orphan." In the early days of Hitler, his Finance Minister approached Rothschild for a large loan. "What are your assets?" "Coal underground and Hitler above ground," the famous banker replied, adding, "I would gladly help you if you could reverse the situation." When a Jew approached the Nazi judge and asked to change his name legally, the judge was skeptical. "You can't fool me. You are Cohen; you will remain Cohen." "Your honor," the Jew insisted, "I want to change my first name from Adolph to Abraham!" Extremely superstitious, Hitler went to a Jewish fortune teller-medium. She told him that he would die on the eve of a Jewish holiday. "Which holiday?" he asked. "Anytime you die, the next day will be a Jewish holiday." A Jew prefers to read the vicious Nazi newspaper *Der Stürmer*. Why? In the honest press, he reads about tragedies, pogroms, round-ups and humiliations while in *Der Stürmer* the articles relate how the Jews own the banks and wield world power. Why is the Warsaw Ghetto like Hollywood? Because of all the stars (yellow armbands) one sees on the streets.[10] However mordant, this levity in the face of annihilation speaks volumes on the uses of humor *extremis*. More research, of course, is needed to explore this important phenomenon.

Jewish humor, write Novak and Waldoks in the most recent study, is substantive. It is about something usually with moral fibre and didactic flavor. As Freud observed, essentially democratic, Jewish humor targets authority and punctures pomposity. It carries a critical cutting edge which disturbs at the same time that it amuses. In the contest of wit, little people frequently win. *Shpritsing* (attacking) dogmas, institutions, celebrities and enemies, Jewish humor does not even spare God.[11] When bloated with daily *tsores*, the Jewish joke purges one with the suddenness and effectiveness of seltzer. It spells relief.

On the flip side of the comic coin, Black humor is equally functional. It serves survival, escape, self-criticism, conflict and control. Arising from an African base, slave humor turned abominable situations, at least psychologically, around. Trickster humor whereby cunning overcomes strength especially appealed to Negro slaves. "You scoundrel, you ate my turkey!" an enraged master charged. "Yassuh, massah," the slave countered, "you got less turkey but you sho' got more nigger." The master was mollified. Osofsky cites the battle of wits:[12]

> Pompey, how do I look?
> O' massa, mighty.
> What do you mean "mighty" Pompey?
> Why massa, you look noble.
> What do you mean by "noble"?
> Why, sar, you look just like one lion.
> Why Pompey, where have you ever seen a lion?
> I see one down in yonder field the other day, massa.
> Pompey, you foolish fellow, that was a jackass.
> Was it massa? Well you look just like him.

Who was really foolish? One slave boasts to another that he can cuss his master out whenever he so desires. Evidently, it makes him feel good. His friend tries it and his massa tore him up. "Where was he standin'?" "Right there in front of me." "That's the wrong way. When I cuss my massa out he's up at the big house and I'm in the field near the creek."[13]

The comedy of avoidance—some might term it evasion—worked effectively. Afro-American humor, until recently, resided underground. The messages were dressed in animal tales. In-group humor spanned double meanings, word-play, play-element, self-deprecation, aggression against the Man, and the swapping of insults. In the "Dirty Dozens" one chanted:

> I fucked your mama
> Till she went blind.
> Her breath smells bad
> But she sure can grind.
>
> I fucked your mama
> For a solid hour.
> Baby came out
> Screaming "Black Power!"
>
> Elephant and the Baboon
> Learning to screw.
> Baby came out looking
> Like Spiro Agnew.
>
> I fucked your mother on an electric wire.
> I made her pussy rise higher and higher.

The counterpointers scored too:

> At least my mother ain't no cake—
>   Everybody gets a piece.
> At least my mother ain't no doorknob—
>   Everybody gets a turn.
> Least my mother ain't no railroad track,
>   Gets laid all around the country.
> Least my brother ain't no store;
>   He takes meat in the back.

There are clean dozens too:

Your father's drawers have so many holes in them that when he walk they whistle.
Your house is so small that roaches walk single file.
Your family is so poor the rats and roaches eat lunch out.[14]

Clean or dirty, these verbal jousts have sparked scholarly controversy.

Radcliffe-Brown was the first to explain "the joking relationship as an institution by which a person is expected, sometimes required, to make fun of another who, in turn, is required to take no offense." These joking relationships, Radcliffe-Brown found, were prevalent among tribal societies in Africa, Asia, Oceania and North America. They arise when people are in ambiguous relationship to each other.[15] John Dollard viewed the dozens — indeed, he was the first social scientist to examine this phenomenon — as a "valve for aggression in a depressed group." They provide a safe substitute for physical violence. Abrahams disagreed. He saw the dozens as a ritual designed to liberate black adolescents from their mommas as a way of resolving acute Oedipal and identity problems. Levine, on whose brilliant book much of the foregoing analysis rests, finds weakness in all single-cause interpretations. He notes two principal functions in the ritual of insult: training in verbal facility and training in self-discipline.[16]

Do we slip the yoke, as Ralph Ellison contends, when we change the joke? By playing the American buffoon, the Negro gained certain benefits in slavery. After slavery, however, choices were available. Despite societal constraints, or because of them, many Negro entertainers continued to play the stereotyped role. They struck a Faustian bargain. Whites, at one end, figured that as along as the Negro seemed funny he was not dangerous. Thus, the Negro's laughter, Margaret Butcher observed, "was often contrived and artificial" rather than natural and spontaneous. Either as clown or brute beast (Sterling Brown detected five other stereotyped roles in American literature), the Negro was locked into white fantasies. These roles probably assuaged white guilt rendering the appearance — as tranquilizing as it was false — that blacks were happy.[17]

Industrialization coupled with urbanization sent shock waves through 19th-century America. First the minstrel show and later the vaudeville show helped mass audiences to cope. This brave new world rested on an old ideological base, namely, the Protestant Ethic. Success depended on order, industry, cleanliness, punctuality, frugality. One had to delay instinctual gratification. Sublimation, however, was no guarantee of success. Fear of failure was a persistent concern. Projecting their fear and fantasy onto blacks, whites fashioned an anti-self. Epitomizing lust, passion, and license, blacks objectified the distance between societal norms and man's natural self. The principal comic mode, to wit, travesty, turned on the disparities between actor and costume, position and name, life and language. Slaves had mighty names. Stage Negroes used ornate language studded with malapropisms. They engaged in social pretense. In the minstrel show, Jim Crow travestied the rural black and Jim Dandy burlesqued the urban Negro. Real people took on minstrel dimension. Intellectuals may have regarded Marcus Garvey a parody of Jim Crow while the "Black Moses," argues Huggins, viewed W.E.B. DuBois as a Jim Dandy. To Americans who were everybody and nobody, a jumble of masks, a kaleidoscope of costumes, a bundle of uncertainties, life mirrored art.[18]

The man who helped to make the mold of the minstrel mask was a mass of contradictions. Joel Chandler Harris was born in 1848, a bastard. His mother worked as a servant. He became an apprenticed printer at age thirteen. Lonely, shy, insecure, he turned for solace to Negroes. The Uncle Remus stories which Harris stole were published in 1880. Fortune followed; fame too. Strangely, Harris did not sense the schizoid qualities of his work. Uncle Remus represents polarities in the Negro psyche. Brer Rabbit celebrates the code of survival. Profoundly anti-Christian, the code stresses slickness, deceit, evasiveness, and ruthless self-interest. If one wants to know what thoughts reside behind the black mask, the animal tales, properly interpreted, provide a better clue than spiritual or sorrow songs.[19] Harris was neither the first nor the last white who ventured into black territory for psychological comfort and material gain. Cultural theft had paid huge dividends.

For the black performer, on the other face, blacking up with burnt cork provided a rite of exorcism. If blacks on stage represented the anti-self and its spectrum of values, namely, indulgence, indolence, and ineptitude, whites assumed the mask too in quest of catharsis. Audiences howled as they perceived the incongruity between affectation and actuality. The laughter of derision served to put the pretender in his place. Black artists wanting a piece of the entertainment pie insisted, despite Ernest Hogan's best-selling tune, "All Coons Look Alike To Me," that real coons, as Walker and Williams billed themselves, could do it better. Not only did commercial considerations encourage blacks to parody whites who were parodying blacks in the minstrel mode, but, Robert Bone contends, the mask served as a way of distancing the super-ego's middle class values from the dark recesses of the id.[20]

Blackface liberated and chained Bert Williams. Born in Antigua, West Indies, in 1874 or 1875 depending on what source one cites, Williams grew up in fairly comfortable circumstances. Failing health prompted his father to move to Riverside, California, in 1885. Only a mediocre student, despite superior intelligence, Williams pursued a career in show business. Teaming up with George Walker in 1893, Williams soon became one of America's premier entertainers. Not only did the Walker association prove pivotal; so did the use of burnt cork. As Williams confided: "Then I began to find myself. It was not until I was able to see myself as another person that my sense of humor developed." Like clown white, the black mask permitted Bert Williams to achieve distinction. Stifled as a man, he crested as a comedian. Williams poked fun at societal institutions:

churches, marriages, funerals. As a wise-fool he uttered
common sense. As a Jonah man, Williams portrayed the
black *shlemazl*. He sang:[21]

> My luck started when I was born
> Leas' so the old folks say
> Dat same hard luck's been my bes' frien'
> To dis vary day.
> When I was young, Mama's friends —
> > To find a name they tried
> They named me after Papa — and de same day papa died, fo'

> > I'm a Jonah, I'm a Jonah Man,
> > My family for many years would look at me
> > And den shed tears.
> > Why I am dis Jonah
> > I sho' can't understand,
> > But I'm a good substantial, full-fledged
> > Real, first-class Jonah Man.

Originally, the straight man to Walker's comic, Williams,
as Jim Crow, the slow rural black, stole the show from
Walker as the urban Jim Dandy. Steeped in the Protestant
Ethic gospel according to Booker T. Washington, Williams
wanted to "elevate the black man." Shuffling along, bat-
tered by a heartless world, he never succumbed to self-pity.
But his humor turned, on and off stage, to melancholy.
"It's no disgrace to be a Negro," Williams confessed, "but
it is very inconvenient." Although he earned much money,
he had to sleep in segregated hotels, ride freight elevators,
and act solo after his partner succumbed to paresis, an
advanced stage of syphilis.[22] One of his best bits involved
a fish peddler who climbs a mountain to sell fish to white
folks. "No, we don't want no fresh fish to-day." Buried in
a landslide, he spots a little man on top beckoning. "So I
sez to myself: 'Praise God, that w'ite man is done changed
his mind.' So I climbs back again up the mountain, seven
thousand feet high, till I comes to the plum top and w'en
I gits there the little w'ite man is standin' there waitin' for

me. He waits till I'm right close to him befo' he speaks. Then he clear his throat and he sez to me, he sez: 'And we don't want none to-morrow either.'" In another bind because of bad times, he is forced to take a job in a circus. Cornered in a lion's cage, unable to escape, he falls to his knees in prayer. "And this Bengal tagger leaped toward me and jus' as my heart was gettin' ready to stop for good, that tagger took and leaned over and I heard him whisper right in my ear, 'Don't be skeered, pal. I'm colored same as you.'"[23]

Pulling laughter from pain is a common trait of both black and Jewish humor. Williams mastered this process. He chanted:[24]

> When life seems full of clouds and rain
> And I am full of nothin' but pain,
> Who soothes my thumpin,' bumpin', brain?
> Nobody!
>
> When winter comes with snow and sleet,
> And me with hunger and cold feet,
> Who says "Here's twenty-five cents, go ahead
>         and get something to eat?"
> Nobody!
>
> When summer comes all cool and clear
> And my friends see me drawin' near
> Who says "Come in and have some beer?"
> Nobody!
>
> When I was in that railroad wreck
> And thought I'd cashed in my last check,
> Who took that engine off my neck?
> Not a soul!
>
> I ain't never done nothin' to nobody
> I ain't got nothin' from nobody, no time.
> Until I get somethin' from somebody, some time
> I'll never do nothin' for nobody, no time.

After Walker's death in 1910, Williams began to drink more heavily and plunged into chronic depression. W.C. Fields, no mean drinker in his own right, remembered Williams as "the funniest man I ever saw and the saddest man I ever knew."[25] Well-read, highly articulate and painfully funny, Bert Williams had to score comic points in this kind of dialogue:[26]

> A man is brought before the judge for chicken stealing and sentenced. The white judge is curious: how could he steal chickens with dogs in the yard? "Hit wouldn't be of no use, judge, to try to explain things to you all, if you was to try it you would as like as not get your hide full of shot an' get no chickens either. If you want to engage in any rascality, judge, you bettah stick to de bench whar you am familiar."

About marriage, a favorite target: "If you have two wives, that's bigamy, if you have many wives, that's polygamy, if you have one wife, that's monotony." Actors' Equity refused to accept dues from Williams. He remained in a constant stage of exile "from the white culture," Ann Charters writes, "from which he was barred because he was a Negro; and from his Harlem neighbors and theatrical acquaintances, because he remained at heart a West Indian."[27] Poor health and excessive drinking extracted their toll; his heart gave out on March 4, 1922. He was only forty-seven. As he shuffled along presumably to the great fish-fry in the sky, many mourned. Paul Laurence Dunbar may have unintentionally contributed the most appropriate epitaph for Bert Williams when he wrote:

> We wear the mask that grins and lies
> It hides our cheek and shades our eyes —
> This debt we pay to human guile:
> With torn and bleeding hearts we smile.[28]

Mr. Dunbar knew whereof he sang. He too put on the minstrel mask when he composed lyrics such as "Who Dat Say Chicken in Dis Crowd" and "Hottest Coon in Dixie" for blackface vaudeville. That tradition lingered like a haunted refrain. In the ensuing years on stage and radio as well as on celluloid, blacks appeared to be locked into the stereotypical performance as coons, bucks, Toms, fools, and tragic mulattoes. Mantan Moreland, Stepan Fetchit, Eddie "Rochester" Anderson, Bill Robinson, Hattie McDaniel, Butterfly McQueen et al. etched comic portraits on the silver screen. This strange — indeed shameful — interlude is described by Leab and Bogue and need not be detailed here. Suffice it to say, the Civil Rights Movement whipped things around reversing a deplorable long-term trend. Dick Gregory helped launch what Arnez and Anthony aptly call "third stage image-creating public humor."[29]

To be sure, the reversals engineered by Dick Gregory and the other black comedians who followed are as laudable as they are funny. Nevertheless, certain disturbing elements persist. Third-stage comedians did not eliminate the "tar baby" with the bathwater. At the risk of sounding prissy if not priggish, I find the continued use of "nigger" disquieting. Redd Foxx as junk-man often borders on turf happily vacated by Amos 'n' Andy. Most of the recent TV sit-coms, especially the enduring Jeffersons, are not much better. Castration themes can be found in many jokes purveyed in these programs and by stand-up comics. Redd Foxx boasts of a Negro securing the first athletic scholarship awarded to Ole Miss. He was a javelin catcher. Flip Wilson's Geraldine is the real killer. Esther Rolle's Florida scores the most points and in the great ascent George Jefferson is cut down by his wife Louise. Whites are vulnerable, too. How, for example, did Tarzan acquire his jungle call? Redd Foxx asserts that one day when Tarzan was swinging through the trees, Jane called for help. "Grab vine," he grunted. She missed; instead she grabbed him by the balls. "Aaahooooo!" Destructive urges, indeed death wishes, manifest in George Walker and Bert Williams, appear resurgent among contemporary black comics. Godfrey Cambridge went to an early grave (with *Bye Bye Braverman*); George Kirby fiddled with hard drugs; and Richard Pryor barely avoided a *Götterdämmerung* funeral pyre free-based from ether and cocaine.[30]

In the 1917 Ziegfeld Follies, Bert Williams starred in a skit with Eddie Cantor as his effeminate, blackfaced son. Eddie of the goggled eyes and the frantic whoopie called Williams "Papsy." The son of Sambo, the Jewish comic hid behind the minstrel mask. Thus, black and Jew made the comedic scene together: the objects of a common linkage in dark laughter. Other Jewish entertainers followed this suit. The most famous, of course, was Al Jolson. Born in St. Petersburg, Russia, in 1886, Jolson and his family settled in Washington, D.C., where his father worked as a cantor. Adjustment to life in America proved difficult. Jolson wound up in a Catholic home for troubled youths in Baltimore which also housed future baseball immortal Babe Ruth. He tried odd jobs: one as a singing waiter. He was a mediocre performer until in 1904 a valet suggested that he use blackface. The rest is fable as well as history: Bert Williams went down; Al Jolson went up.[31]

Behind the mask, many forces — aggression, nostalgia, guilt, loneliness, anxiety — coalesced. As Stanley White shows in his provocative article, Americans wanted, indeed quested, for an emotional release from the daily assaults unleashed by urban society on the old order. Entertainers like Cantor and Jolson pandered to wishfulfillment which conjured up a mythical South where whites ruled, black mammies took care of things, and Negro children frolicked from sunup to sundown. Jolson had inherited a Jewish blue note. Fusing this somber, cantorial strain with vibrant, sometimes demonic, energy, Jolson captivated audiences all over America. Whether he sang of the Old South in

"Swanee," or unrequited love in "After You've Gone," or grief in losing one's "Sonny Boy," Jolson struck a responsive chord in his listeners. *Yiddishe shmalts* larded with blackface sentiment proved a formidable recipe. This method cooked for Sophie Tucker, Eddie Cantor, George Jessel as well as for Al Jolson.[32]

Pulsing with a coarse vitality, Jewish comedians had sharpened their skills in the streets. They mimicked hoity-toity teachers, snarling rabbis, fat cops. Since fellow Jews owned and operated many theaters, careers in comedy were open to talent. Many worked as teams initially. Weber and Fields, Gallagher and Shean, Smith and Dale spring quickly to mind. Soon they acquired confidence, developed *khutspe* and started to stand up or sit alone by the telephone. Listen to George Jessel:[33]

> Hello momma, this is George who sends you the check each month. I'm sitting with Wendell Wilkie, no momma, not Mendel. He talked about the Four Freedoms. What did he say about our neighbors — the four Friedmans? I am going to browse in an art gallery. Yes, it's respectable. I'll bring Whistler's mother home for the living room. No room: she'll have to sleep with sister Anna. It's a picture. I also picked up a Rubens. A sandwich? No a painter. You want him to paint the kitchen?

Aggression alternates with embarrassment in this routine. The Americanized son plays off the immigrant mother. Momma's mistakes evoke exasperation as well as recognition.

Alfred Kazin observed that great writers did not establish "the Jew in the national consciousness as a distinctly American figure..." Rather this contribution was a collective effort embracing the Marx Brothers, Eddie Cantor, Al Jolson, Fannie Brice, George Gershwin. Two traditions attracted the Jewish artist: the blackface strain and the European operetta. Blackface had a brassy, lowdown, earthy quality in opposition to bourgeois mentality. On the other ear, European operetta sounded mellow, genteel. Most gravitated to the black culture because it granted freedom from conventional restraints and served as the American libido. This attraction occurred at a time when pundits were lamenting the "decline of the West" and poets were raining metaphors of sterility on their respective "wastelands." Thus, a coarse, vibrant ethnic humor and music — pastiche in Ronald Sanders' arresting formulation — appealed to vast American audiences.[34]

Rarely reflective, Jewish entertainers used Yiddish accents, dialect stories, unabashed sentiment, gritty jokes, frantic energy — all, Irving Howe charges, "spin-off from immigrant experience." The Marx Brothers, for example, plunged into "gleeful nihilism." Fortified with S.J. Perelman scripts, they assaulted all institutions with "ruthless deflation" — a staple of Jewish humor. No one — profession or person — remained safe from their demolition derby, least of all Margaret Dumont, stolid symbol of WASP sterility. As Hitler mounted his diabolical crusade for world hegemony, *sha-sha!* (Be quiet! Don't make waves!) benevolence led to the disappearance of Jew from American popular culture. Jews, like blacks, had become almost invisible. Radio had celebrated, Philip Roth reminds us, Jack Armstrong, the "All-American Goy." The dream girl was a blonde *shikse* "nestling under your arm whispering love, love, love, love!"[35]

When the Jew as entertainer resurfaced after World War II, he fused several baser metals: *shnorer* and *shlemiel* types from the *shtetl* and the Catskill *meshugener* (crazy), that "wild irresponsible disconnected buffoon who oscillates between the frantic edges of obscenity and tearful sentimentality." Jewish vulgarity "busted loose" from genteel wraps. Stand-up comics from 1950 to 1970 emitted snarling references to Jewish mothers. Shame still made their comic pump. Only this time, the needle-trades assumed a more malicious and savage style. Not only the dirty underwear in the closet proved embarrassing but their identifying evasions, as Lenny Bruce pontificated ("I'm proud to be Jewish means that I made the adjustment."), also triggered self-contempt. They suffered, Howe states convincingly, from a moral duality. The gaudy glitter — gold dust if you will — of making it was at bottom: *drek* (shit). Always "overwhelmingly social," Jewish humor had an obligation: to foster spiritual values and group cohesion in the face of constant materialist temptation.[36] Rovit, Howe, Altman — all astute critics — conferred low grades in their reports of Jewish entertainers. Rovit complains that Jews have failed to produce a Charlie Chaplin, a Mark Twain, a Sinclair Lewis. Why? Because they adapt too easily. Silent on major controversial issues, Jewish humor, in contrast to its black counterpart, has accepted, without struggle, the middle-class belief system. Intelligence, so revered at one time, now receives denigration. Even Woody Allen, smart enough to know better, trumpets the uselessness of intellectual activity. He quips about the courses he took in college prior to dropping out, namely, Truth, Beauty, Advanced Beauty, and Intermediate Truth. Futility attends academic effort. One hip girl using the rhythm method could not keep the beat. The boy most likely to succeed becomes a junkie. He marries a junkette. Woody gives them silverware — sixteen spoons.[37]

Perhaps the most important comic in the post-war period, Lenny Bruce, became a junkie indeed. Before self-destructing on a toilet bowl which some might see as a fitting climax, he developed a unique, cogent kind of humor that shocked as it amused. Drawing on folk sources, black as well as Jewish, Lenny "slew sacred cows and paraded their carcasses before our astonished eyes," to borrow Sarah B. Cohen's vivid description. He had a strong impact on contemporary comics, especially blacks. Red Foxx, for example, loved him:[38]

> Lenny Bruce was the greatest human being I ever met. He was honest. He said things that were not convention to say. But they

need being said and Lenny was the first to say them. He was crucified for telling the truth. He was a great influence on me.

Foxx's "Fuck Kate Smith" routine may have been inspired by a Bruce bit wherin the "Mad Magid" (according to Irving Howe) offered a choice to test the primacy of imperatives: race vs. sex. Choosing between Lena Horne and Kate Smith (Bruce also pitted Harry Belafonte against Charles Laughton), most men would share Lenny's preference for lovely Lena (and handsome Harry).[39] Lenny Bruce also inspired Richard Pryor, George Carlin, Robert Klein, not to mention Norman Lear. From a hack comic early in his career, Bruce became a "speechifying comic Jeremiah." Frenzied resentments bubbled to the surface in his elaborate, spontaneous *shpritses*. He went beyond the fringe of stand-up comedy which Maurice Yacower defines as [40]

> essentially Jewish. The performer stands alone and without a prop before a crowd of strangers. By his wit he attempts to forge a sense of community with them. By his brain and humor he tries to gain their acceptance, the laughter that denotes approval... Despite his strangeness and alienation, he must persuade them that he is one of them... So he stands alone in front of a silent and alien audience, spinning out his line of self-deprecating patter or charming cheek (chutzpah). The stand-up comedian is the eternal outsider, the Wandering Jew.

Instead of a hearty, honest, loving image, Bruce's sweeping gestures, Yiddish phrases, and fierce sense of moral outrage inextricably link him to the Jewish tradition. Beyond the pale, his flights of fantasy took off from suppositions of *what if*[41]

> ...the Lone Ranger was making it with Tonto and Silver?
> ...Hitler was made Chancellor of Germany by central casting?
> ...Sophie Tucker was really a nymphomaniac with the hots for Puerto Rican busboys?
> ...Christ and Moses returned to earth?
> ...the Jews killed Christ because he refused to become a doctor or a lawyer?
> ...American religions incorporated to sell by way of Madison Avenue?

Bruce as Jewish humorist is treated elsewhere by this writer in detail. Irving Howe provides the best succinct analysis:[42]

> Humor of this kind bears a heavy weight of destruction; in Jewish hands, more likely self-destruction, for it proceeds from a brilliance that corrodes the world faster than...it can remake it. A corrupt ascetic is a man undone... He became a *magid* (preacher) without a message, a martyr without a cause. He fell back, deeply back, into a Jewish past neither he nor his audiences could know much about—a reborn Sabbatai as stand-up comic.

Before self-destructing with a little help from the law, he provided ample food for comic thought which subsequent humorists, black as well as Jewish, digested.

Most Jewish comedians seek status, success, *shikses*. They crave love and fear death. Woody Allen reflects:[43]

> Life is a concentration camp. You're stuck here and there's no way out, and you can only rage impotently against your persecutors.
>
> It's not that I'm afraid to die. I just don't want to be there when it happens.
>
> Death is an acquired trait.
>
> Death...is one of the worst things that can happen to a Cosa Nostra member and many prefer simply to pay a fine.
>
> It is impossible to experience one's own death objectively and still carry a tune.
>
> Death is one of the few things that can be done as easily lying down.
>
> The thing to remember is that each time of life has its appropriate rewards, whereas when you're dead it's hard to find a light switch.
>
> I do not believe in an afterlife, although I am bringing a change of underwear.
>
> History will dissolve me.
>
> Why are our days numbered instead of lettered?
>
> Yea, I shall run through the valley of the shadow of death.

Woody's obsession with ultimate concern is shared by another leading American Jewish comic artist. Mel Brooks wants to live forever. His 2,000-year-old man is Jewish and therefore vulnerable to "hostile man...nature and God," "I really wailed. I could hear my antecedents. I could hear 5,000 years of Jews pouring through me." "Death," Brooks knows, "is more of an enemy than a German soldier."[44]

Dread and death evoke high anxiety. Brooks prefers to "swing, shout, and make noise!" Humor is "another defense against the universe." Brooks affirms: "Let's not mimic death before our time comes! Let's be wet and noisy!" In *The Producers*, Brooks reduces the horror that was Hitler with an extended joke. In *Blazing Saddles*, a super-macho black sheriff restores law, order, and laughter to a frontier town. This new genre, the Jewish Western, is replete with vulgarity, effusiveness and in-jokes as in the reference to Yiddish-speaking Indians: *Zey zaynen shvartses — loz zey geyn!* (They're blacks — let them go!). The use of Yiddish is a means to preserve a dying voice, a fading culture.[45]

Humor pressed from the comic vineyards of Woody Allen and Mel Brooks is never sour grapes. Rather it invites comparison with Paul Tillich's Protestant theology: both are Existential philosophies of ultimate concern. Preoccupation with death as one *leitmotif* alternates with joyful, one is tempted to say Dionysian, affirmation. Though rooted in *tsores* that appear to be timeless, our subject is a comedy of affirmation and continuity with a "fluid connection to history."[46] As a cultural force, blacks and Jews have imparted renewed vitality to a slumping America. Through their humor, lubricating as well as abrasive, they have recharged our nation's machinery. Tuned in we hear the electric hum of their talent while they have turned us on.

Put another way, the comic as ethnic provides a much needed tonic, or is it enema?, for the ailing if not sterile WASP *corpus*. Peter Schrag's epitaph — the Decline of the WASP — may be a bit premature. From the perspective of the body-politic, humor has proved more conservative, perhaps even reactionary, than radical. Little change, Christopher Wilson argues, can ever result from a process which, contrary to popular belief, is rarely anarchic and subversive. Instead, jokes are potent instruments in preserving the status quo. The effectiveness of "protest humor" may in fact be illusory. Ridicule, according to empirical studies, "is directed downwards and laterally through a hierarchy." For every Lenny Bruce stand a multitude of Jack Carters; in lieu of Dick Gregory, there are too many Jimmy Walkers. Since the professional comic is a social success and potential role model, deviancy must be stifled if not "dynomited." Richard Pryor fears that they [the establishment] will try to kill Dick Gregory as they did Lenny Bruce. Whatever the reasons for paranoid scenarios, it is necessary to point out that the self-ridicule inherent in both black and Jewish comedy eases the relationship between bigot and victim. Witness Archie Bunker. We laugh with Archie — as much as we laugh at him. Thus, inequities and inequalities are maintained and bigotry's face is softened. Wilson concludes on a somber note: "Through its pleasures and personal utility, humor recruits and bribes us to become laughing conservatives."[47]

Clearly, derisive laughter may indeed buttress the social order. Humor, in larger measure, is a defense against life's finite limits. We may wax witty at death not so much in Promethian defiance but more to dull the edge of fear at twilight time. In their quest for survival coupled with social justice, unable to reject their destiny, blacks and Jews adjust. When they cannot adjust, they revolt. When the oppressed are unable to revolt, they laugh.[48] Since the rupture of the Black-Jewish alliance on the Civil Rights front and in other vital causes, the humor of exclusion and the wit of aggression have gained primacy. What two authors recently described as a "bittersweet encounter" has turned into a relationship of sour gripes. As racism and anti-Semitism fester, progressive-minded persons from each group fall into despair. Gone are the days of the New Deal coalition.[49]

Despair, however, must be transcended. In summary one turns for solace to Sigmund Freud. The good doctor writes:[50]

> There can be no question of an antithesis between an optimistic and pessimistic theory of life; only the simultaneous working together and against each other of both primordial drives, of Eros and the death drive, can explain the colorfulness of life, never the one or the other all by itself.

Freud, of course, sensed the prevalence of Thanatos leading inexorably to a tragic view of life. Bruno Bettelheim, from whom this coda is borrowed, concedes that in the end the death drive triumphs but as long as there is life in us we can struggle on the side of Eros. For Eros to succeed and Psyche to rejoice, Bettelheim concludes, we must live and love well.[51] We also need positive laughter. The humor of blacks and Jews serves Eros. Comedians from both cultures have affirmed life against adversity. They have kept the faith of their people aglow like a phoenix in the ashes.

## REFERENCES

Footnotes, for the most part, will appear in sequential order at the end of the paragraph or section to cite salient sources within the paragraph or section.

1. William Schechter, *A History of Negro Humor in America* (New York: Fleet Press, 1970); p. 128 contains a variant of the opening joke. A priest asks a Negro: "Are you a Catholic?" He responds: "Lord no, ain't I got enough trouble just being colored?" The confluence of humor and aggression is the subject of

Gershon Legman, *Rationale of the Dirty Joke: An Analysis of Sexual Humor* (New York: Grove Press, 1968), p. 9.

Nathan Hurwitz, "Blacks and Jews in American Folklore," *Western Folklore* 33:4 (October 1974), pp. 301-04, 306-09, 318-24.

2. Many of the jokes used in this paper are found in a variety of sources. The wording, therefore, is rarely identical. Although I have changed words here and there, I have tried to maintain the basic form without sacrificing content or spirit. For example, Howard J. Ehrlich, "Observations on Ethnic and Intergroup Humor," *Ethnicity* 6:4

(October 1979), pp. 394-95 uses the name "Horowitz" instead of "Cohen" as do Gert Raeithel, *Lach, wenn du kannst* (Munich: Kindler Verlag, 1972), p. 172, and this writer.

The Kuhn-Loeb joke is found in Hurwitz, "Blacks...," p. 306.

3. Irving Howe & Eliezer Greenberg, eds., *A Treasury of Yiddish Stories* (New York: Viking Press, 1965), p. 26.

4. I have used the language *verbatim* of Joseph Boskin, "Protest Humor: Fighting Criticism with Laughter," *Bostonia* 54:5 (December 1980), p. 49, who borrowed an earlier version from Donald C. Simmons, "Protest Humor: Folkloristic Reactions to Prejudice," *American Journal of Psychiatry* 120 (December 1963), p. 567.

5. Boskin, "Protest...," pp. 52-53. *Talis* is a prayer shawl worn by men for morning prayer. *Tefillin* are phylacteries, small leather boxes (containing parchment strips) held in place by thin leather throngs on forehead and upper left arm.

6. For the Snow White joke and other "goodies" see Joseph Boskin, "Black/Black Humor: The Renaissance of Laughter," in Werner Mendel, ed., *A Celebration of Laughter* (Los Angeles: Mara Books, 1970), pp. 152-58. A true *mayven*, Boskin provides a veritable cornucopia of pertinent jokes for intelligent folks. In addition, his bag teems with sparkling commentaries.

Simmons, "Protest...," p. 569.

7. The first scholarly treatment of this important phenomenon can be found in Antonin J. Obrdlik, "'Gallows Humor'—A Sociological Phenomenon," *American Journal of Sociology* 47:5 (March 1942), pp. 709-16. See also

Irving Kristol, "Is Jewish Humor Dead? The Rise and Fall of the Jewish Joke," *Commentary* 12:5 (November 1951), pp. 432-36.

Rabbi H.R. Rabinowitz, *Kosher Humor* (Jerusalem: R.H. Hochen's Press, 1977), pp. 44-49.

William Novak & Moshe Waldoks, eds., *The Big Book of Jewish Humor* (New York: Harper & Row, 1981), pp. 80-82.

8. Maurice Samuel, *The World of Sholem Aleichem* (New York: Alfred Knopf, 1944), p. 189.

9. Stephen J. Whitfield, "Laughter in the Dark: Notes on American Jewish Humor," *Midstream* 24:2 (February 1978), p. 51. Whitfield, combining brevity, soul, and wit, is brilliant.

10. Rabinowitz, *Kosher*, p. 44-49

Emmanuel Ringelblum, *Notes from the Warsaw Ghetto*, edited and translated by Jacob Sloan (New York: McGraw Hill, 1958), pp. xxvi, 22, 68-69, 84-85.

11. Novak & Waldoks, *Big Book*, pp. xx-xxii.

12. "The less turkey...mo' nigger" retort issues from several sources including Joseph Boskin, "Goodby to Mr. Bones," *New York Magazine* (May 1, 1966), p. 85.

Gil Osofsky, ed., *Puttin' on Ole Massa: The Slave Narratives of Henry Bibb, William Wells Brown, and Solomon Northrup* (New York: Harper & Row, 1969), pp. 22, 23. Osofsky cites other examples of funny irreverence. As he lay dying, one master heard from a "faithful servant": "Farewell massa! Pleasant journey: you soon be dere — all de way down hill!"

13. Norine Dresser, "The Metamorphosis of the Humor of the Black Man," *New York Folklore Quarterly* 26:3 (September 1970), pp. 216-17.

14. Lawrence W. Levine, *Black Culture and Black Consciousness: Afro-American Folk Thought from Slavery to Freedom* (New York: Oxford University Press, 1978), pp. 346-47.

15. Christopher Wilson, *Jokes: Form, Content, Use and Function* (London: Academic Press, 1979), p. 88. See also

A.R. Radcliffe-Brown, "On Joking Relationships," *Africa* 13 (1940), pp. 195-210.

16. John Dollard, "The Dozens: Dialectic of Insult," in Alan Dundes, ed., *Mother Wit from the Laughing Barrel: Readings in the Interpretation of Afro-American Folklore* (Englewood Cliffs: Prentice Hall, 1973), pp. 279-80, 290; see also the introduction, especially p. xiii.

Roger Abrahams, *Deep Down in the Jungle... Negro Narrative Folklore from the Streets of Philadelphia* (Hatboro, Pa.: Folklore Associates, 1964), pp. 49-59.

Roger Abrahams, *Positively Black* (Englewood Cliffs: Prentice Hall, 1970), p. 41-42.

Levine, *Black*, pp. 350-58 contains a luminous discussion of this controversy and offers his own interpretation.

17. Sterling A. Brown, "Negro Character as Seen by White Authors," *Journal of Negro Education* 2 (April 1933), pp. 180-201.

Morris Goldman, "The Sociology of Negro Humor," unpublished dissertation, New School for Social Research, 1960, p. 170.

Phillip Sterling; ed. and collector, *Laughing on the Outside: The Intelligent White Reader's Guide to Negro Tales and Humor* (New York: Grosset & Dunlap, 1965), p. 22; see Redding's thesis on p. 18.

18. Nathan I. Huggins, *Harlem Renaissance* (New York: Oxford University Press, 1971), pp. 249-71; p. 274 provides a consummate analysis. See also

Albert F. McLean, Jr., *American Vaudeville as Ritual* (Lexington: University of Kentucky Press, 1965), pp. 24-26, 109, 114, 135-36.

Robert Toll, *Blacking Up: The Minstrel Show in Nineteenth Century*

*America* (New York: Oxford University Press, 1974), pp. 228, 245, 254-56, 259, 262, 274.

19. Robert Bone, *Down Home: A History of Afro-American Short Fiction from Its Beginning to the End of the Harlem Renaissance* (New York: G.P. Putnam's & Sons, 1975), pp. 24-26, 27-29.

Bernard Wolfe, "Uncle Remus and the Malevolent Rabbit," in A. Dundes, *Mother Wit*, p. 527, observes that in Harris's first book, Rabbit appears twenty-six times. In his twenty encounters with Fox, Rabbit, symbolizing the Negro, whips him in nineteen. When pitted against the strong, namely, Wolf, Bear, and Fox, Rabbit invariably wins. Other weaklings, Buzzard, Bullfrog, and Terrapin consistently beat the Fox.

20. Toll, *Blacking Up*, pp. 247-48.

Robert Bone, *Down Home*, pp. 59, 60-61. Though overly committed to his pastoral thesis, Bone deserves more credit than he receives. As recently as 1950, many — if not most — black comics on the TOBA or "chittling" circuit still blackened up. Even after the NAACP applied pressure, one resisted the new look. Johnny Hudgins confessed: "I feel so naked out there." Harlem audiences at the Apollo found the burnt-cork comics appealing which Malcom X found appalling. See John Schiffman, *Uptown: The Story of Harlem's Apollo Theatre* (New York: Cowles Book Company, 1971), pp. 124, 126. [TOBA = Theater Owners Booking Association, also known by clients as "Tough On Black Actors"]

21. Ann Charters, *Nobody: The Story of Bert Williams* (New York: Macmillan, 1970), pp. 15-19, 21-28, 71.

Robert Toll, *On With the Show: The First Century of Show Business in America* (New York: Oxford University Press, 1976), p. 123.

22. Langston Huges & Milton Meltzer, *Black Magic: A Pictorial History of the Negro in American Entertainment* (Englewood Cliffs: Prentice Hall, 1967), p. 58.

William McFerrin Stowe Jr., "Damned Funny: The Tragedy of Bert Williams," *Journal of Popular Culture* 10:1 (Summer 1976), pp. 5-11.

Charters, *Nobody*, pp. 95-97.

23. Levine, *Black*, pp. 360-61.

Charters, *Nobody*, p. 106. There is a comparable Jewish tiger in Hitler's circus. Common to oppressed people, these "crossover" jokes particularly appeal to Jews as well as blacks. See

Nathan Ausubel, *A Treasury of Jewish Folklore* (New York: Crown Publishers, 1949), pp. 442-43.

24. Charters, *Nobody*, pp. 9, 135-37.

25. Mabel Rowland, ed., *Bert Williams: Son of Laughter* (New York: English Crafters, 1923), p. 128.

26. Ibid., pp. 182-83.

Levine, *Black*, p. 361.

27. Charters, *Nobody*, p. 139.

28. As quoted in Nancy Levi Arnez & Clara B. Anthony, "Contemporary Negro Humor as Social Satire," *Phylon* 29:4 (Winter 1968), pp. 339.

29. Ibid., p. 340. The portraiture of blacks in film is canvassed in Daniel J. Leab, *From Sambo to Superspade: The Black Experience in Motion Pictures* (Boston: Houghton Mifflin, 1976).

Donald Bogle, *Toms, Coons, Mulattoes, Mammies and Bucks* (New York: Viking Press, 1973).

Gary Null, *Black Hollywood: The Negro in Motion Pictures* (Secaucus: Citadel Press, 1975).

30. William Schechter, *History*, pp. 196-97.

Redd Foxx & Norma Miller, *The Redd Foxx Encyclopedia of Black Humor* (Pasadena: Ward Ritchie, 1977), p. 234.

Jack Kroll & David T. Friendly, "Richard Pryor, Bustin' Loose," *Newsweek* (May 13, 1982), pp. 48-54.

31. Robert Oberfirst, *Al Jolson: You Ain't Heard Nothin Yet!* (San Diego: A.S. Barnes, 1980), pp. 22-24, 28-37, 79-81. Highly uncritical and conspicuously worshipful, this book does, however, convey relevant biographical data. The prose consists of pure syrup. Why include Al Jolson in this paper? Jolie, as he was affectionately called, thought of himself as a comedian. See

William Cahn, *The Laugh Makers: A Pictorial History of American Comedians* (New York: G.P. Putnam's Sons, 1957), p. 126. Moreover Jolson projects a striking counterpoint to another Follies' figure, namely, Bert Williams.

32. Stanley White, "The Burnt Cork Illusion of the 1920's in America: A Study in Nostalgia," *Journal of Popular Culture* 5:3 (Winter 1971), pp. 531-43. On p. 543 White comments: "All that mattered was to evoke the image of the once servile black for an emotional outlet in a dehumanizing, disjointed age — the mammy for security and comfort, and the Negro male for ridicule and jest. Whereas the Negro's body had once been in bondage, now it was his personality that was enslaved to satisfy the white man's immediate psychic needs."

Irving Howe, *World of Our Fathers* (New York: Harcourt, Brace, Jovanovich, 1976), pp. 562-63.

33. Howe, *World*, pp. 556-62.

McLean, *American Vaudeville*, p. 144.

Theodore Reik, *Jewish Wit* (New York: Gamut Press, 1962), p. 85 contains the George Jessel telephone routine.

34. Alfred Kazin, "The Jew as American Writer," in Abraham Chapman, ed., *Jewish American Literature* (New York: New American Library, 1974), pp. 589-90.

Ronald Sanders, "The American Popular Song," in Douglas Villiers, ed., *Next Year in Jerusalem* (New York: Viking Press, 1976), pp. 197-203.

35. Howe, *World*, pp. 565-68.

Phillip Roth, *Portnoy's Complaint* (New York: Bantam, 1969), pp. 164-165.

36. Earl Rovit, "Jewish Humor & American Life," *American Scholar* 36:2 (Spring 1967), pp. 237-44.

Leslie Fiedler, *Waiting for the End* (New York: Stein & Day, 1964), pp. 67-68.

"Lenny Bruce at Carnegie Hall," February 4, 1961, United Artists Record, UAS 9800. Bruce equates "pride" in Judaism with "adjustment"—not "happiness."

Nat Hentoff, "Yiddish Survivals in the New Comedy," in Chapman, *Jewish American Literature*, pp. 691-92.

37. Rovit, "Jewish Humor," p. 245.

Howe, *World*, pp. 565, 568-70.

Sig Altman, *The Comic Image of the Jew: Explorations of a Pop Culture Phenomenon* (Rutherford: Fairleigh Dickinson University Press, 1971), pp. 191-196, 199-205.

Maurice Yacowar, *Loser Take All: The Comic Art of Woody Allen* (New York: Frederick Ungar, 1979), pp. 17-18.

38. Altman, *Comic Image*, pp. 189, 191.

Albert Goldman, "What Lenny Bruce Was All About," *New York Times Magazine* (June 27, 1971), pp. 16, 18, 19, 20, 22.

Albert Goldman, *Ladies and Gentlemen–Lenny Bruce* (New York: Random House, 1974) is both exhaustive and exhausting. See also

Frank Kofsky, *Lenny Bruce: Comedian As Social Critic and Secular Moralist* (New York: Monad Press, 1974), pp. 72-73 shows that Bruce tapped black and Jewish folk sources.

Foxx, *Encyclopedia*, p. 235.

39. John Cohen, ed., *The Essential Lenny Bruce* (New York: Ballantine Books, 1967), pp. 26-27.

40. Altman, *Comic Image*, pp. 189-191.

Schechter, *History*, p. 194.

Howe, *World*, pp. 572-73. Robert Klein admits: "I was inspired to the hilt by Lenny Bruce" as quoted in

Joan Bennet, "Standup Comedy: Roles Replacing One Liners," *New York Times*, Section 2 (June 30, 1974), p. 35.

Yacowar, *Loser*, p. 213.

41. Hentoff, "Yiddish Survivals," p. 692.

Robert Alter, "Defaming the Jews," *Commentary* 55:1 (January 1973), pp. 80-81.

Walter Blair & Hamlin Hill, *America's Humor: From Poor Richard to Doonesbury* (New York: Oxford University Press, 1978), p. 516.

Cohen, *Essential Lenny*, pp. 41, 52-75, 133-39, 142.

42. Joseph Dorinson, "Lenny Bruce, A Jewish Humorist in Babylon," *Jewish Currents* 35:2 (February 1981), pp. 14-19, 31-32.

Howe, *World*, p. 573.

43. Eric Lax, *On Being Funny: Woody Allen and Comedy* (New York: Charterhouse, 1975), pp. 224-25. Other observations include: "Dying doesn't make you thirsty. Unless you get stabbed after eating herring... Also there is the fear that there is an afterlife but no one will know where it is being held."

Yacowar, *Loser*, p. 215.

44. Maurice Yacowar, *In Method Madness: The Comic Art of Mel Brooks* (New York: St. Martin's Press, 1981), p. 51. Though illuminating, this book does not match Yacowar's brilliant effort, earlier, in presenting the comic art of Woody Allen.

Kenneth Tynan, "Profiles: Frolics of a Short Hebrew Man," *New Yorker* (October 30, 1978), pp. 65, 68-69, 80, 92.

45. Yacowar, *In Method*, pp. 6, 17, 52. The key to Mel Brooks's comedy is the phrase : *Loz mikh aroys!* ("Let me out!")

46. Boskin, "Protest Humor," p. 51 cites Sharon Weinstein's apposite metaphor: "fluid connection with...history...".

47. Christopher Wilson, *Jokes: Form*, pp. 228-29; comics with a radical perspective — I share Richard Pryor's fear — are often silenced. See also

Schechter, *History*, p. 194.

Gert Raeithel's first-rate paper, originally delivered at the 1980 IPA Conference and later published, makes a comparable point from another vantage, namely, that humor carries one away to "aloofness." Such a mind-set is less than conducive to either social action or political change. See his "American Humor As an Experience of Growth," *American Humor* 7:2 (Fall 1980), pp. 4-6.

48. The formula is from Albert Memmi, *The Liberation of a Jew*, translated by Judy Hyun (New York: Orion Press, 1966), pp. 53-54; a similar statement issues from a Yiddish proverb: "When you're hungry, sing; when you hurt, laugh." as cited in Leo Rosten, *Leo Rosten's Treasury of Jewish Quotations* (New York: McGraw Hill, 1972), p. 7.

49. Two authors who chronicle Black-Jewish relationships are Robert G. Weisbord & Arthur Stein, *Bittersweet Encounter* (Westport: Greenwood Press, 1970). See also

Richard Krickus, *Pursuing the American Dream: White Ethnics and the New Populism* (Garden City: Anchor Books, 1976), pp. 278, 295, 296.

50. As quoted in Bruno Bettelheim, "Reflections: Freud and the Soul," *New Yorker* 58:2 (March 1, 1982), p. 92.

51. Ibid., p. 93; at its best, Black humor represents, writes Saunders Redding in Sterling, *Laughing*, pp. 17-19, "an escape into pride and dignity," while Jewish humor betokens a transcendence of destiny. To the call of Joyce O. Hertzler, *Laughter: A Socio-Scientific Analysis* (New York: Exposition Press, 1970), pp. 215-16 for "positive laughter," we reply "Amen" from our corner or, if you will, "Right on!"

**HÄGAR THE HORRIBLE** By DIK BROWNE

# JAMES WATT'S *CRIPPLE*

## Reinhold Aman

The word *cripple* is rarely used today as a direct insult ("You cripple!") or descriptively ("He's a cripple."). It is too strongly loaded with emotional and negative connotations. In addition, the two voiceless stops $k$ and $p$ make this word sound hard and nasty.

Thus it was like a slap in the face when we heard and read that former Interior Secretary James Watt used *cripple* in a joke that backfired and brought about his resignation. At a breakfast meeting of some 200 lobbyists, Watt was talking about his five-member review commission on coal-leasing. Trying to ridicule the excesses of affirmative action, he joked that his panel had "every kind of mix you can have. I have a black, I have a woman, two Jews and a cripple." (Associated Press, 21 Sept. 1983; *Time*, 3 Oct. 1983, p. 14)

Watt did not use *disabled* or *handicapped*, the euphemisms we have become accustomed to, but the brutal-sounding *cripple*. We are not used to hearing honest language any more.

Commission member Richard Gordon, a professor at Pennsylvania State University, was disturbed by Watt's choice of words: "I am the Jew and the cripple, if you want to call someone who has a paralyzed arm a cripple." (AP) Senator Robert Dole, whose right arm was left paralyzed by a machine-gun burst during World War II, told Watt that as far as he could recall, "no one had used the word 'cripple' in 30 years. Modern folk use words like 'disabled'" (UPI, 27 Sept. 1983). Violinist Itzhak Perlman, a polio victim who requires crutches, was strongly offended and said that cars became crippled, not people. "It means can't do anything, broken down, at a standstill." (UPI)

Is a person with a paralyzed arm or with unusable legs a *cripple*? According to some of the definitions (see "Offensive Words in Dictionaries"), yes. If we accept the broader definition, "disabled or deficient in some way," there are 36 million *cripples* in the USA (UPI), including 4.3 million students aged 3-21 (*USA Today*, 11 Nov. 1983, p. 1).

The original meaning of *cripple* was 'a lame person or animal,' as can be seen from its origin, Old English *crypel*, akin to *creep*, 'to move along slowly or bent over.' Mr. Perlman's interpretation of *cripple* is understandably influenced by his affliction and by the taunting he must have suffered, but he is not correct according to standard usage. I have never heard a traffic report about "crippled cars"—they are usually called "disabled vehicles." *Crippled* does not mean "can't do, broken down, at a standstill."

Senator Dole may not be as modern as he thinks he is. As euphemisms are wont to do, *disabled* and *handicapped* have taken on the negative connotations of *crippled*, if not worse (mentally, visually, etc., handicapped). Edward Kennedy Jr., whose right leg was removed to save him from bone cancer eleven years ago, does not like these two terms. Instead, he prefers "physically challenged" as his own euphemism for the euphemisms (*WF*, 18 Febr. 1985, p. 2). But "physically challenged" is too veiled; it is so far removed from reality that it is meaningless. When I (working in an oil factory) had to move 55-gallon oil drums by hand, I was "physically challenged" but not crippled. Surely, such sugar-coating of ugly reality helps those afflicted with the specific infirmity (and their family members) to cope, but ultimately it is senseless, because in a few years "physically challenged" will have absorbed the negative connotations of "crippled" and will have to be replaced by yet another euphemism. (At some other time, I will report on related attempts by some librarians to suppress officially another "ugly, cruel" word, *leprosy* and to replace it by "Hansen's disease," in the same spirit as *mongolism* is being replaced by "Down's syndrome.")

Super-Yente and comedian Joan Rivers — formerly a *comedienne* — worked Watt's lapse into her performance at the 1983 Emmy Awards (UPI, *MJ*, 26 Sept. 1983, pp. 1 and 6). She asked Eddie Murphy, her co-host, what his religion was. When he replied, "Catholic," Rivers said:

> Great. You're a Catholic and a black. I'm a woman and a Jew, and if you had a limp, we could be the committee appointed by James Watt. He's an idiot!

Paul Valentine of the *Washington Post*, quoted in the *MJ* (2 Nov. 1983, p. 17), offers a substantial, thought-provoking defense:

> There are some smug omissions in the compendium of forbidden words that the Eastern Liberal Establishment is busily assembling in the wake of Jim Watt's laryngeal sins.
>
> While assorted moral tone-setters are wringing their hands over the public utterance of "cripple" and "wetback" and even "homosexual" by Watt and other heathen, they happily go on preserving their own lexicon of pejorative stereotypes.
>
> They are too numerous to list in their entirety, but they include *Okies, Californians, Midwesterners, Moonies, hard hats, holy rollers, Bible thumpers, snake handlers, tobacco spitters, hillbillies, rednecks* and a vast swarm of lesser freckle bellies and peckerwoods who roam the liberal landscape...
>
> Critics washed Watt's mouth with soap for saying "cripple" when he should have said "handicapped." ... If the word-police get their way, a whole new range of references will be stricken from the language. *Codger, crone* and *gaffer* would have to go so as not to offend the elderly. *Idiot, lunatic, moron* and *imbecile* likewise would certainly have to be excised...

The peremptory condemnation of words, as words, leaves no room for considering the context in which those words are spoken. Yes, words — *Scotch, nigger, redneck, WASP* — may be said in insult or derision, but they may more often be said in irony or sarcasm, in pathos or in metaphor, with no intention of diminishing the person mentioned. In fact, the intent may be just the opposite: to exalt or uplift...

Stifling the use of words as a protective gesture is unhealthy in two ways: It fails to eradicate the underlying hatred or scorn, if such there is, that the speaker may harbor for a category of people, and it reduces the richness of the language in which our thinking is embedded... Jim Watt did not intend to insult Jews, blacks, women or handicapped people when he described the composition of his coal-leasing study commission. What he did try to do, in his own artlessly sarcastic way, was to ridicule irrelevant tokenism in public service. Irrelevant tokenism is always worth ridiculing. Even the tokens would acknowledge that...

For more information on *cripple*, see my "Offensive Words in Dictionaries" in this volume.

# ADS FOR TV EXECUTIONS

## Charles Chi Halevi

The recent efforts by a condemned criminal to get his execution televised gave rise to a plethora of protests and support — but all for the wrong reasons.

The problem with positions urged by both bleeding heart liberals and right wing neanderthals is that they fail to take into account the victims of capital crimes, whose death leaves them unable to support their families. Revenge may be sweet but it doesn't buy meat.

But what if we televised executions, and then sold the advertising spots to the highest bidders? The profits could provide an annuity for the victim's family, thus enabling the criminal to repay society and his victim.

Of course this would require some enabling legislation. The bill we envision could be called *Gory Advertising Sells Products*, better known by its initials: **GASP**.

Under **GASP** a condemned criminal's execution would be televised and ads sold to those companies that would benefit the most from such a market. If the execution is by electrocution, one natural advertiser would be the local electric company. If it's by gas chamber, then of course the gas company would get the nod. Should a firing squad be required, then the Winchester and Colt companies will want to get a shot at it.

There would be other advertisers, certainly. Funeral homes would find a natural market, and so would insurance companies who even now take great delight in reminding us to take care of our loved ones after we're gone. No doubt organized religions will want to discuss life after death.

Once **GASP** catches on, strange phenomena will be observed in American society. Calvin Klein will come out with a line of designer blindfolds, and more shaved heads will be seen on Main Street USA than can be accounted for by Krishna converts. Shrouds will be chic, just as camouflage outfits gained popularity again after the invasion of Grenada.

A regular TV series of executions could be launched, perhaps entitled "Saturday Night Dead." A music video by Michael Jackson would be the perfect accompaniment; with minor alterations, "Beat It" could be changed to "Heat It" and include the chorus:

> *It doesn't matter*
> *If you broil or fry,*
> *They'll watch it on TV*
> *And then buy, buy, buy.*
> *So heat it, heat it...*

For mass executions the Beach Boys could sing that surfing standard "Hang Ten."

Naturally these "live" shows will have some inherent problems. Ponder the plight of the poor producer whose star performer gets a last-minute reprieve, leaving the show with a lot of dead air to fill.

One way to solve this dilemma is to have a spare condemned person waiting in the wings. Soon, however, even they would be used up and advertisers looking for new blood will put pressure on legislators and judges to dispense the death penalty for shoplifting, making an illegal U-turn and keeping library books overdue.

They'll also petition to have executions made as colorful as possible, which means a return to burning at the stake and guillotining. Besides a renewed audience interest and higher Nielsen ratings, such a move would open the way for still more advertisers, such as Open Pit BBQ Sauce, Gillette and Head & Shoulders Shampoo.

True, the fainthearted will decry this solution, but their protests will die down as audiences are treated to theatrical entertainment reminiscent of the good old days of public hangings, when people brought their children and picnic lunches to enjoy the show and learn a lesson.

Constitutionally, there may be only one flaw in **GASP** — the "cruel and unusual punishment" experienced by the executed "performers."

After all, what could they possibly do for an encore?

### TO MY CRITICS

When I am in a sober mood
  I worry, work, and think.
When I am in a drunken mood
  I gamble, fight, and drink.
But when all my moods are over,
  And the worst has come to pass,
I hope they bury me upside down,
  So the world can kiss my ass.

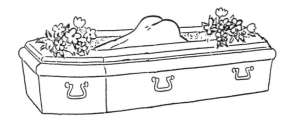

# MORE TRADE NAMES
# OF AMERICAN CONDOMS

## Sir Maurice Sedley, *Bart.*\*

Rubber dubbing within the American condom manufacturing industry continues unabated. Twenty-three newly identified brand names fall into three of the previously identified general categories (*Maledicta* 5:47-49): *Aggression* — 8; *Hedonism* — 12; *Morphology* or *Shape* — 3.

| AGGRESSION | HEDONISM |
|---|---|
| *Banzai Bliss* | *Contact* |
| *Bareback* | *Diamond* |
| *Blazes* | *Double Play* |
| *Conquer* | *Fuji* |
| *Die-Hard* | *Glide* |
| *Round Up* | *Glow* |
| *Swashbuckler* | *Oriental Touch* |
| *Thunderfuck* | *Sensations* |
| **MORPHOLOGY** or **SHAPE** | *Slimscore* |
| *Decca-Stud* | *Super Score* |
| *Snugs* | *Waves* |
| *Wrinkle* Chapeau *Hard* | *Yield* |

The augmented *N* of 75 names breaks down as follows into general categories:

| | | | |
|---|---|---|---|
| **Aggression:** | N = | 14 | 19% |
| **Hedonism:** | N = | 41 | 55% |
| **Morphology or Shape:** | N = | 9 | 12% |
| **Neutrality:** | N = | 7 | 9% |
| **Protection or Security:** | N = | 4 | 5% |

An analysis of the eight newly identified aggressive condom names indicates that seven of them imply a potentially violent assault on the feminine form, while one is openly defiant of femininity.

**Banzai Bliss**: The male as a fanatical, saber-waving, shouting soldier charging across the field of Aphrodite to achieve victory over a feminine adversary. The name implies that the "attack" will be delightfully successful.

**Bareback**: The male as a rough and ready horseman riding his feminine mount with a minimum of preliminaries.

**Blazes**: The male as an arsonist setting the female aflame with passion — the feminine form seen as a building to be torched by the fire of masculine passion.

**Conquer**: Woman as military objective to be subjugated.

**Die-Hard**: Male defiance in the face of certain loss of erection upon achieving orgasm upon the female body. Also, the name of a long-lasting battery.

**Round Up**: The male astride his "horse of passion" going after his female "heifer" to rope, bulldoze, tie and brand her.

**Swashbuckler**: The male as a saber-waving, rope-swinging sea-dog boarding the female's "vessel" afloat on the sea of passion.

**Thunderfuck**: The male as a noisy, Zeus-like divinity shooting his divine lightening into the female's yielding body. The picture on the package shows a Superman-like figure with a lightening bolt in one hand — both the name and the picture smack of grandiosity.

### HISTORICAL NOTE

Chapter VIII of the classic study of Himes on contraception provides the first scholarly history of the condom.

Fallopius (1564) is credited with first describing the condom in European medical literature. The term *condom* first appears in England, in 1717, in Turner's treatise on syphilis, but to date, the etymology of the term remains unresolved. [*See* William Kruck in our Bibliography. –*Ed.*]

1926 was the red-letter year for the American condom industry when Youngs Rubber Company of Trenton, New Jersey, introduced the "Trojan" brand.

In 1931, Youngs commissioned the first marketing study of the condom. It was researched by Herman W. Smith who made a tour of twenty counties of Western Florida and purchased condoms at the following locations: 211 gas stations, garages, auto supply houses; 80 restaurants, cafés, soda fountains, lunch counters; 33 pool halls and barber-shops; and 40 grocery stores, newsstands and shoe-shine stands.

In his 267-page report, Smith identified 47 different brands of condoms, e.g., **Aggression**: *Cadets, Hercules, Man-O-War, Samsonites, Vikings*; **Hedonism**: *Carmen, Cleo-Tex*; **Protection or Security**: *Bobbies* (English Policemen), *Dred-Not* (perhaps a pun on *dreadnaught* — the guns of the big warship are "covered"), *Sûreté*; and reported that both the retailing and wholesaling of the product was chaotic.

The report inspired Youngs to lead a "moral crusade" against the random sale of condoms, and began supporting local option statutes to restrict the sale of condoms to drugstores. Long Beach, California, became the first American municipality to pass such legislation, and it was soon followed by a host of other American cities. The success of these local option statutes made the condom industry both respectable and profitable in the United States.

## REFERENCES

*Adam & Eve Shop-By-Mail Catalog.* Carrboro, N.C., 1982.

Hejno, John. "The Contraceptive Industry Facts and Figures on America's Least Known About Business," *Eros* (New York), Summer 1962, pp. 13-15.

Himes, Norman E. *Medical History of Contraception.* New York: Gamut Press, 1963. Reprint of 1936 original ed.

Kilpatrick, John W. "The Condom Conundrum: An Etymological Exploration with a Hitchcock Ending," *Eros*, Summer 1962, p. 16.

*Romeo Catalog.* Chapel Hill, N.C., 1981.

# KAKOLOGIA

## A CHRONICLE OF NASTY RIDDLES
## AND NAUGHTY WORDPLAYS

### Reinhold Aman

#### INTRODUCTION

Like cunnilingus, editing and publishing "Kakologia" is a lonely and unappreciated labor of love, but someone has to do it. I have apologized for this material offensive to many readers in the preceding two volumes of *Maledicta*.

However, I have received many positive reactions to this part of our journal from folklore scholars and others who believe, as I do, that this kind of material must be chronicled — as it reflects society — and preserved in this permanent home. In fact, those who support these collections are much more outspoken than the few lamenters:

> Sod the bastards who object to "Kakologia." How long, oh Lord, before people accept the notion that this is an example of freedom of speech? ... Censorship is nothing more than the desire to be rid of something with which you are uncomfortable. The people who want you or anyone else to publish just what they can handle are the same people who, secretly, would like to put all of "them" back on a boat to wherever "they" came from. They are the people who want to deal with a problem by hiding from it. (Joe McConnell)

But then there is the occasional complaint that makes me squirm, knowing how unfair and nasty much of the material is to various groups. The lengthy kakological "Howard University Law School" piece in the last volume (7:308-311) brought a complaint from an anthropological linguist:

> Obviously, bad taste is your bread and butter, but as a purveyor? The piece is hard to justify. I know a fair number of urban blacks, workers and professionals. The lawyers don't talk that way, and nobody lives that way.

I responded that it was a contrived composite of many anti-black stereotypes, but that there are in fact blacks who act and talk the way they were depicted in that piece, and that he might have led too sheltered a life in academia to know real life. He replied that he wasn't too sheltered, that his wife has been teaching for 18 years in a big eastern city's black ghetto, and that his son-in-law was black, continuing:

> I think the flashy car / flashy clothes part of the stereotype faithfully reflects Pimpsville, which is far from an exclusively black preserve. And the welfare fraud part is more part of a rightist stereotype than it is of real life... But my problem is with the genuineness of the data, its empirical qualifications. In the "Howard U" case the item looks suspiciously like something cooked up to further the bias of an individual. If so, it does not provide genuine data relevant to verbal aggression in the large. The piece makes me wonder about your criteria for exclusion... It may be made up to satisfy some individual's hatred.

My answer was that the piece was a genuine example of folklore, photocopy humor, Xeroxlore: not a single person's work sent to just one recipient but circulating widely, and repeatedly photocopied, as one can tell by the condition of the material. I also explained that my major criterion for inclusion was as follows: the material has to have been photocopied repeatedly and has to circulate in several states to be considered "folklore" fit for publication.

Regardless of its academic merits and nastiness, the piece is rather clever and very well done. It crams most anti-black stereotypes into the format of a law examination, similar to the fake Job Applications for blacks, Mafia members, etc., that have been circulating widely for years. The original was no doubt the work of a lawyer probably associated with the government, as few laymen would know the legal and bureaucratic topics and language used; it originated probably in the greater Washington, D.C., area or northern Virginia, and was composed about ten years ago (Jackson Five concert clue). It was then reworked by others (Biology section, which doesn't match the previous). I'm certain that a trained folklorist can do a better analysis of this item.

Similarly offensive material published by established folklorists also is attacked and defended. Witness the "Auschwitz Jokes" published by Alan Dundes with Thomas Hauschild in *Western Folklore* (October 1983, pp. 249-60). Judith Samuel was deeply insulted and criticized that journal for publishing that article which she called a "useless...excuse for scholarship." In the next issue of the *California Folklore Newsletter* (December 1984, p. 3), Joseph Holman defended Professor Dundes's work with words applicable to our work, too:

> As a Jew, I too am offended and shocked by the "Auschwitz jokes" themselves, but as a folklorist I feel strongly that they are deserving of attention and analysis. To condone censorship of certain topics because one finds them racist, sexist, crude, or otherwise objectionable seems to me to strike at the heart of social scientific research. It is only by bravely facing and studying human expressions which appear horrifying or disgusting that we can hope to understand why people think and behave in ways which strike others as illogical or cruel.

Ethnic jokes and negative reactions to them keep making the news. The following examples should suffice to illustrate this topic:

• Polish-American groups became angry when they learned that a book of Polish jokes was buried in a time capsule on the Longmeadow (Mass.) town green during the town's bicentennial celebration. Officials of the Historical Society bowed to pressure from Julie Strzempek,

Zignon Muszynski and others, dug up the capsule, and removed the book. (*MJ*, 12 Oct. 1983, pt. 2, p. 8).

• There is a time and place for such jokes, but teachers should have more brains than to share such material with children who, godnose, have enough problems growing up: In 1982, a Paulsboro, N.J., graphic arts teacher of a high school with 26% blacks passed out a list of jokes aimed at Poles, Italians, Jews, American Indians, blacks, and other ethnic and racial groups. In 1983, he passed around the well-known "Nigger Application for Employment" form. The NAACP is now trying to remove him from the school. (*Philadelphia Inquirer*, 25 April 1983, p. 3-B; contributed by Suzanne Zappasodi)

• In Milwaukee, Wisconsin, one grade school teacher was fired and another suspended for distributing a racist leaflet at an alternative school for handicapped or emotionally disturbed students. Both teachers, who are white, had given a racist bogus job application for Jesse Jackson to an emotionally disturbed black student, who was to give it to other white teachers. (*MJ*, 22 Feb. 1985, pt. 2, p. 5)

• Wisconsin Representative Louise Tesmer told an ethnic joke in the Assembly while arguing against legalized gambling. It dealt with three mothers bragging about their sons: the German is a lawyer and makes $50,000 a year; the Jew is a doctor and earns $100,000 a year; and the Italian mother's son, who earns $100,000 a week, is a 'sports mechanic': "He fixes the baseball game, he fixes the basketball game, he fixes the races." Tesmer later apologized. (*MJ*, 13 Oct. 1983, pt. 2, p. 3)

• Local and other laws are being introduced to stop ethnic jokes ("harassment"): California employers with five or more regular employes now can be fined under a recent law forbidding the telling or posting of ethnic jokes, slurs, and graffiti. (*MJ*, 11 Aug. 1982, Accent, p. 5)

• A national coalition of nearly 20 ethnic groups has

been formed to fight ethnic stereotyping in the media. They support a bill (HR 3105) introduced in the House in May 1983 by Rep. Mario Biaggi seeking the creation of an Office of Ethnic Affairs within the Federal Communications Commission to deal with ethnic and racial stereotyping and ridicule. During the last nine months of 1983, the FCC received 595 complaints, including a 700% increase in complaints against FM radio stations with call-in shows in which listeners made racial or ethnic slurs. (*MJ*, 14 March 1984, pt. 2, p. 2)

• The Irish in Britain are fighting the stereotypes of being drunken, violent and stupid. (*International Herald Tribune*, 17 March 1983, p. 4; contributed by Jess Nierenberg)

• The Portuguese community in general, and the New Bedford (Mass.) Portuguese specifically, are upset by the news media who unfairly targeted the hard-working, law-abiding citizen by persistently identifying the "Big Dan's Bar" rapists as "Portuguese immigrants." (*MJ*, 31 Aug. 1983, Accent, p. 1)

While in the preceding cases only words are used as weapons, there is much more lethal ethnic, racial and religious hatred in this world that cannot be stopped by law. Physical harm and death are widespread:

• In Lawrence, Mass., violence spread for two days through the six-block Tower Hill area, where scores of Hispanics and whites hurled ethnic insults, rocks and fire-bombs against each other. (*MJ*, 10 Aug. 1984, p. 1)

• The violence in Northern Ireland and the Middle East continues.

• Beginning on 12 February 1983 and lasting ten days, thousands of people were killed in bloody religious and ethnic battles in Assam, India. Hindus fought Moslems; Hindu Assamese battled aboriginal tribespeople; Bengali-speaking Hindus fought Assamese; Assamese slaughtered Moslem Bengalis. Seventeen villages were burned to the ground; men, women and children were massacred; 250,000 are homeless. Among the causes were the hates, tensions and suspicions of 10,000 tribespeople and Assamese living in refugee camps. (*MJ*, 1 March 1984, Accent, p. 5)

• In Sri Lanka, dozens of people were burned, stabbed, hacked and bludgeoned to death in this country's latest orgy of ethnic rioting between the minority (Hindu) Tamil and the majority (Buddhist) Sinhalese populations. (*MJ*, 28 July 1983, p. 1; *Time*, 22 April 1985, p. 32)

It's not easy being a "deviation from the norm," whether by one's easily detectable "ethnic" looks, name, accent, or by skin color, creed, dress, food. At least in the USA most "deviations" don't get killed for being different. Perhaps we should put up with the ethnic, racial and religious "jokes," accepting them as safety valves through which much anti-out-group hostility is drained off, instead of suppressing them, causing the universal human dislike for "others" to explode in murderous rages...

## DE-ETHNICIZING ETHNIC JOKES

As pointed out in previous volumes, the same jokes about stupidity are used to put down the Irish in England, the Italians, Poles, and blacks in the USA, the East Frisians in Germany, the Minnesotans in Iowa, etc. Wishing to use such jokes without slurring specific ethnic groups, two writers have used different methods: Elizabeth Claire, in her *What's So Funny? A Foreign Student's Introduction to American Humor* (1984) just calls the targets *Ethnics* (p. 100). Paul Dickson, in his *Jokes* (1984) invents the word *Funistradans* (p. 162), while acknowledging Jeffrey Goldstein's objection to using fictitious nationalities in such jokes that lose their punch by being de-ethnicized. My preference is to use the actual ethnic groups, not only because of the inappropriateness of assigning certain shortcomings to other groups (e.g., Polish *fool* jokes turned into pointless jokes about Iranians who have different shortcomings), but also because the de-ethnicized jokes falsify reality by not chronicling honestly which ethnic groups are the target at what specific times and places. Claire's solution is necessary for her young and impressionable audience, and Dickson's solution may have been his personal or the publisher's choice, but we who record such material in scholarly publications must not weasel out.

### REASONS FOR ETHNIC JOKES

I do not wish to get too deeply into the reasons for ethnic jokes. While I and others reflect on the causes, I believe that this topic is for trained sociologists and psychologists (if the latter ever leave the poor rats alone and turn to humans) who can publish their findings in their journals. Gordon Allport's *The Nature of Prejudice* and Prager & Telushkin's *Why the Jews?* provide many insights.

Some of our readers have shared their thoughts on this problem. The following excerpt from a letter by Ingrid Banholzer (Germany) illustrates that our readers don't just laugh but also think:

> I've thought about the reasons why certain groups are discriminated against. Surely only because they are different from the masses. The masses are ignorant. They want all people to be the way they themselves are; everything else makes them insecure. Insecurity is the reason why the masses discriminate against and laugh about those who look and think different. It's not so much that the masses are vicious: it's their insecurity that makes them dangerous and aggressive.

### NEW GENRES

Two new genres have been observed. Examples of the first type were contributed by Joel Bonn (Montréal, Canada) and the users of Henry Birdseye's computer bulletin board. Examples of the second type were submitted by readers in California and Virginia.

### (A) TARZAN AND JANE

If Tarzan and Jane were Jewish, what would Cheetah be?
— *A fur coat.*

If Tarzan and Jane were Italian, what would Cheetah be?
— *The other woman.*

If Tarzan and Jane were Polish, what would Cheetah be?
— *The gifted child.*

If Tarzan and Jane were Vietnamese, what would Cheetah be?
— *Dinner.*

### (B) HIRE THE...

Richard Barton submitted these two heard in San Francisco:

*As the Conservatives say, "Hire minorities — they're a great tax shelter!" and As the Liberals say, "Hire minorities — it's so gratifying to patronize them!"*

Paul Runey also sent such an example: *"Hire the handicapped — they're fun to watch!"* [1]

Parkinson's disease struck Professor Michel Monnot at age 38, but he has not lost his sense of humor, telling me

---

[1]Mr. Runey, of Richmond, Virginia, a former paratrooper, has been a paraplegic for 26 years. Like another paraplegic friend in Las Vegas, he likes to use gallows humor to cope with his difficulties and derides the bureaucrats' and sociologists' euphemism *catastrophically injured.*

this riddle: *What does the Parkinsonian say to the guy with whom he has just completed a deal? "Let's shake on it!"* [2]

## ED GEIN DEAD

Ed Gein, who inspired macabre jokes (see *Maledicta* 7, pp. 281-83), died 26 July 1984, at age 77, after having spent 27 years in mental hospitals. Wisconsin's most notorious murderer was also the inspiration for Hitchcock's *Psycho*.

## NEW JOKE TOPICS IN 1984 AND 1985

### WEST GERMANY

Among West Germans, three joke topics were current during 1984-85: (1) bumbling Chancellor Kohl, (2) more vicious anti-Turkish jokes, and (3) the investigations into the alleged homosexuality of General Kießling.

The Kohl jokes are quite harmless, making fun of his intellectual dullness and ignorance of English. The following samples are from the Munich newspaper *AZ* of 28 April 1984, p. 4, submitted by Prof. Gert Raeithel:

England's Maggie Thatcher invites Kohl to a pub, where she orders a dark (*dunkles*) beer, and he has a light one (*helles*). She proposes a toast, "To your health!" Kohl replies, "To your dunkles!"

Reagan, Kohl and Chernenko arrive late at a meeting. Reagan apologizes, "I am sorry." Chernenko, "I am sorry, too." Kohl, "I am sorry three."

---

[2]Dr. Monnot, a *Maledicta* contributor and personal friend, will fight the negative image of those afflicted by Parkinson's by walking from Minneapolis to Los Angeles, beginning his walk on September 14, 1985, and arriving in L.A. on January 31, 1986. Tax-free contributions to fight this disease may be sent to: Northfield Hospital Parkinson's Fund, Northfield, MN 55057.

Some anti-Turkish jokes, contributed by Bob L., Stuttgart:

What's the difference between the Jews and the Turks?
— *The Jews have it behind them.*

How does a Turk commit suicide?
— *By smelling his armpit.* (This joke is told in Israel about the Georgians; see MAL 7:284)

What's a Turkish Mercedes?
— *A 1968 Ford Taunus.* (A car as worthless as an old Rambler)

What's the difference between a disaster and a catastrophe?
— *When a planeload of Turkish guest workers crashes, that's a disaster. When it lands safely in Frankfurt, that's a catastrophe.*

If a bomb fell on Turkey, how many people would be killed?
— *Two. The rest of them live in Holland.*

The last one was sent by a Dutch reader. In other countries with many Turkish guest workers such anti-Turkish jokes are told, too. This punctures the balloon of some American folklorists who, blinded by prejudice, use these jokes for their anti-German speculations.

In December 1983, the top-ranking West German NATO general Günther Kießling was unceremoniously dismissed on the grounds that his alleged homosexuality had become a security risk (*Financial Times*, London, 19 Jan. 1984, p. 2). The proceedings were as bungled by the German government officials and blown out of proportion by the media vultures as was President Reagan's Bitburg cemetary visit by their American counterparts. The German media reported the latest allegations and denials *ad nauseam*, and soon "Kießling jokes" appeared. Here are a few, submitted by Ingrid Banholzer:

How did Kießling change the German Army's salute?
— *The soldiers now have to blow a kiss.*

According to Kießling, what's the difference between a Four-Star Hotel and a Four-Star General?
— *You enter a Four-Star Hotel from the front.*

When asked to name four European rivers, which ones did General Kießling name?
— *"Main, Rhein, Inn, Po."* (Four actual river names, but in this order they sound exactly like German *Mein' rein in Po*, "Mine [penis] into [the] behind.")

### USA AND CANADA

In the USA and Canada, in addition to the ongoing AIDS jokes, there were several productive topics during 1984 and 1985: the mass murder at McDonald's restaurant; the

Massachusetts poolroom rape, the Baby Fae heart transplant, the Union Carbide disaster in India, Indira Gandhi's assassination, Michael Jackson's Glove, the Mondale-Ferraro candidacy, the Marvin Gaye murder, Miss America (first black and the lesbian photo scandal), as well as locally in New York City, jokes about Hasidic Jews and militant feminists. But the largest outpourings of sick and sickening riddles was caused by the Ethiopian famine, which we recorded separately (see Christopher's article). Incidentally, while in Cologne, Germany (summer 1985), I inquired whether Ethiopian jokes were told there. A few circulated, but most of these had been told two and three years ago as "Rhodesian" and "Biafran" jokes.

For the first time, we have also been able to gather several anti-WASP jokes.

The latest topic is Rock Hudson, dealt with in the AIDS jokes below.

### A.I.D.S.

What do you call someone with herpes and AIDS?
— *An incurable romantic.*

Why don't feminists get AIDS?
— *Because they're too tight-assed.*

What do gay alligators get?
— *Gator-AIDS.*

What do you call gay lawyers?
— *Legal AIDS.*

What do you call black faggots in wheelchairs?
— *Cool AIDS.*

What do you get from listening to San Franciscan gays?
— *Hearing AIDS.*

Why don't gays whisper in each other's ears?
— *Because they don't want to get hearing AIDS.*

What do they call the restroom in a gay bar?
— *First AIDS station.*

How did the minister get AIDS?
— *He didn't clean his organ between hymns.*

What does AIDS stand for?
— *Another Infected Dick Sucker.*

What does AIDS stand for?
— *¡Adiós, Infected Dick Sucker!*

Have you heard of the new AIDS movie?
— *It's called "Germs of Endearment."*

Who brought AIDS to the USA?
— *Some asshole.*

What's the breakfast specialty at the gay hotel?
— *AIDS Benedict.*

FOREIGN
AIDS

From the private
collection of a
famous cartoonist

How do you know that your garden has AIDS?
— *When you find that your pansies are dying.*

What are Rock Hudson's friends happy about?
— *That they didn't get "a Piece of the Rock."*

Why is Prudential Insurance losing a lot of customers?
— *Because nobody wants "a Piece of the Rock."*

Why was Rock Hudson's auto insurance cancelled?
— *Because he's been rear-ended too much.*

What new movie are Sylvester Stallone and Rock Hudson doing?
— *Rambutt.*

What's the difference between Staten Island and Rock Hudson?
— *The first is a ferry terminal, the second a terminal fairy.*

Dr. Casper Schmidt heard the following one in South Africa (*VIGS* is the Afrikaans acronym for AIDS):
>  *Waarvoor staan VIGS?*
>  — *Vinger-In-Gat Sindroom.*
>  What does AIDS stand for?
>  — Finger-in-asshole syndrome.

## MASS MURDER AT McDONALD'S

The McDonald's massacre and jokes about it had a special impact on me: a few weeks before the shooting, my wife, daughter and I had eaten at that restaurant, after coming back from Mexico. When I read the news and saw the television reports, I thought, "Holy shit! That was close! This could have been the end of *Maledicta*."

John H., Seattle, reported 28 July 1984 that the mass murder of 21 people and wounding of 15 at McDonald's restaurant in San Ysidro, California, by James Huberty, on July 18, inspired such riddles as:

*What's the "McDonald's Special"?*
*— For $29.95, you get a Big Mac, a McHelmet, and a McVest.*

He also reported that these jokes appeared on the "Jokes" section of the UNIX Users Netnews, but the San Diego node of this computer network disabled this section for one month following the massacre, apparently because the locals found such sick humor intolerable at that time.

Lewis T., New York, heard the following one in New York:

*What did the gunman say when he walked into McDonald's?*
*— McFreeze!*

It is eerie that in March 1984, three months before the McDonald's massacre took place, the following riddle was recorded on Henry Birdseye's computer bulletin board in Colorado:

*How do you kill 200 Mexicans on Thanksgiving?*
*— Blow up a McDonald's.*

After the mass murder, Douglass Cross and George Cory even composed a song about it, "I Left My Heart in San Ysidro," published by the Surrealist Workers Party in Sheridan, Wyoming. John S. in Washington, D.C., sent a copy.

The following jokes were posted on the Colorado BB on 20 August 1984:

*Have you heard about the new McDonald's going up?*
*— It has Golden Archers.*

*What are the new items on the McDonald's menu?*
*— Dead McMuffins and Dead Macs.*

*Have you heard about the Big Mac Attack?*

*What's the newest on McDonald's menu?*
— *Duck.*

*Have you heard the new McDonald's ad?*
— *"Burger King cook their hamburgers over fire.*
*We cook ours under fire."*

As reported by Gerd L., Berlin, McDonald's is also the setting of a joke in West Germany. The Turkish guest workers and their food are the targets:
*Wie heißt der Manager der McDonalds Filiale in Istanbul?*
— *Izmir Übel!*
(What's the name of the manager of the Istanbul branch of McDonald's? — "Man, do I feel sick to my stomach!" Izmir, a city in Turkey, sounds like colloquial German for *ist mir*.)
Another harmless McDonald's riddle:
*Did you hear that McDonald's now offer venison balls on the menu?*
— *They are under a buck.*
See also the McDonald's joke in the Ethiopian riddles.

## BIG DAN'S POOL HALL RAPE

After the Bedford, Mass., gang-bang, where a woman allegedly was raped repeatedly on a pool table by Portuguese immigrants, the following song was circulated about Fall River, Mass., a nearby town, equally ethnic and seedy. Received in June 1984 in a plain brown envelope by N. K. in Rhode Island, who passed it on to me. M.C.I. stands for "Massachusetts Correctional Institution." The song is a parody of Jimmy Dean's "Big John."

## FALL RIVER POOL

Was the sixth of March in eighty-three
All she really wanted was a drink for free.
She told her mom she's goin' for smokes,
Never really thought she'd be gettin' six pokes
   *(Chorus)*
     At Big Dan's, Big Dan's, Big Dan's, Big Bad Dan's, Big Dan's.


The bar was dark, the men were dirty,
She finally raised her skirt 'bout eight thirty.
Victor and José and the other poor fools
Were playin' a new game called Fall River Pool
     At Big Dan's, Big Dan's, Big Dan's, Big Bad Dan's, Big Dan's.


Well, she brought 'em to trial, she stated her views.
'Bout half a dozen Portagees who chalked their cues
The court was tough, but so's the street
Her mama always said, "Be careful what you eat"
     At Big Dan's, Big Dan's, Big Dan's, Big Bad Dan's, Big Dan's.


The jury came back, said "Guilty of rape"
The immigrant community all went ape.
The judge said, "Boys, she turned some tricks,
But ya shoulda known better than to dip your sticks"
     At Big Dan's, Big Dan's, Big Dan's, Big Bad Dan's, Big Dan's.


The bar's a bake shop, the patrons said "Bye."
Six boys are servin' eight-to-ten at M.C.I.
But they'll be out as soon as they're able
And never go near another seven-hole table
     At Big Dan's, Big Dan's, Big Dan's, Big Bad Dan's, Big Dan's.


The only riddle I received is the following:

*What has 6 pockets, 4 legs, and smells like fish?*
*— The pool table in Al's Bar, New Bedford, Conn.*

Prof. Elaine Chaika commented on this rape in her "The
Force of Linguistic Structures on Cultural Values: Some
Distinctions, as Exemplified by the 'Big Dan' Rape Case,

in *Interfaces* 11/3 (1984), pp. 68-74. This useful essay is marred by her ultra-feminist, if not ignorant, verbiage: "Portuguese, like English, evinces in its vocabulary a belief that women are primarily sex objects," p. 68. On pp. 71-72 are several Portuguese terms contrasting the male and female as to sexual conduct, intelligence, and marital status.

### BABY FAE HEART TRANSPLANT

What's the fastest-moving land animal?
— *A scared baboon on a bicycle pedaling past the Loma Linda hospital.*

Did Baby Fae have a rejection?
— *No. She chocked on a banana.*

What were Baby Fae's first three words?
— *"Ba na na."*

Did they finally get Baby Fae off the respirator?
— *Yes, but now they can't get her off the chandelier.*

How did the staff know Baby Fae was having trouble?
— *Her heart stopped going "LUB-dub, LUB-dub" and started to go "ba-BOON, ba-BOON."*

What do you say to an infant who had a canine heart transplant?
— *"Baby, STAY!"*

Who delivered Baby Fae's eulogy?
— *Marlin Perkins.* (Or *King Kong*)

## UNION CARBIDE - BHOPAL GAS DISASTER

What is the new theme song of Union Carbide?
— *"Ten little, nine little, eight little Indians."*

How do you make the perfect Manhattan?
— *Get Union Carbide to build a plant right in the middle of Harlem.*

What do you call 500 Bhopal residents that have had their breasts removed?
— *The Indian Nippleless 500.*

Who knocked off more Indians than John Wayne?
— *Union Carbide.*

What's Union Carbide's newest product?
— *Dot remover.*

## INDIRA GANDHI ASSASSINATION

Who won the National Hockey League Player of the Month award last month?
— *Indira Gandhi. She stopped twelve shots in five seconds.*

Why should Indira have changed her deodorant earlier?
— *Because her Right Guard let her down.*

Who finally stopped smoking this week?
— *Indira Gandhi.*

What's the East Indian Telephone Company's song?
— *"Reach out, reach out and torch someone."*

## MICHAEL JACKSON'S GLOVE

Jackson's gimmick of using only one glittering glove not only inspired hundreds of thousands of little chickenbrains to buy an overpriced Michael Jackson glove, but also kindled the imagination of quipsters as to what had happened to Michael's other glove:

Where did they find Michael Jackson's other glove?
— *Between Brooke Shield's breasts.*

Where did they find Michael Jackson's other glove?
— *In Boy George's trousers.*

What did Brooke Shield's gynecologist find?
— *Michael Jackson's other glove.*

Similarly, in a Mimi Pond comic strip in *NL* (July 1984, p. 70), the female who made a man out of Jackson is examined by her gynecologist next day who finds a glove in her vagina.

## MONDALE-FERRARO CANDIDACY

Joan Rivers spoke at a lunch honoring Nancy Reagan at the Republican convention in Dallas. The audience of about 1,800 women applauded ("if somewhat warily") her "somewhat tasteless barb" about Walter Mondale and Dolly Parton (Fritz & Tits, the three biggest boobs in the Whitehouse, which we published earlier in 7:299). *Time*, 3 Sept. 1984, p. 39.

Did you hear that Mondale was arrested for speeding?
— *He was caught doing 69 with his Ferraro.*

Why did Mondale want to replace Geraldine Ferraro with Vanessa Williams?
— *Because Vanessa proved that she could lick bush.*

What did Mondale say the day after the Democratic Convention?
— *"But I told you I wanted a Ferrari!"*

What do Reagan and Mondale have in common?
— *They both have a bush for vice president.*

Why did Mondale pick a woman for his vice president?
— *He was jealous that he didn't have his own bush.*

What has four legs and two tits?
— *The Democratic Twat.*

Who's on the Democratic ticket in 1984?
— *Fritz and Tits.*

Who is running for the Democratic Party?
— *Wally and the Beaver.*

## BLACK MISS AMERICA

What's the new Miss America theme song?
— *"Here she be, Miss America."*

Knock-Knock. — *Who's there?* — Ida. — *Ida who?*
— I da new Miss America.

Have you heard about the new Vanessa Williams postage stamp?
— *You have to lick it in front.*

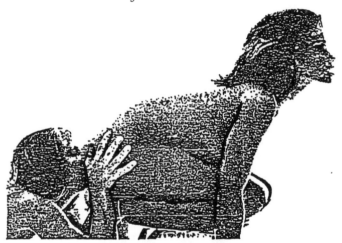

# ORDER YOURS TODAY!!
## *Miss America Duck Call*
### BACKDOOR ENTERPRISES
#### Box 2
#### Brownhole, Miss.

The above illustration, here reduced, circulated soon after the photos of Miss Williams appeared in the Sept. 1984 *Penthouse*. In a bogus news story in *National Lampoon* (Nov. 1984, p. 20), Miss Williams defended those photos: "There's nothing dirty or obscene about the human body," she said. "I just felt I could make an artistic statement by rubbing my steamy snatch on the quivering tongue of a big-titted white bitch."

## MARVIN GAYE MURDER

What was the last thing Marvin Gaye's father said to him?
— *"This is the last 45 you'll ever hear."*

Whom has the Ku Klux Klan picked as their Man of the Year?
— *Marvin Gay, Sr.*

## ANTI-HASIDIM

In New York City, the "backward" Orthodox Hasidic Jews are ridiculed by "modern," secularized Jews and by Brooklyn blacks who live in close proximity to the Orthodox Jews. The following riddles were collected by a male Jewish school teacher and a female black white-collar worker and student:

What does a Hasidic woman have between her legs?
— *Labia menorah.*

How many Hasidim does it take to change a lightbulb?
— *Two. One to consult the rebbe, and another to call a shabes-goy.*

Why is the Hasidic birthrate dropping?
— *Because the rebbe won't let them pork.*

Why don't Hasidic Jews shave?
— *To make up for their wives' heads.*

Why does a Hasidic boy let his hairlocks grow down to his balls?
— *So he can polish his sister's shaven head.*

Why do Hasidic Jews wear such big hats?
— *So they'll have a place to shit if there are no kosher toilets.*

When does a Hasidic Jew bathe?
— *When he goes walking in the rain.*

What's black, stinks of herring, and won't shake hands with you?
— *A Hasidic Jew.*

### ANTI-FEMINIST

Name a feminist revolutionary.
— *Leon Twatsky.*

When does a feminist smile?
— *When you turn her upside-down.*

How many feminists can escape from a burning building?
— *I don't know, but let's find out at the next N.O.W. convention.*

What's the ultimate feminist sexual fantasy?
— *A vibrator that lectures on Marxism.*

### ANTI-WASP

What's a macho WASP?
— *One who jogs home after getting a vasectomy.*

How can you tell a WASP widow?
— *She is the one in the black tennis outfit.*

What do you call a WASP who didn't go to college, doesn't work for his father, and believes in social causes?
— *A failure.*

What do WASPs consider "slumming"?
— *Visiting Aspen in the summer.*

How does a WASP define "blowjob"?
— *Having to blow out more than five candles on a cake.*

What's the difference between a WASP and a black taking a shower at the gym?
— *The WASP gets out of the shower to take a piss.*

What's a WASP's idea of being open-minded?
— *Dating a Canadian.*

### OTHER TOPICS

Other well-publicized topics and natural disasters produced few riddles:

What was the last sound heard in southern Bangladesh?
— *"Surf's up!"*

What are the two favorite movies in Bangladesh nowadays?
— *Splash* and *Gone with the Wind.*

What's the name of the new Bernhard Goetz television game show?
— *Maim That Coon.*

What's the difference between a sparrow and an Iowa farmer?
— *The bird can still make a deposit on a John Deere tractor.*

## GENERAL

What do you get when you cross a Cabbage Patch doll with the Pillsbury dough boy?
— *An ugly, squatty broad with a yeast infection.*

What's the difference between a vomiting pygmy and Jane Fonda?
— *A runt that does spit-ups and a cunt that does sit-ups.*

What do Claus von Bühlow and the Jolly Green Giant have in common?
— *Both have millions tied up in vegetables.*

What's in an Jewish fighter pilot's survival kit?
— *A burnoose and a clip-on foreskin.*

How did Billie Jean King die?
— *She was found face down in Joan Rivers.*

How did John De Lorean get arrested?
— *He tried to move a lot of snow and the government caught his drift.*

What do you call a female peacock?
— *Peacunt.*

What did the husband do when he heard that his wife had an affair with his best friend?
— *He rushed home and shot his dog.*

How do you say "Preparation H" in Italian?
— *Innuendo.*

What's the difference between "kooky" and "kinky"?
— *With kooky you use a feather. With kinky, the whole bird.*

What do you get when you cross a hooker and a computer?
— *A fucking know-it-all.*

How do Pinocchio and Barbie make love?
— *She sits on his face and says, "Tell a lie, tell the truth, tell a lie..."*

What's the difference between mononucleosis and herpes?
— *You get mono from snatching a kiss, and herpes from kissing a snatch.*

What do you call nuts on a wall?
— *Walnuts.*
What do you call nuts on a chest?
— *Chestnuts.*
What do you call nuts on a chin?
— *Blowjob.*

What did the three gays do who attacked a woman?
— *Two held her down while the third did her hair.*

What are the three things a Texan hates?
— *A nigger with a knife, a Mexican with a gun, and a Yankee with a U-Haul truck.*

What's a "Good Ole Boy"?
— *A Jew from New York who moves to Texas, marries a Mexican, adopts a black child, then moves back to New York.*

Who killed David Kennedy?
— *Syringe Syringe.*

How do you get the Jackson Five into a Volkswagen?
— *Two in the front, two in the back, and Michael rides in the ashtray.*

What do you call Arnold Schwarzenegger engaging in auto-eroticism?
— *Onan, The Barbarian.*

What did Stevie Wonder say when Eddie Murphy asked if he could imitate him in his act?
— *"I don't see why not."*

What do you call a dead nigger in a parking lot?
— *A speed bump.*

What's the difference between a proctologist and a bartender?
— *A proctologist takes care of only one asshole at a time.*

What's a proctoscope?
— *A long tube with an asshole at each end.*

What's flat and pink and smells like pussy?
— *[Stick out your tongue]*

Why is your boss like a diaper?
— *He's always on your ass and full of shit.*

What do you call a black Smurf?
— *Smigger.*

Why do dogs lick their balls?
— *Because they can.*

What do you get when you cross a Jew and a bear?
— *Yentl Ben.*

What do you call Barbra Streisand's pubic hair?
— *Yentl floss.*

# ANNOUNCEMENTS

Announcements by the Editor, accomplishments by our members, and other noteworthy information *not* related to our specialty.

• Dear Readers: Please put your address (at least your name and ZIP code) on order blanks, etc. Making me copy your address from your check takes time and may cause problems if you have two addresses.

• The Fifth National **WHIM** Conference will take place March 28–April 1, 1986, at Arizona State University, Tempe, AZ 85287. Theme: *American Humor.* Deadline for submitting papers is 1 Jan. 1986. Send title, one-page abstract and $35 registration fee to the indefatigable conference organizer: Prof. Don Nilsen, English Dept., ASU.

• **TAASP**, The Association for the Anthropological Study of Play, will hold its meeting jointly with WHIM, 29 March to 1 April 1986, in Tempe, Arizona. Contact Prof. Frank Manning (Anthropology Dept., Western Ontario University, London, Ontario N6A 5C2, Canada) for more information. **Gershon Legman** will deliver the keynote address "Pecker-Pool and Cockalizers: Erotic Folk Elements in the Humor and Play of Adolescents" at the TAASP meeting. Mr. Legman is interested in further speaking engagements during his visit to the U.S. If interested in inviting him for a lecture, please contact him at La Clé des Champs, F-06560 Valbonne, France.

• Osmond Beckwith's *Vernon: An Anecdotal Novel* (1981, 195 pp., $10.00) covers the early part of a man's life—birth to age 17—centering around a boy's acquiring personhood and learning to distinguish the self from all others. As the boy is "typical," many male readers will see themselves in Robert Parsons growing up in rural America after the turn of the century. The author offers his novel to our readers for $6.00 postpaid: P.O. Box 328, Wharton, NJ 07885.

• Professor Jan Brunvand (English and Folklore, University of Utah) has published two interesting and amusing collections of stories told widely and even reported by newspapers as true: *The Vanishing Hitchhiker: American Urban Legends and Their Meanings* (1981) and his *The Choking Doberman and Other "New" Urban Legends* (1984).

• The Rev. Asa Sparks (Pumpkin Press, 604 Pumpkin Dr. SW., Decatur, AL 35603) has published a series of inexpensive booklets for youngsters, such as *The Boy Who Would Not Be A Frog, The Girl Who Loved Frogs, God Says I'm OK*, and *Sex and the Single Saint.*

• Branden Press (Box 843, Brookline Village, MA 02147) recently reprinted Friderike Maria Zweig's *Greatness Revisited.* Essays by Stefan Zweig's wife centering on Salzburg and American impressions of this literary and artistic couple. Professor Harry Zohn (Brandeis University) edited this work and wrote the introduction. Paperback, 152 pp., $7.95.

• John Campbell (Patrick's Press, Box 291, Columbus, GA 31902) has published three big quiz books: *Campbell's High School/College Quiz Book, Campbell's Potpourri I of Quiz Bowl Questions* and *Campbell's Potpourri II of Quiz Bowl Questions.* The books are 318 to 535 pages long, with questions from many fields, including nicknames of gangsters, outlaws and entertainers.

• In 1982, Professor George Monteiro published *The Coffee Exchange: Poems.* Some 60 personal prose poems — snapshots of Portugal and the people loving, hating, praying, swearing — by an American of Portuguese extraction visiting his ancestral homeland. 77 pages, $4.19. Gávea-Brown Publications, Center for Portuguese and Brazilian Studies, P.O. Box 0, Brown University, Providence, RI 02912.

• John Thorne has been publishing a series of culinary pamphlets on dill, pizza, rice & beans, basilico, British pub grub, English muffins, onion soup, chowder, and other delicacies. These well-done, inexpensive publications appeal to anyone who likes to cook. Write to him for more information at Jackdaw Press, Box 371, Essex Station, Boston, MA 02112.

• Elias Petropoulos, who recently returned from Berlin to Paris, has begun a new album, this time featuring pictures of 5,000 gravestones he photographed in Berlin. — His Greek-language photo-album *Courtyards in Greece* was published in Athens by Phorkys, in 1983. It contains a two-page English summary by John Taylor. — In the same year, he published 202 copies of an album dedicated to the memory of the 60,000 Jews killed by the Nazis in Saloniki, with 140 rare photos, post cards, and designs. Petropoulos has donated all copies of this

French/English edition of *Les Juifs de Salonique / The Jews of Salonica* to the major libraries around the world.

• The International Society for General Semantics, publishers of *ETC.: A Review of General Semantics*, also puts out a four-page newsletter, *Glimpse*. Write to Russell Joyner, Executive Director, ISGS, P.O. Box 2469, San Francisco, CA 94126, for a sample back issue of *Glimpse*.

• André Bacard edits the *Affirmist Newsletter*. Its main function is to inform members of the Affirmist Roundtables, a group founded in San Francisco in 1983, of their successes in providing a positive voice in our cynical world. More information available from Mr. Bacard, Box 1851, Novato, CA 94948.

• Professor Frank Nuessel (Modern Languages Dept., University of Louisville, Louisville, KY 40292) has been publishing a series of unusual linguistic post cards, some showing the word "peace" in several languages, others featuring unusual postage stamps, including a Polish one of Esperanto's Zamenhof.

• *The Middle East & South Asia Folklore Newsletter* has been published since Spring 1984. It informs researchers of all aspects of folklore of these regions. For more information write to the editors, Dwight Reynolds or Benedicte Grima, Dept. of Folklore & Folklife, 415 Logan Hall, University of Pennsylvania, Philadelphia, PA 19104.

• Professor William A. Douglass has been editing *The Basque Studies Program Newsletter* for several years. In the June 1985 issue, Linda White discusses the difficulties of creating a Basque-English dictionary ("Doing a Dictionary," pp. 6-9). More information: Basque Studies Program, University of Nevada Library, Reno, NV 89557-0012.

• Under his pen name "James Morton," Robert Throckmorton has published *The Picnic in the Woods*, a whimsical rhymed nonsense story featuring a prepubescent maiden. 48 pages, $3.60 (foreign addresses = $4.60). Write to Dr. R. Throckmorton, 1267 Douglas Drive, Las Vegas, NV 89102

• In 1985, Professor Brigitta Geltrich-Ludgate edited and published *Spoofing!: "Slightly Naughty!" An Anthology of Folkloristic Yarns and Such*. Vol. 2, No. 1. Paper, typescript, 42 pp., $5.00. The material is harmless, clean, for undemanding youngsters: Little Wisdoms, Miscommunications, Plumbing, Religious Sermons, Jokes, Riddles. For the kiddies: stuff about Boy-girl conflicts, Nutty Adults, Pixies & Fairies, etc. Available from Creative with Words Publications, P.O. Box 223226, Carmel, CA 93922. She is also collecting material for her next volume and asks for submissions.

• Ethnology and Folklore bookseller Elliot Klein (New York City) has opened a European branch: 21, rue Saint-Jacques, F-75005 Paris, France.

• Michael and Gwenola Neal sell literary and scholarly periodicals and books, new French books, and undertake bibliographical and literary searches. They can be reached at: 16, résidence le Bosquet, F-91940 Les Ulis, France.

• Dr. Henry Burger's **The Wordtree: A Transitive Cladistic for Solving Physical & Social Problems** (1984) is a revolutionary dictionary. It groups all words by their effect on the environment, using transitive verbs only. Each word is binarily divided into its sub-process, such as *to surprise + to menace = to frighten*; *to frighten + to hallucinate = to bugbear*. Scientists like this approach, humanists react with horror. Upon seeing this work, some London traditionalists "almost had instant convulsions" or "ran screaming to their studies." The Hierarchy section arranges the 24,600 transitives from simple to complex, the Index alphabetizes them. One can trace any word (process) back toward its components (causes), or forward toward its effects. This system is quite rigid, and unusual, forced coinages take one aback, e.g. *to jackiegleason*. The total quarter-million words include 90,000 words of instruction and theory. The typesize is quite small (readable, but not for browsing); thus the 380 large, crammed pages are the equivalent of 1,755 "normal" pages. Available for $149 from Wordtree, 7306 Brittany, Merriam, KS 66203-4699.

• Prof. Larry E. Seits (English Dept., Waubonsee Community College, Sugar Grove, IL 60554), has edited or co-edited four volumes of *Papers of the North Central Names Institute*. Available are vols. 1-4 (1980-83), each around 100 pages, containing the papers read at these meetings and treating such topics as Illinois place names, street names, and railroad names. Volume 5, *Festschrift in Honor of Virgil Vogel*, is edited by Prof. Edward Callary (English Dept., Northern Illinois University, DeKalb, IL 60115).

# colorful speech

Examples of colorful speech taken from written and oral sources: insults, slurs, curses, threats, blasphemies, similes, comparisons, etc. Contributions are welcome and credited. We prefer short, clever, witty, creative, concrete examples. Always identify your source (person or publication).

• **My cock was as straight and rigid as a Wehrmacht officer's spine.** (*NL*, Jan. 1985, p. 42)

• As one testicle said to the other: **Don't mind that asshole behind you. We're working for the prick up front.** (Heard by Ebert Waldorf)

• Humor consultant Malcolm L. Kushner, who has **a smile that could sell used snuff**, said that "data-processing managers are **dull schmucks.**" (*Time*, 25 March 1985, pp. 8, 10)

• **Noisier than two skeletons fucking on a hot tin roof, with brass bras on.** (Folklorist Steve Poyser. Contributed by Simon Bronner)

• John McEnroe, the bratty tennis champ pictured as cute on his BIC razor commercials, "is **as cute as a razor nick.**" (Melvin Durslag, *TV Guide*, 28 Jan. 1984, p. 28)

• In Letters from the Editors, those who say "I could care less" are advised either to use the correct form, "I couldn't care less", or to use alternatives, such as, **Who gives a rat's ass, you puke-faced gargoyle?** (*NL*, Oct. 1984, p. 80)

• **You're as plain as cornbread — You look like the cross between a booger and a haint** [bogeyman; ghost] **— You're as ugly as a mud fence stuck with tadpoles — You wouldn't last any longer than a snowball in hell**

235

— **You're as dull as a froe** [a wedge-shaped cleaving tool], and **You're as useless as a milk bucket under a bull.** (From W.K. McNeil's "Folklore from Big Flat, Arkansas" in *Mid-America Folklore* 12/2 [Fall 1984], pp. 27-30)

• In 1983, Louisiana Governor Edwin Edwards bragged that he could not lose the election to David Treen unless he was **caught in bed with a dead girl or a live boy.** (*Time*, 11 March 1985, p. 29)

• Comments about a female coal miner: **She's got dust on the bust and coal in the hole.** — When she smokes a cigarette, **her face looks like a pig's ass with a piece of straw on it.** (Overheard in a Michigan saloon by Fred R.)

• From an article by Dave Tynan about a Hollywood stars' dentist: "Without a good set of choppers, **you can't do dick-shit** in this town, not even dog-food commercials." — "Starlets **so hot you couldn't fiddle them with an asbestos condom.**" — "He's a **doughnut poker.**" [homosexual] — "Cigarettes yellow your tooth enamel. In a few years those pearlies of yours will **look like fog lights on the freeway.**" (*NL*, Oct. 1984, pp. 29-30)

• Sister to her younger brother who had just spat at her: **Save the rest to grease your cock in case a skunk comes by you want to screw.** (From Ann Beattie's *Falling in Place*, 1980, p. 4. Contributed by Catherine Felgar)

• **Everyone uses me as a pissing post.** (Complaint by a Wisconsin journalist to the Editor, 1982)

• **That girl is uglier than a hatful of assholes.** (*NL*, June 1982, p. 40)

• **Your request is as welcome as a premature ejaculation.** (Editor to a pushy author who demanded that his article be published immediately)

• **The best part of you ran down your momma's leg.** (Lee Marvin in the movie *Death Hunt*, 1981. Contributed by Len Ashley)

• **She has a cunt like a torn overcoat pocket.** (Comment about a large woman by Kurt Schweitzer to the Editor at a Milwaukee ethnic festival, July 1982)

• **You're slicker than snot on a doorknob** and **She's hotter than a fresh-fucked fox in a forest fire.** (Contributed by Robert Parrott)

• **You're as slick as deer guts on a door knob.** (From a letter to the Editor, from Fred R.)

• Dana was back in town, **looking as greasy as a snake in a barrel of snot.** (Comment in a letter about a mutual friend. Contributed by Chris Starr)

• For a fellow who's supposed to be an engineer, S.W. is **as dumb as a hoe handle.** (Contributed by Chris Starr)

• **If she was any dumber, you'd have to water her.** (Leo Hayes about a barmaid. Contributed by Robert Balliot)

• **It's raining like a (double-cunted) cow pissing on a flat rock.** (Contributed by Scott Beach, David Hibbard, and Elbert Waldorf)

• **He's so dumb he thinks cunnilingus is an Irish airline.** (German author Arno Schmidt. Contributed by Basil

Schader. Also in use in the USA. The actual name of the airline is *Aer Lingus.*)

• **I wouldn't piss in his ass if his guts were on fire.** (Contributed by Tim Hawley)

• **I bet she could do squat thrusts on a fire hydrant.** (Comment about a "whorish-looking" woman at a bar, overheard by Gordon Wood)

• **Go blow your tits off!** Australian equivalent of U.S. "Stop shitting me! I don't believe you!" (Told to the Editor by an Australian fellow-traveler on the Orient Express, 1982)

• **He's loose as a whore's crotch** and **He plays as tight as a tomtit's arsehole.** (Heard during poker games in a Middlesex, U.K., hospital by Patrick Debenham)

• **He's balder than Buddha's balls.** (Contributed by David Govett)

• **You double-revolving, interlocking and interfornicating brass-bound son-of-a-bitch!** (Frequent utterance by a Chief Boatswain Mate, U.S. Navy; heard by William Wortman)

• **You illegitimate son of twin-retarded African bastards!** (North Carolina, early 1900s)

• Pete Hamill is **one of the vilest maggots ever to bore holes in carrion.** (Joe S., commenting on the anti-Hamill poem in MAL 5:45-46)

• **She can suck a golf ball through a garden hose.** (Comment about a fellatrix, overheard by Sanford Gorney)

- **He's so dumb he couldn't talk a two-headed pig out of a corncrib.** (Contributed by Fred R.)

- **That truck couldn't pull a sick whore off a pisspot.** (Current with long-haul truckers in the late 1940s. Contributed by George Monteiro)

- **That's so bad it would gag a maggot in a gut wagon.** (Used in the 1940s. Contributed by Tim Hawley)

- **She's got tits like slaters' nail bags.** [Two large, stiff, hard leather bags filled with a few pounds of nails, slung crosswise over each shoulder.] — **She's got a cunt like a bill-poster's bucket.** — **She's got a face like a blind cobbler's thumb.** (Describing a monumentally large and ugly woman. All heard in the British Army, ca. 1970, by Alan Bird)

- **He's jumping around like a fart in a mitten.** (Contributed by M.L. + T.L. Sherred)

- **May you have the fattest geese and no teeth, the finest wine and no palate, the prettiest wife and no sex organ! (God forbid!)** (From the Yiddish. Contributed by Sherri Pine)

- **Smirking like the pig that et the baby's diaper.** (Joyce Harrington in "Sweet Baby Jenny," in *The Year's Best Mystery & Suspense Stories 1982*, p. 107. Contributed by Bruce Rodgers)

- **When I was twenty, my dick be hard as Chinese 'rithmetic.** (Richard Pryor in HBO's "Comedy Store's 11th Anniversary Show," July 1983)

- I lived in a town so small **the only thing open all night**

**was my girlfriend's legs.** (From *Easy Rider* magazine, unknown date & page. Contributed by Al Pergande)

• **Your breath smells like wild wolf pussy.** (Favorite remark of Howard, a Chicago black, mid-1950s. Contributed by his barracks-mate Joseph Duchac)

• **She took directions like a pig takes to garbage.** (Steve Martin in the 1982 movie *Dead Men Don't Wear Plaid*.)

• **This sheila bangs like a shithouse door in a gale.** (Australian comment about a sexually capable woman, probably created by writer Barry Humphries. Contributed by Gareth Hughes)

• I know you are **busier than a toothless beaver in a log jam.** (From a letter to the Editor by Norman Handelsman)

• He was **busier than a one-armed paperhanger with crabs.** (Contributed by Robert Goodwin)

• **I'm as busy as a blind queer at a wiener roast.** (Clyde H., in his letter to the Editor)

• If I ordered a dozen sons-of-bitches and they just sent me Harold, I wouldn't feel that I had been shortchanged. (A professor discussing a colleague; overheard by James Walters)

• At other times [he] sounds **as outraged as a satyr with a suppressed orgasm.** (Donald Kramer, in his article on *Maledicta* in "Par for the Curse," *MD* magazine [Nov. 1983, p. 165], describing your Editor's writings)

• Anyone who says that the shark is not a dangerous

animal is **as full of shit as a blocked toilet in a Mexican bus station.** (*NL*, May 1983, p. 51. Contributed by Gert Raeithel)

• **We call him "scrotum" — he's something between a prick and an arsehole.** (Contributed by Robert Penprase)

• **A crow shit on a log, and the sun hatched him.** (Armenian expression of disdain. Contributed by Albert Kalo)

• He's such a chronic worrier that **the skin of his forehead is like that of a chilled scrotum.** (Contributed by Henry Moehring)

• That apartment was so dirty that there were **fart stains on the wall.** (Disgruntled landlord describing the condition of one of his vacated properties. Contributed by Robert Th.)

• I feel **as frustrated as a eunuch masseur.** (Comment by Bob Buckie, Saudi Arabia, in a letter to the Editor)

• **I want it so quiet in here I could hear a rat pissing on cotton.** (Army officer to his men. Contributed by Stephen Gregory)

• **He's got a nose like somebody's elbow.** (From Lindsay Maracotta, *The Sad-Eyed Ladies: Life, Love & Hard Times in the Singles Scene*, 1977, p. 29. Contributed by Martha Cornog)

• **A blowjob is the sincerest form of penis envy.** (The Wiz, Flushing)

• The size of the screen on the Osborne computer can best

be described as **cretin-friendly**, but as I always say, **a bird in the hand is better than a pustule on your glans.** (Jerry Cerwonka, in a letter to the Editor)

• Most computer programs and their manuals are **as "user-friendly" as a syphilitic whore.** (Editor, to colleague upset by idiotic manuals)

• **I would drag my bare balls over forty miles of ground glass to finger-fuck her shadow!** (College student, 1958, leering lustfully at a photograph of Kim Novak. Contributed by Peter L.)

• The Australian price of my *Bawdry* book is $A14-95, which is currently about US$13.60 — but the exchange rate is **up and down like a whore's drawers** at the moment. (Don Laycock, in a letter to the Editor)

## A BIG COCK AND A LEAKING MOUTH

*It is a bad habit for children to have a meal walking about with a rice bowl and dropping grains of rice here and there.*

*This colour picture story book of children's life is written down for the purpose of helping the children to get rid of this bad habit. The illustrator vividly expresses the contents with plenty of children's interest and temperament.*

大公鸡和漏嘴巴

姚正平写　　朱延令画

少年儿童出版社出版

40 开　　15 页

0.11 美元

(From the 1981 catalog of the Shanghai Publishing Company)

# DEAR & DAMN EDITOR

Authentic excerpts from our readers' mail, stroking or slamming your Editor. Also, questions asked by several readers.

¶ I read the whole new issue in one night and was forced to tell my friend, "Not tonight, dear, *Maledicta* just came today. So you don't get to." —Janet, Kansas

¶ The new volume is simply marvellous. Much to my wife's annoyance, it kept me in stitches three nights running. As we read a lot in bed, it irritated her no end. —John, Ontario

¶ MAL is late again? Well, if you are behind in your work it's understandable — even prostitutes get a little behind in their work. —David, New York

¶ I would really be happy if you could write a book on insults for 10, 11, 12, 13 year olds. I am 11. —Shannon, Georgia
*Are you listening, writers? There's a wide-open market for you.*

¶ When my boyfriend breaks up with me, which is quite often, he calls me a "cunt" in public. I hate it. What exactly is a cunt? —Marsha (34), California
*While many women hate this word, some use it neutrally or endearingly, as they have informed me. It's that part of your body for which your creep of a boyfriend comes back. No, it's not your armpits, but you're getting warm.*

¶ I'm enclosing a page from the reprint I'm working on. I hope it looks OK to you. If it doesn't, tough shit. Just where in the hell do you come off being critical in the first place, huh? Why don't you just take a triple lip-lock on

243

my love-muscle, motherfucker! (I'm anticipating your negative reaction. Does everybody drift off into this delightful
language in their letters to you?) — Tim, Missouri

*Many do, and it chagrins me sometimes. I can write reams and
talk for hours without using* fuck, shit, cunt *or* balls *once; but,
somehow, this language is expected of me (see Eileen's letter, below).
Here is an example of such a letter from a renowned folklorist who
sent it 15 April 1985, the day I declared "National No-Cuss Day"
in an Associated Press story published throughout the country:*

> Hey, Rey, you old fart, just what the fuck do you think you're doing,
> running shit like this in the local paper? This pisses me off. Boy,
> once you mother-fuckin' bastards get your name in the paper, you
> think you're goddamn experts on everything. Take your "No-Cuss
> Day" and shove it where the sun don't shine. Of all the cocksucking,
> cuntlicking, asshole ideas I've ever heard of, this is the most
> unfuckinbelievable. — Have a nice day, M., Pennsylvania

¶ Who would have thought–looking at your work–that you
would be such a charming gentleman? — Eileen, Massachusetts

*I'm not sure about this "charming gentleman" stuff, but you touch
upon an important point: the ancient confusion of the messenger with
the message (messengers who brought good news were rewarded; those
who brought bad news were punished or killed). The main reason
for publishing photos of Uncle Mal in this journal is to show people
that I'm not a disgusting, filthy old pervert who hangs around in
parks with candy in his raincoat pockets, trying to lure children into
his allegedly porno-filled home. I have to keep fighting this wrong
mental image people form from reading news reports about my work
or* Maledicta. *The real R.A. is not like his personas. In fact,
people who don't know what I'm doing have often asked whether
I'm a priest (or a rabbi, when I had a beard). One doesn't have
to be a beaver to study Canadian fauna, nor a homosexual to publish
gay glossaries. And one doesn't have to be foulmouthed to study and
publish vulgarities. Your reaction is not uncommon, though; when*

*I meet new friends in New York, Texas, California, and various European countries, the reaction usually is, "What a surprise! I expected you to be much wilder, nasty-mouthed, vulgar. But you are so quiet, such a nice person." This embarrasses me, naturally, thus I have to use a few goodies to show them that I'm not all that saintly. The point is: don't judge a book publisher by his cover. What if I published medieval religious poetry but kept neat sheep in my shed?*

¶ I suppose there is plenty of foul language in your publication. As you know, the passage in the Lord's Prayer "Thy Kingdom come" (which I knew by heart at the age of 6) forbids such language. Our world today is full of foul language, and the chance of having the Kingdom are vanishing rapidly. I therefore decline to read your publication as the Lord will not dwell in unclean tabernacles. —Frank, California

*Dear Clean Tab: Read Burke's* The X-Rated Book: Sex and Obscenity in the Bible. *Or the Bible (im-)proper, from which this book quotes chapter & verse. That'll stain your tabernacle!*

¶ It's always a pleasure to speak with you and to read your cards, letters and journal. If it weren't for your nasty rag, the only thing I'd have to look forward to is a possible yearly blowjob from my old lady. —H., Colorado

¶ It's good that MAL is an annual. I've been catching up on parts of vol. 7 that I didn't do justice before. —Lillian, Pennsylvania

¶ I read, and re-read, and re-read all the Maledicta material I have…journals, fliers, letters. I treasure them all. —Norma, California

¶ I saw you on television not long ago and frankly, my

dear chap, if I had a hound that looked like you, I'd shave his derrière and make him walk backward. —Robert, New York

¶ I'm looking forward to your next annual. Routinely, after each volume has been read, the office conversation (with or without the patients' ability to answer) centers on the items presented. Keep up the good work. —Don (dentist), Maryland

¶ My entire collection of MAL is sequestered in my boss's office. From there, I hear sounds of chortles, guffaws, snorts, and snickers. And in times of stress, my boss mutters imprecations in strange and outlandish languages. —Jude, Pennsylvania

¶ The new volume has just arrived. Jesus! The fuckin' thing is almost as thick as my dick! I damn-near ruptured myself carrying it to the kitchen to circumcize the bubbly envelope. —Scott, California

¶ Contrary to your advice, I have not saved a quarter of the volume to be read every three months; that takes far more willpower than I have. *Maledicta* is an eloquent testimony to how much a single, dedicated individual can accomplish; it puts to shame most journals issued by editorial boards and backed up with platoons of typists, layout specialists, subscription staff, and the like. I've seen statistics reporting that the average article in a technical journal is read by two to three people (including the authors!)—a fate few *Maledicta* articles need fear. —Ross, New Jersey

*I appreciate your good words, coming from one who—in addition to being employed full-time as a scientist—also puts out a demanding language journal as a Ma & Pa operation. (Mine is just a Pa operation, by the way; Ma isn't a Maledictaphile.)*

¶ More and more I have come to realize the depth of cacademic opposition to genuine, humane scholarship. The last cacademic to whom I showed MAL solemnly advised me *not* to list my *Maledicta* articles on my résumé, because it would be "unseemly for a scholar." This from a married woman who spent the faculty Christmas party fondling every *schwanz* in sight. — S., New York

¶ Dear Liederhosen: Don't ever have a deadline! Anticipation is part of the pleasure. — Natalie, Rhode Island
*I've told you a dozen times already, it's Lederhosen! If there were such a thing, Liederhosen would mean "songs-pants." When I wore Lederhosen as a boy in Bavaria, I didn't have enough to eat to be musical. Perhaps you're confusing me with Mario Lanza who used to sing "With a song in my pants"...but I digress. No, I won't have any deadlines. It'll be slow good, as Heinz says.*

¶ My only worry is that, now that *Maledicta* is becoming an empire, the gentlemen from Wall Street will arrive with their checkbooks and demands for "mass appeal." Please remain as thorny as that other great American humorist and, scholar — also a fat, four-eyed, squareheaded pickle-stabber — H.L. Mencken. — Fred, New York
*Fear not. I'll always remain (t)horny. Since 1978, there have been repeated attempts by biggies to mass-market our material, either by "cleaning it up a bit" or by putting out* The Best of Maledicta. *The former I'll refuse to do to my dying day; but the latter is a possibility, as it would increase readership of the Real Thing through those who found out about MAL through a popular anthology.*

¶ What a surprise! You are incredible. Here is my article, all beautifully laid out and printed while I was gone, and I haven't done a thing. *Mon dieu*, thank you so much for so much dedication and what must have been exhausting work. — Michel, Minnesota

*Thanks. But it isn't necessary to address me as* mon dieu; mon rédacteur *will do. You're one of the rare authors who appreciate all the work I do to transform their often sloppily typewritten, mistake-riddled, difficult copy into as aesthetic a piece as I can. There seems to be an inverse correlation between the typesetting difficulty and the author's appreciation. Many authors of godawful stuff (complicated foreign languages, fancy layouts) never bother to send a note of appreciation or even subscribe, which at times pisses me off. So, an occasional good letter like yours makes up for the anal-retentive ingrates.*

¶ MAL is a real infusion of sanity and joy into my life... I hope this time the enclosed draft in U.S. funds will be honoured by your bank. I'm no lover of these screwy institutions, from the snotty and/or brain-damaged bitches who masquerade as tellers to the constipated assholes who run them. — Paul, Ontario

¶ I know what you're going to say when you receive this letter: "Lost the $#&%! order form! Doesn't use the return envelope! This letter isn't folded right! Writes sloppy! Bad English! Can't spell! Didn't eat his carrots! Drives too fast! Hates furry, cute animals! Spits on the sidewalk! Doesn't flush the john! Reads dirty books! Needs a bath! Watches too much MTV! Has zits!" So what? My checks don't bounce! — Al, Florida

*Ah, my years of educating readers are paying off. At least you now know your shortcomings and may be on your way to become civilized. But next time you visit me, don't pick your nose or other body parts! And stop kneading your earwax into little balls! And get rid of that smegma! And write again soon, but legibly.*

---

### MATHEMATICS
The heat of the meat + the mass of the ass = the angle of the dangle.

# ELITE MALEDICTA

"Bad words" *spoken by* or *said about* famous people, the so-called elite. Contributions are welcome and credited. Full bibliographical documentation is required. Where known, report these essentials: **WHO** (maledictor) said **TO WHOM** (target) **WHAT** (actual words), **WHY** (cause of utterance), **WHEN** (time), **WHERE** (place), **CONSEQUENCES** (fines, arrest, dismissal, injury, murder, suicide, etc.), and **BACKGROUND**. See my "Words Can Kill" in this volume for more information.

• Franklin Roosevelt's Interior Secretary Harold Ickes, known for his sharp tongue, once said of Huey Long, governor of Louisiana, that he had **halitosis of the intellect.** (*Time*, 11 July 1983, p. 7)

• President Teddy Roosevelt, who was no pussyfooter, once called the President of Venezuela a **pithecanthropoid,** referred to George Bernhard Shaw as a **blue-rumped ape,** and denounced the Populist Senator William Peffer as a **well-meaning, pinheaded, anarchistic crank, of hirsute and slab-sided aspect.** (*Time*, 20 June 1983, p. 24)

• In June, 1984, presidential aspirant Fritz Hollings referred to his fellow aspirant John Glenn as **this joker.** He also called budget director David Stockman a **pathological finagler.** (*Time*, 20 June 1983, p. 24)

• Speaker Tip O'Neill called President Reagan **Herbert Hoover with a smile.** (*Time*, 20 June 1983, p. 24)

• During the 1984 campaign, President Reagan called Walter Mondale **Vice President Malaise.** (*Time*, 20 June 1983, p. 24)

• Black Muslim leader Louis Farrakhan, angered by black *Washington Post* reporter Milton Coleman's disclosure (via a colleague) of Jesse Jackson's *hymie* and *Hymietown* indiscretions, called Coleman a **no-good filthy traitor.** (*San José Mercury News*, 10 April 1984, p. 7-B. Contributed by Bruce Rodgers)

• President Reagan, usually self-controlled in public, *exploded in anger and profanity* at Democratic congressional leader Bill Alexander (Ark.) who refused to support the President's MX missile and suggested that Reagan submit a balanced budget. An unnamed Reagan adviser said of Alexander, **"this guy would make the pope cuss."** (*Los Angeles Times, MJ*, 30 March 1985, p. 3)

• Comedienne Joan Rivers upset hundreds of people during the 1983 Emmy Awards by calling Interior Secretary James Watt an **idiot** for his *cripple* joke, as well as for insulting the late Joan Crawford, jokes about herpes, homosexuals and prostitutes, and for saying that "they always wanted me to sit in the **goddamned** audience." (UPI, *MJ*, 26 Sept. 1983, pp. 1, 6)

• "The good thing about masturbation is you don't have to dress up for it." Truman Capote. (Lawrence Paros, *The Erotic Tongue*, p. 103)

• Nancy Kissinger, wife of former Secretary of State Henry Kissinger, faced criminal charges for grabbing the throat of Ellen Kaplan on 7 February 1982 at the Newark, N.J., airport. Kaplan had been distributing pro-nuclear literature there and directed "a personal slur" at Henry when he walked by. A judge later acquitted Nancy of the assault charge, ruling that she had reacted in a "spontaneous" and "somewhat human" way by grabbing Kaplan's neck for slurring Henry. The *MJ* did not report the actual slur in its 3 March 1982 edition (p. 2), nor did the *WF* on 11 June (p. 2). The *MJ* of 10 June (p. 2), reporting the acquittal, finally explained that it was "a homosexual remark." The normally straighter-than-thou Paul Harvey, on his radio news of 5 March, reported Kaplan's slur against Henry as "**Do you sleep with young boys?**"

• When Claus von Bülow's former lover, Alexandra Isles, was his current lover, she was also dating New York critic John Simon, which Simon calls a lie. Von Bülow's current girlfriend, Andrea Reynolds, says that Simon comes from the "outhouse" section of Europe. Simon, demonstrating his usual flair for name-calling, pronounced von Bülow and Reynolds "**disgusting creeps, revolting garbage — two swine.**" (*WF*, 25 May 1985, p. 2). [Simon was born in Subotica (formerly Maria-Theresiopel), a Yugoslavian city near the Hungarian border.] )

• Cable Network chief Ted Turner, who had been interviewed over several weeks by *Playboy* contributing editor Peter Ross Range, became upset by the journalist's questions aboard an airplane whether Turner planned to force people to come up to his standards. Turner interrupted him in mid-sentence with "**I'm sick as hell of you,**" snatched his tape recorder and smashed it to the cabin floor, kicked his tape bag into the cockpit door, and, swearing and shouting, stomped on the tapes. (UPI, *MJ*, 26 June 1983, p. 2)

• Gwynne Dyer, a Canadian foreign affairs columnist, reports that North Korean leader Kim Il Sung's embassy will send you six feet (two meters) of the leader's collected works just for the asking. According to Dyer's report on the writings, "Kim Il Sung apparently not only created the world, but he also built all the mountains, fertilized all the flowers and **screwed all the sheep in it.**" (The *Record*, Québec, 18 June 1982, p. 5. Contributed by Clifton Merritt)

• Tennis ace (*or* ass) John McEnroe produces a steady record of physical and verbal abuse. During the 1983 French Open, in Paris, he called an official an **utter moron** and a **French frog.** He was fined $3,000 by the Men's International Pro Tennis Council for, among other things, "ball abuse." At Wimbledon, England, he was fined $500 for verbal abuse. At the U.S. Open in New York, McEnroe was fined $1,850 for throwing sawdust on a spectator and for abusing an umpire and a ball. In Sydney, Australia, he paid a $1,500 fine for abusing officials. (*TV Guide*, 28 Jan. 1984, pp. 27-29)

• From a letter in *NL*, May 1985, p. 8: "**John fuckin' McEnroe...you dickless piece of shit!**"

• Québec Premier René Lévesque called Claude Ryan, opposition leader, a **liar.** Ryan responded that Lévesque was a **liar and an imbecile.** (Wes Darou, "Personality and Verbal Abuse," unpubl. paper, ca. 1981, p. 23)

• According to Tom Shales, *Washington Post* TV critic, Senator Jesse Helms (N.C.) frequently attacks the media, usually citing the CBS News. CBS employees are asking themselves whether Helms "is a character out of *Seven Days in May* or out of *Li'l Abner*, that is, a **dangerous loony** or just a **colorful loony.**" (*MJ*, 13 March 1985, Accent, p. 9)

• On an experimental talk show in Berne, Switzerland, the host opened his monolog by referring to President Reagan as an **Arschloch**, German for "asshole." The host was fired. (*The Progressive*, March 1982, p. 19. Contributed by Ivan Kramoris)

• When Bob Jones III, president of Bob Jones University in Greenville, S.C., heard that the State Department had denied a visa to Northern Ireland's inflammatory Rev. Ian Paisley, Fundamentalist Jones called Secretary of State Alexander Haig a **tyrant of the worst sort, a monster in human flesh, and a demon-possessed instrument to destroy America.** He then issued a statement with this curse: "I hope you will pray too that the Lord will smite him hip and thigh, bone and marrow, heart and lungs and all there is to him; that He shall destroy him quickly and utterly." (*Houston Post*, 3 April 1982, p. 12-A. Contributed by Gordon Wood). [We will soon report on the source of this malediction, the complete "Papal Curse."])

• "Pëtr Tchaikovsky was **as gay as a tree full of chickadees.**" (Contributed by Richard Barton. [A chickadee is a *crestless titmouse*.])

• One reason why cartoonist Pat Oliphant voted for Reagan was to protest the Democrats' choice of "a **turkey** like Walter Mondale." (*MJ*, 17 July 1985, Accent, p. 11)

• When golf champion Watson made a birdie on the 18th hole, his colleague Nickolaus greeted him on the green by saying, "You **son of a bitch**, you're something else." (*Chicago Sun-Times*, 21 June 1982. Contributed by Ken Grabowski)

• In a statement, Italy's Red Brigades terrorists called kidnapped U.S. Brig. General James L. Dozier "**a Yankee pig.**" (AP, *MJ*, 20 Dec. 1981, p. 1)

• *Playboy*'s Hugh Hefner, in a story on the "Top 10 Insufferable Celebs" by Hugh Mulligan, is called "**The pipe-puffing prophet of pretentious porn.**" (AP, *MJ*, 12 Oct. 1982, pp. 1-2)

• "If the Rev. Louis Farrakhan had been born white, I have little doubt he would have become the Imperial Wizard of the Ku Klux Klan." (Columnist Sydney Harris in the *Detroit Free Press*, 29 Nov. 1984, p. 13-B. Contributed by Marie Helfrich)

• Former Philadelphia mayor Frank L. Rizzo was annoyed by KYW-TV's reporters who were setting up cameras outside his home, preparing to film a report on the cost of having Mr. Rizzo's home guarded by police officers. Mr. Rizzo broke some of the camera equipment and threatened reporter Stan Bohrman: "I wouldn't talk to you under any circumstances. Get away from me. I'm a private citizen now. Look, **creep**, get out of here... **You're a coward, a yellow sneak. You're a crumb, a creep, a coward and a lush.**" (*New York Times*, 20 Nov. 1980, p. B-7. Contributed by Leonard Ashley)

• After his release from a 10-day stay in a Tokyo jail for having taken 7.7 ounces of marijuana into Japan, Beatle Paul McCartney engaged in self-abuse when telling reporters on his flight to Amsterdam, "I have been a **fool**. What I did was **incredibly dumb**. My God, how **stupid** I have been." (*MJ*, 27 Jan. 1980, p. 2)

• Television producer David Susskind on former President Jimmy Carter: "Carter is **incompetent, arrogant, insulated, provincial and unknowing**. He is a **pious fraud**. The **pietistic humbug** is intolerable." (*Time*, 3 Nov. 1980, p. 42)

• During the 1980 presidential campaign, Ronald Reagan called President Jimmy Carter **incompetent**, and Carter said that the Republicans were "spreading **horse manure.**" (*MJ*, 23 Oct. 1980, p. 1)

• Hoven, S.D., priest Leonard A. Nemmers, who distributed campaign literature at his church's parking lot, later apologized to former Sen. George McGovern, but McGovern, defeated in the election, sent Father Nemmers a letter instead: "...if I had to pick the **No. 1 candidate for the biggest ass** in South Dakota in 1980, you would win hands down." (*MJ*, 8 Jan. 1981, p. 2)

• Two Florida senators astonished visitors by exchanging angry words and gestures under the Senate's press gallery in Tallahassee. Sen. Dempsey Barron, whose "Dempseycrat" coalition was planning a parliamentary assault on the presidency, said to Senate President W.D. Childers, "You **little shit**, I'm going to **whip your ass** and throw you out of the Senate right now." Childers, who is at least six inches shorter than Barron, retorted: "You're going to do *what*?" and moved within inches of his antagonist, who obliged by repeating his insult and threat. At that point, burly Sen. Edgar Dunn, a former college football lineman, wheeled Childers around and marched him into the president's office. (*Miami Herald*, 2 June 1981, p. 1. Contributed by Matilda Ruffin)

• Lyndon B. Johnson commented perceptively on the press in *Hubert*, by Edgar Berman: "They're like kids — unless you **whack them across their ass** once a day, they'll run all over you. They're **slanted as an old cowshed**, but where they really **get their rocks off** is on that editorial page... Those **smart-ass** columnists are **as whorish as the highblown Washington lawyers and bankers.** I could **have**

**their peckers in my pocket** any time — if I cared. But who wants them? Give me the headline writer, the photo editor and the cartoonist, and you can have all the editors and columnists you want." (Contributed by Peter Metzger)

• Barbara Davis Hyman, daughter of Bette Davis, told *USA Today* in an interview that "from the time I was four, the only form of address he [Gary Merrill, Bette's former husband] ever used with me was **'You little slut!'**" (21 May 1985, p. D-2)

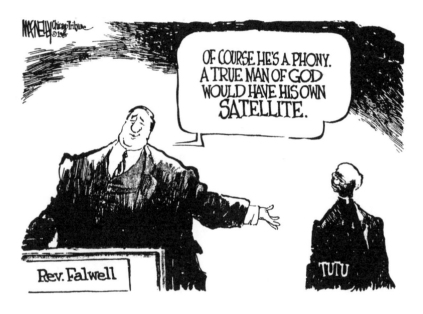

## HOW TO SUBMIT MATERIAL
## FOR ALL DEPARTMENTS

Always use *separate* sheets or cards for *separate* items, adding your name and ZIP Code (or country) to each item. Type or print legibly. Also, always provide complete bibliographic documentation of your source, and a copy of the item, if possible.

# FEEDBACK

Responses to **QUERIES** published earlier. The numbers identify the volume and running number of the query; e.g., Query 4.14 is the 14th query in volume 4.

### 4.13 DEROGATORY NEWSPAPER NAMES

*Aurora Beacon-News* (IL): Aurora Be-Confused

*Bedford Sackville News* (Nova Scotia): Badford Sexville News

*Chicago Sun-Times* (IL): Chicago Slum-Times. (Large black readership)

*Columbus Dispatch* (OH): Columbus Dogpatch

*Dallas Morning News* (TX): Dallas Morning Snooze

*Dallas Times Herald* (TX): Dallas Times Horrible, Dallas Crimes Herald

*Halifax Chronicle Herald* (Nova Scotia): Halifax Chronicle Horrid

*Herald-Telephone* (Bloomington, IN): Horrible-Terrible

*The Lantern* (Ohio State University student newspaper): The Latrine

*St. Louis Globe-Democrat* (MO): St. Louis Globe-Demagogue

*U.S. News and World Report* (magazine): Useless News and World Distort

Contributed by: Simon Bronner, Leo Dombrowski, Thomas Emig, Chuck G., Sanford Gorney, Douglas Quine, Larry Seits, and Jenny Wade.

### 4.14 I READ *MALEDICTA* BECAUSE...

¶ No other journal gives me the joy that MAL does. I don't know you and have only the editorial *persona* from which to draw conclusions, but I wish to thank you for the innocent delight which fills my heart when I read your stuff. —Michael, Nova Scotia

¶ I have to tell you of my joy, and that of my friends, of knowing MAL. To spend a day without smiling or laughing is to lose a day irretrievably. You contribute to life. — Marie, France

¶ I find MAL entertaining, informative, educational, and just plain fun to read. — Jude, Pennsylvania

¶ MAL is the ultimate "Fuck you!" As a little-esteemed former academician, I used to explain to my students: "The ability to say 'Fuck you' without resorting to crude obscenity, *that* is the mark of the educated person." Uncle Mal, you shore do sing it purdy. — Eli, Illinois

¶ I read MAL for information, inspiration, education, entertainment, when I don't feel like working, and when I do feel like working. — Victor, North Carolina

¶ As an artist, I enjoy the creativity of MAL. Also, one of my great interests is cultural anthropology. Speech tells everything and should not be lost, as so much of the past has been, including creative expression. — David, Massachusetts

¶ MAL is the best source there is for what people actually do with language, no holds barred. — Tom, Illinois

¶ In a world where feminists, Marxists, behaviorists, and other vermin are doing their damnedest to denature and geld human speech, MAL flings in their wimpy faces the divine power of language in its last unassailed bastion — vituperation. — Joseph, New York

¶ I find in MAL material which is simply not available anywhere else. — Leonard, Iowa

¶ Because I'm interested in language and communication. — John, Pennsylvania

¶ I read MAL because I'm a high school teacher of English who can't use taboo words in class. But I can savor them in your publication. —Douglas, Louisiana

¶ I find MAL fascinating: it's a kind of outlet for something I don't feel free to use in my daily life, so I can at least read about it. —Louise, Québec

¶ MAL is the magazine I have always been longing for. It dares say what others only think. —Bengt, Sweden

¶ It is a source of constant joy—and I have said so on Irish radio. —Hugh, Ireland

¶ It provides periodic mental massage that my cramped brain greatly appreciates. —John, Dictrict of Columbia

¶ I have long been interested in slang and obscenities in other languages. I read MAL for education and entertainment, which is what enlightenment is all about. —Brett, South Carolina

¶ Because Uncle Mal was my professor at the University of Texas and because I enjoy it. —Ben, Texas

¶ I read MAL because my fat form really bounces from laughter. What joy to let loose, even at age 75 and as a great-grandmother. —Emily, California

¶ MAL gives me many hours of enjoyment and many useful bits of information which I have derived from its pages over the years. —Tom, California

¶ Having MAL, even without reading it all, is like having gas in your tank, even if you never go anywhere. It gives me a feeling of security. —Vivien, New York

¶ As a human sexuality teacher, I get a great deal of material from MAL to entertain and to offend. It always makes me laugh. I also read it at required cacademic meetings. It makes them more palatable — my colleagues think I'm laughing at their shit. — M., California

¶ I read MAL because it's fun. Also, as a sociobiologist, I study behavior and communication, and sex and violence; verbal aggression is among the most interesting forms of violence. My doctoral thesis was on the defensive behavior of social wasps, and often when they buzzed their wings in warning, I seemed to hear a very small, high-pitched "Fex off! Fex off!" — Chris, Philippines

¶ We enjoy the opportunity to purchase long-lasting and intellectually stimulating gifts for those of us who are thought of as offensive perverts by those who are too stupid to recognize creativity in its highest form. — Karen & Arthur, Illinois

¶ Through my reading of *Maledicta, Benedicta!*, and other writings and publications of yours, I have validated for myself the legitimacy of the use of verbal aggression. I was brought up to avoid ever using profanity, obscenities, and vulgarities. As a consequence, for most of my life, I have been handicapped by an artificially incomplete vocabulary. Thanks to you and some other events in recent years, I can now apply the words and expressions no matter how "dirty" or "offensive" they may be, when called for by the situation. — John, New Jersey

*I have received similar comments from a Canadian lady and a South African physician about the liberating effects of our publications. But here is a letter in which the reader explains why he does not like to read our journal:*

*Maledicta* makes too many references to things that I know nothing about and therefore I don't understand them. If I understood more of it and therefore could appreciate the wordplays or allusions or humor, I'm sure I would read it with a glee. But for me, if I lose way more than I win, well, is that fun? Is that what discretionary reading is all about? I took one course about word derivation in college but barely got through. The prof didn't have the slightest idea how to communicate whatever he might have known about words and language. Forgive me for not reading your journal any more. — Scott

*I have urged Scott not to limit himself to reading only what he knows. Now he's back in our fold and on his way to become one of the most astute people in Arizona.*

## MISCELLANEOUS NICKNAMES
(See MAL 5:321-22)

### INHABITANTS

Baltimore, MD: **Baltimorons**; Cedar Rapids, IA: **Bunnies** ("See der rabbits"); Chicago, IL: **Chicagorillas**; Louisville, KY: **Louisvillains**; Omaha, NE: **Omahogs**. From H.L. Mencken, via *Word Ways* (Aug. 1983, p. 151).

### ACADEMIC INSTITUTIONS

Ball State University, IN: **Ball U**

Barnard College, NY: **The Barnyard**

Bunsenville Community High School (BCHS), IL: **Big Chunks of Horse Shit**

Brandeis University, MA: **Brand-X University**

Carroll College, WI: **Carnal College** (Named during Prank Day)

Duquesne University, PA: **The school that was built on a bluff and run that way ever since.** (Built on a high bluff overlooking the Monongahela river)

Kishwaukee Community College, IL: **Tractor Tech**

Michigan State University: **Moo-U** (Located in dairy country)

New Mexico State University (NMSU): **Enemas U**

Ohio State University: **O-khuy-o State University** (*khuy* means "prick" in Russian)

Pace University, NY: **Piss U**

St. George's University Medical School, Grenada: **Last Chance U** (Last chance to become a physician, as seen by students denied admission in U.S. schools. *WF*, 26 Oct. 1983, p. B-3)

University of Waterloo, Ontario: **Water-in-the-loo U**

Waubonsee Community College (in Sugar Grove, Illinois, on Highway 47): **Our Lady of Highway 47, University of Sugar Grove, Wau-Wau Tech**

Wayne State University, MI: **Wayne Snakes U**

Contributed by: Peter Benner, Robert Fritz, Chuck G., Paul Madarasz, Perry Plouff, Joe S., Larry Seits, Lewis Tanner, and Editor.

## BUILDINGS

In the Washington, D.C., area, the Pentagon is known as the **Pentagoon**. — Stanford University's Tower has been known for at least 38 years as **Hoover's Last Erection**, as Pres. Herbert Hoover was one of Stanford's benefactors. — University of Pittsburgh's Cathedral of Learning is known as **The Heights of Ignorance** and **The Two-story Building with a Hard-on**. — The Church of the Holy Sepulchre in Jerusalem, *el-Kiama* (Arabic for 'resurrection'), is contemptuously mispronounced **el-Kamama**, "the dunghill," by Jews, who were not allowed in the church until 1967. From *Jerusalemwalks*, a travel book by Nitza Rosovsky, NY, 1982, pp. 54-55. — "The Towers," a tall student apartment building at the University of Wisconsin in Madison, is known as **Tokyo Towers** because most residents are JAPs (Jewish American Princesses). —

The official abbreviation for the Salem, Oregon, State Office Building is **S.O.B.**

Contributed by: Susan Aman, George Gleason, Bruce Rodgers, Jude Stackpole, William Reitwiesner, and Editor.

## COMPANY NAMES

**CBS News**: *Shabby Ass News.* — **Chevrolet**: *Shove it or it lays.* — **FORD**: *Found On Road Dead, Fix Or Repair Daily,* and *Fucked-Over Rebuilt Dodge.* — **IBM**: *Itty Bitty Machines,* and the Editor's own coinage, *Infernal Bloodsucking Monopoly.* — **TWA**: *Teeny Weeny Airlines.*

Contributed by: Hortense Fritz, Robert Fritz, Ken Grabowski, Peter Maher, John Spragens, and Editor.

## ETC.

The acronym of the American Association for Southeast European Studies, *AASES*, is pronounced "asses" and was mistakenly typeset as **ASSES** in *Balkanistica* 4. — **CIA** stands for *Creeps In Action*, according to Bill Maxwell in the TV show *The Greatest American Hero*, 3 March 1982. — In Washington political circles, *Common Cause* (a public interest group) is often referred to as **Common Cunt**, because of the well-known propensity of its female lobbyists to sexually service Congressmen and Senators in exchange for their votes on key issues.

Contributed by: Robert Fritz, Charles G., Joseph S., and an anonymous Georgetown University professor.

## CANADIANA

All following items were submitted by John Robert Colombo, Toronto:

*AIRLINES:* **CPA** = Canadian Pacific Airlines, now called CP Air: *Can't Possibly Arrive* or *Come Push Along.* — **PWA** = Pacific Western Airlines: *Please Wait Awhile* or *Pray While Aloft* or *Probably Won't Arrive* or (since its purchase by the Alberta government under Peter Lougheed) *Peter Wants*

*All.* — **TCA** = Trans-Canada Air Lines, the forerunner of today's Air Canada: *Two Crashes Apiece.*

*CITIES:* **East York** (a Toronto, Ont., borough): *Least York.* — **Edmonton**, Alberta: *Deadmonton, Alta.* In use before its 1970s oil wealth. — **London**, Ontario: *London the Lesser.* Used in the 19th century to distinguish it from London, England. Brendan Behan considered the city's name an "impertinence in itself." — **Scarborough** (a Toronto borough): *Scarberia.* — **Toronto**, Ontario: *Tomato, Can.* Said to have been favored by Ezra Pound in his correspondence with Ernest Hemingway and Morley Callaghan.

*POLITICAL:* **Grit**: Traditional name for a Liberal in Canada. When Conservative John Diefenbaker won in 1957, a journalist dubbed this victory *Gritterdämmerung,* "Twilight of the Grits." — **Tory**: Traditional name for a Conservative in Canada. The party is either *No-Torious* (according to Liberals) or *Satisfac-Tory* (according to Sir John MacDonald, the first Tory. — **CCF** = Co-operative Commonwealth Federation, forerunner of today's NDP. Because of its basis in rural Canada, urbanites dismissed it as *Canadian Cow Farmers,* and Leftists, wary of Communists infiltrating the organization, said the initials stood for *Come, Comrades, Forward.* — **FLQ** = Front de Libération du Québec, a terrorist group responsible for the October Crisis of 1970, said to stand for *Families Leaving Québec.* — **NDP** = New Democratic Party. A democratic socialist party, the initials have been taken to mean *No Dreams of Prosperity* or *Never Dies Politically.* — **P.Q.** = Parti Québécois, the separatist administration in Québec. Said to stand for *Pack Quickly* or *Panic in Québec.*

*PROVINCES:* **Alberta**: *Saudi Alberta.* Because of the high-handed attitude of this oil-rich province. — **Nova Scotia**: *Nova Scarcity.* Because of rough times experienced by this maritime province.

*RAILROADS:* **CNR** = Canadian National Railways, now

CN: *Certainly No Rush* or *Collects No Revenue.* — **CPR** = Canadian Pacific Railroad, now called CP: *Can't Pay Rent* or *Can't Promise Returns* or (alluding to the coolies who constructed it) *Chinese Pacific.*

*MISCELLANY:* **Petro-Canada** (nationwide oil company owned by the Canadian government): *Pierre Elliott Trudeau Ruined Our Canada.* — **RCMP** = Royal Canadian Mounted Police: *Roman Catholic Members of Parliament,* a sort of unofficial federal lobby (1940s use).

### 4.11 GENITAL PET NAMES

**Dildoheaded Peckerworm**: Name for penis by a doctor's woman friend. He creates new ones for every new relationship, such as **His Highness** and **Her Holiness**, **Prince Everhard of the Netherlands**, **Jesse James** (who is doing a stickup), **Sputnik** (who likes getting into **Orbit**), and others.

**Handmaiden**: Used by a 39-year-old white male in private conversation with his penis; "hand" because of its use during masturbation, and "maiden" because it is a surrogate for a female. Among friends, he calls it **Jocko** "because of its humorous sound."

**Homer**: Used by a white 17-year-old homosexual in Minneapolis. He refers to "Homer" in the third person and addresses his penis directly during sex. No explanation known for this naming.

**Simba**: Comedian Robin Williams, in an HBO television program, referred to his penis as "Simba," accompanied by an elephant's trumpeting. Based on the phallic trunk.

**Special Purpose**: Used in the Steve Martin movie *The Jerk* (1979). Martin's mother earlier had told him that he had a special purpose, which Martin thought was the name for his penis. When Bernadette Peters later says to Martin, "My mother wants me to marry someone with a special purpose," Martin replies, "I *have* a Special Purpose!"

**Tomorrow**: A Wisconsin man calls his girlfriend's genitalia "Tomorrow", because she never comes.

**Trouble**: Name for vagina used by a Tennessee couple. The husband tells his wife: "I'm going to get into trouble." When she has her period, she replies: "You've got to stay out of trouble for a few days." Also used by a Manhattan stock broker who used to leave the Biltmore Men's Bar at about 8 p.m., on his way to his mistress, telling his friend that he wanted "to get into trouble."

**Winston**: Used by a 10-year-old white male in California. "Winston tastes good," (like a cigarette should).
Contributed by: Dennis, Joe, Larry, Len, Ray, and Editor.

### 3.6 RIDICULING PLACE NAMES

Adams-Morgan (section of Washington, DC): **Madam's Organ**

Atlanta, GA: **Hotlanta**

Bad Axe, MI: **Bad Ass**

Barre, VT: **Gay Barríe**

Birmingham, AL: **Possum City** (heavy black population)

Bloomington, IN: **Blooming-Gulch, Gloomington**

Bordentown, NJ: **Boredomtown**

Camden, NJ: **Condom**

Charlottesville, NC: **Harlotsville**

Coral Gables, FL: **Moral Gables** (blue laws and locals' attitude)

Cupertino, CA: **Pukertino**

Detroit, MI: **Detriot**

Erie, PA: **Dreary**

Furth im Wald, Germany: **Furz im Wald** ("Fart in the Forest")

Kansas City, MO: **Kansas Shitty**

Los Angeles, CA: **Ellay, Ex-LAX, Hellay, Lost Angeles, Louse Angeles, Smogville**. All by *San Francisco Chronicle* columnist Herb Caen, who is now embarrassed about these nicknames, having seen L.A. recently. (*MJ*, 13 Aug. 1984, p. 2)

Montpelier, VT: **Montpeculiar**

Mountain View, CA: **Mountain Phew**

New York City: **Big Horse Apple, Nueves Jerkes** (many Hispanics)

Niagara Falls, NY: **Nigeria Falls**

Orlando, FL: **Borlando** ("The only city that starts with a zero and ends with a zero")

Philadelphia, PA: **Dellafilthia**

Portland, OR: **Porthole**

Redwood City, CA: **Deadwood City** ("because nothing ever happens")

Rochester, NY: **Crotchfester, Rottenchester**

Roselle Park, NJ: **Roselle Pits**

Schenectady, NY: **Disconnectady**

Sunnyvale, CA: **Slummyvale**

Tampa, FL: **Tampax**

Topeka, KS: **Two-Pecker**

Tustin, CA: **Disgustin, Tunaville** (common). ("This town is about as exciting as a plain tuna sandwich on white bread.")

West Cornwall, CT: **West Cornhole**

Windsor, Ontario: **Windsewer**

Contributed by: Janet Bernstein, Paul Cox, Donna "Honey-Chile" Ellingson, Larry Feign, Chuck G., George Gleason, David Hibbard, George Krotkoff, Paul Madarasz, Greg Page, Albert Pergande, Fred Reed, William Reitwiesner, Fred Sawyer, Jonathan Scoville, Lewis Tanner, Larry Thompson, Suzanne Zappasodi, and Editor. – An earlier listing appeared in 4:299.

----

An older woman, who had kept her heart condition a secret from her husband, reveals to him slyly on their wedding night, as they are taking off their clothes: "I have acute angina." — "I sure as hell hope so, 'cause you sure have ugly boobs!"

# Miscellany

This is material from the Maledicta Archives, collected by the Editor or contributed by our readers. Contributions are welcome and credited. Full documentation and a copy are requested. Give all essentials known (see introduction to **ELITE MALEDICTA**).

### MALEDICTAPHOBIA

**Maledictaphobia**: the excessive, unreasonable, childish fear of so-called bad words. Commonly afflicted by this mental disorder are cacademoids, cacademish professors of anthropology, linguistics, psychology, and sociology, as well as prudish editors, book reviewers, popular word gurus, British poetasters and similar would-be intellectuals. (Ambrose Bierce, eat your heart out!)

It was most curious to read a very positive, intelligent review of our journal in *Manifest*, a gay publication from San Francisco (No. 24, Sept. 1984, p. 16). The reviewer-editor found the gay and AIDS jokes tasteless, understandably. But even in this laid-back (back-laid?) subculture, the *thing* or *activity* is less objectionable than the *word* for it: "...it's all in the name of uncensored scholarship, but there's something peculiar about an academic journal you'd hide under the bed when your parents visit." In other words, mommy and daddy don't mind that Sonny engages in anal intercourse or fellatio with his lover, but they would freak out if he read *Maledicta*. Ayayay!

### PERHAPS THEY WERE COCKATOOS?

When movie producer Steven Spielberg was a youngster, he kept parakeets as pets. He named them **Shmuck I**, **Shmuck II**, and so on. (*Time*, 15 July 1985, p. 62)

### FUGU OR NOT FUGU?

*Fugu*, a puffer fish eaten by Japanese gourmets who pay

up to $200 a plate, is deadly poisonous when not perfectly prepared. According to columnist L.M. Boyd, there is a Japanese saying: *Those who eat fugu soup are stupid, but those who do not eat fugu soup are stupid, too.* Over 200 fugu eaters died during the last decade from poisoning. (*Detroit Free Press*, 21 Nov. 1984, p. 7-C. Contributed by Marie Helfrich)

### KOREAN MOOSE

American soldiers in Korea (1955-56) referred to their Korean girlfriends as **moose**, from Japanese *musume*, "daughter, girl." The troopers supplied their ladies with goodies from the Sears-Roebuck Co., by airmail. The Sears catalog was known as the *Moose Maintenance Manual.* (Contributed by H.W.C. Furman). John Solt, who verified the Japanese, added that Japanese *musuko*, "son," also means "penis."

### HOW ARE THEY HANGING?

Oriental business signs, shown in the August 1985 *NL*, p. 18, include **AH SIC KOK** (massage), **HUNG LONG** (food market), **FU KING** (restaurant), and **MEI DICK** (barber shop).

### TEA FOR TWO

Marie Helfrich sent me several bags of **FUKIEN BLACK TEA**, produced in Fukien, China. When I told my clean-thinking wifey that I was making myself a cup of this tea, she gave me a dirty look.

### NAUGHTY BITS

In MAL 2:220, I pointed out that some languages use one word to mean "buttocks" or "anus" or "vagina." Similar to U.S. *cock* (meaning "penis" or "vagina," depending on the region), Sanskrit **muska** means "vulva" or "scrotum" or "testicle." (*The Sesquipedalian* II/3, p. 1)

## THIS AD SUCKS

From an advertisement by H-P Septic Cleaning in the Greensheets of a Moundsville (W.V.) newspaper (May 1985): *Why Settle For A Full House When You Can Have A Royal Flush. We'll Take Your Crap!!! Our Number One Business Is Your #2.* (Contributed by John Bordie)

## KLINGONS

The *Boston Globe* (16 March 1977) carried this headline: **Is there a ring of debris around Uranus?** (Contributed by R. Lederer)

## DAMNED IF YOU DO

According to James Hlavac, Louisianans differentiate between a **Yankee** (one who merely visits) and a **damn Yankee** (one who moves there permanently).

## RED-LIGHT HOTEL

In 1873, the people of Lancaster, Wisconsin, wanted a first-class hotel. It would be named after whoever bought the largest block of stock. Jacob Hoar, a very prominent coal and ice dealer, had bought the largest block of stock, but the red-faced committee decided to name the hotel *Stevens House*, after Thaddeus Stevens, another prominent figure. Now, at last, the hotel has been renamed **Hoar House.** (Contributed by Roger Steiner)

## PUBIC RELATIONS

A kinky horror film, originally named *Blood Relations*, was released as **Private Parts.** Some newspapers considered this title unprintable and advertised it as *Private Arts* (Chicago) and *Private Party* (Boston). (*Glimpse*, March 1985, p. 1)

## A PIG BY ANY NAME

Orthodox religious leaders in Israel have sponsored a bill to ban the breeding and marketing of pork. An estimated one million Israelis consume 8,000 tons of pork annually. A standard menu item in many Israeli restaurants, pork is disguised as **white steak**. (*WF*, 9 July 1985, p. 5). A New York Jewish friend told me that Israeli pig breeders also get around certain laws simply by calling pigs "zebras."

## WANNA TALK?

To establish **criminal conversation** (adultery, a tort), you must prove that your spouse had sex with someone else, depriving you of exclusive rights to his or her services. (*Woman's World*, 22 Jan. 1985, p. 7).

## MORMONS DO IT, TOO

"Katlady" of Salt Lake City contributed these Mormon euphemisms: **Bounder** "bastard." — **Flipping** "fucking" (intensifier); also **humming**. — **Gentile** "non-Mormon" (this makes Jews in Utah Gentiles). — **Lamanite** "American Indian." — **Potlicker** "cocksucker." — **Savage** "an uncooperative lamanite" (Mormon pioneer usage). — **Scrud** "shit."

## LOATHE THIS LEG

Manchester football hooligan gangs call themselves *firms*. Tony, a member of such a gang, is a massive, baby-faced man, covered with tattooes from his earlobes to his ankles. His chest reads *Made in England*, and part of his left leg is devoted to racial slurs against Pakistani immigrants. (*MJ*, 23 June 1985, Accent, p. 1)

## CORRECT BODY PART, THOUGH

An American aerospace executive, during a top-level meeting at the Ministry of Defense in South Korea, tried his Korean to ask for the men's room. His Korean hosts reacted with embarrassed silence to his *Ssit bal so?* which means approximately "Where is the nearest whorehouse?" (*San Francisco Chronicle*, 22 April 1985, p. 22. Contributed by Bruce Rodgers)

### NASAL FRICATIVES

*There are peculiarities in the pronunciation of the Eskimo language that cannot be described, but must be acquired by intercourse with the natives.* From Georg von Ostermann, *Manual of Foreign Languages*, p. 313. (Contributed by Nyr Indictor)

### *VAI IN CULO!*

In Catania, Sicily, two armed youths grabbed a salesman and demanded that he hand over all his money. When he gave them 13,000 lire ($6.50), the robbers looked at him in disgust, shouted obscenities, told him to keep it, and fled on their motorcycle. (*WF*, 1 June 1985, p. 7)

### D. J. ENWRONG

The old, passé British poet D.J. Enright clearly suffers from extreme maledictaphobia: "Like his magazine [*Maledicta*], he [Reinhold Aman] seems intent on finding dirt everywhere." (*Verbatim* 12/1 [1985], p. 11) – We do? Methinks agèd Dennis is full of faeces like a Christmas turkey. So that you won't forget his name, here is — since he insists — an all-dirt hint: It's *D* as in *dipshit*, *J* as in *jakes*, *en* as in French *enculer*, "to buttfuck," and *right* as in "I say, old chap, is it in *right*?"

### BUM DEAL

Rumania recently imported a lot of Bibles from the USA. When the books arrived, they were shredded at a Rumanian pulp mill and turned into low-grade toilet paper. However, this religious toilet paper is slick, tough, nonabsorbent, and one can still read much of the print. (*Washington Report*, Aug. 1985, p. 2)

### CUNTPIT, MAYBE?
Headline in *Daily Camera* (Boulder, CO), 18 June 1984: *First all-female cockpit crew flies from Denver.*

### RESPECTABLE SHYSTERS
In the New York metropolitan area, high-class lawyers refer to themselves as *lawyers* and use the term *attorneys* for hacks. Elsewhere in the U.S., it seems to be the reverse: ambulance chasers are *lawyers*, and respectable practitioners are called *attorneys*. (Reported by K.E. Lowenthal)

### USE YOUR DICTIONARY
If people come to you looking for sympathy, tell them they'll find it between *sodomy* and *syphilis*. (Contributed by Richard Barton)

### OVER HERE
Wadley, Georgia, a town of 2,740 people, has "two liquor stores, one red light, and too much swearing," says Mayor B.A. Johnson, who has begun a campaign to rid Wadley of public profanity. He has ordered police to arrest anyone using vulgar language in public. Johnson, 60, a retired high school principal, aims his order at young people who congregate for basketball at a park and who upset neighbors with their foul language. "It's mother this and mother that, and to me that's obscene," he said. (*Orlando Sentinel*, 28 June 1985, pp. A-1, A-9. Contributed by Lenny Frazier)

### OVER THERE
At the same time, the city council of Harderwijk, Holland, has unanimously decided that cursing (*vloeken*) in public was prohibited. Their vote on prohibiting topless and naked

swimming was divided, however. Police inspector Oldenhof stated that enforcement of the prohibition of naked swimming and profanity will enjoy low priority, and that police will only act upon formal complaints. (*Het Nieuwsblad van het Zuiden*, Tilburg, 25 May 1985. Contributed by Ed Schilders)

## DRONES

In a letter to Ann Landers, a reader mentions a rock group called **W.A.S.P.** The initials stand for *We Are Sexually Perverted*. (*WF*, 27 July 1985, p. B-1)

## TUNE-A-MONTH CLUB

As announced in *Come-All-Ye* 6/2 (1985), p. 9, Carolynn Lindeman just published **Women Composers of Ragtime.**

## UNITED DICKS

An ad in *Village Voice* (23 July 1985, p. 37) for **Dicks of America** urges men named Richard to join this organization. For $7.95 you'll get a Dick pin, a Dick sticker, and a Certified Dick membership card. (Contributed by Lewis Tanner)

## BUT WOULD HE LIKE "PIG"?

Branding people with tags like **wogs, slopeheads**, and **gooks** is a convenient way of identifying immigrants and not necessarily racist, according to a high-ranking New South Wales, Australia, policeman. (*NL*, Aug. 1985, p. 33, quoting from the Adelaide *Advertiser*)

## AT LAST!

President Reagan's colon cancer operation brought many medical experts to the boob tube. One fellow from the cancer society told ABC's Dr. Timothy Johnson "how grand it was that we could now use the words **blood** and **stool** on the air." (Ellen Goodman, *Boston Globe*, in *WF*, 19 July 1985, p. 8)

### OUT, OUT, DAMNED DILDO!

John McGrath, who informed me that Goose Bay–Happy Valley, a Labrador twin town, was formerly called Refuge Cove (and "Skunk Hollow" by U.S. Air Force personnel), pointed out that in June 1985 the name of the town **Gayside** was changed to **Baytona** [why not Bayside?]. Dr. Handcock of the Geography department at Memorial University offered his services to choose more suitable names for **Dildo, South Dildo, Dildo Run** and other Canadian place names, which has upset Dildonians. John's friend, Mr. Umelik, suggested that instead the professor change his name to *Manus O'Toole*.

### MEN vs. GAYS

Richard Failla, 44, New York City's first openly homosexual judge appointed to a full criminal court term, said that homosexual men "can aspire to anything any man can aspire to." At his swearing-in ceremony, Failla thanked his "life partner," Dick Gross. (*MJ* 21 May 1985, p. 2)

### WOOF, WOOF!

Larry O'Dowd, 18, of York, northern England, was found guilty of using abusive language and behavior likely to breach the peace. Police Sgt. Fred Taylor testified that a group of youths had blocked a sidewalk, and when he told them to move on, O'Dowd turned and said "meow" to the officer's police dog, a German shepherd. Taylor found this language provocative, and a scuffle ensued. O'Dowd's attorney argued that the word *meow* is not "abusive," but the court ruled otherwise. Member of Parliament Tom Torney protested the sentence and $125 fine: "The next thing you know, somebody will be arrested for saying 'boo' to a goose."

(AP, Nov. 1984, and Carol Frakes's *Purrrrr: The Newsletter for Cat Lovers*, Febr./March 1985, p. 2)

### A PEACE A DAY

Years ago, there was a billboard advertising *Peace* cigarets near the Yokohama–Tokyo highway asking passing motorists, **Have You Had A Peace Today?** (*Spectrum Newsletter*, Winter 1985, p. 8)

### MICTURATING MOTORCARS

The August 1985 *NL*, pp. 25-26, shows photographs of various radiator shop signs claiming to be a great or **the best place in town to take a leak.**

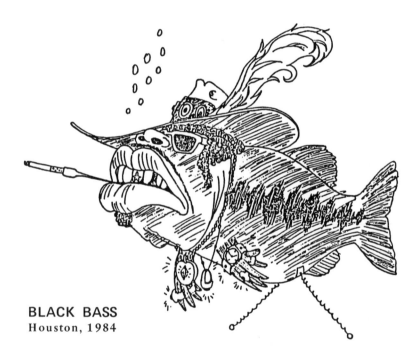

**BLACK BASS**
Houston, 1984

# NEWS

Maledicta-related information *only* on research in progress or accomplished; classroom handouts, questionnaires, bibliographies, etc. Copies of such materials are welcome. Recent articles, books, theses are listed in our **Bibliography**.

- Liliane Kerautret, University of Saarbrücken (West Germany) is writing her *maîtrise* on *Pfälzische Schimpfwörter*. This master's thesis analyzes **personal terms of abuse used in Liebsthal** (Palatinate). She reports that the locals act "as if they were paralyzed" when asked to pronounce the insults. This reaction by the local population to inquiries about their terms of abuse is typical and has been reported by other researchers as well.

- Elias Petropoulos, who keeps churning out works to upset clean-thinking citizens, presently is working on a **study on the enema** and a **lexicon of the arse**.

- Mary Koukoulès, the wife of Elias Petropoulos, is collecting more **offensive Greek verses, sayings, and vocabulary** for another volume like her *Loose-Tongued Greeks*.

- On 20 Oct. 1983, at the meeting of the "Collaborative Professional Group in Foreign Languages" held at the Graduate Center, City University of New York, Professor Allen Walker Read gave a talk about "The Problem of 'Bad Words.'"

- Professor of Psychology Edwin D. Lawson (State University College, Fredonia, NY 14063) is preparing an **annotated bibliography on names and naming.**

- Jean DeBernardi (Chicago) is working on a paper on **Hokkien scolding and swearing.**

• Sgt. Maj. Edward Komac, one of 930 Army bomb disposal experts, is trying to collect **verbal outbursts** unique to members of this most stressful occupation.

• Roy West (1212 Ellsworth St., Philadelphia, PA 19147) has published **Randy McNutty's U.X.A.**, a 24 by 36 inch color map of the USA. It features about 1,200 actual place names ranging from Onancock, VA, to Butternuts, NY, and Titlow, WA. Available from the author for $5.50 postpaid.

• Edward C. Paolella has published various **bibliographies on gay/lesbian studies**, including language. He is particularly interested in receiving clippings or bibliographical information on gay/lesbian issues treated in non-homosexual publications (magazines, journals, newspapers, etc.). He can be reached at: Gay Books Bulletin, P.O. Box 480, Lenox Hill Station, New York, NY 10021.

• Professor Roger Phillips (Milwaukee, WI) is working on a large and unique **Thesaurus of Sexual Language.**

• Professor G.R. Simes (Sydney, Australia) has begun work on his **Dictionary of the Language of Sex and Sexuality in English, on Historical Principles.**

• Professor Leonard Ashley (Brooklyn College, NY) has almost finished his **Dictionary of Sexual Slanguage**, to be published by Stein & Day.

• Professor Christoph Harbsmeier (University of Oslo, Norway) is preparing a **Historical Dictionary of Chinese Obscenities.**

• William Hewitt, a medical researcher and writer (Whittier, CA), has collected over 2,500 sexual words from the clinic, street, and erotic writings for a possible **Sexicon.**

• Dutch journalist Ed Schilders (Tilburg, Holland) has a 400-page manuscript for a proposed **Dictionary of Copulation**, to be called **Coïre**. It treats every aspect of this topic, from posture names to folklore and copulation through the ages.

• Professor Michael K. Smith (Psychology Dept., University of Tennessee, Knoxville, TN 37996) teaches "Linguistics 2000: Language, Linguistics, and Society," in which he treats such topics as **taboo words, euphemisms, and slang** from a linguistic and psychological perspective. Students find this course a welcome change from purely prescriptive Puritanical classes. They are required to do a class project, collecting and analyzing original data.

• Professor Arne Holtdorf (University of Tübingen, West Germany) conducts a *Hauptseminar* on terms of abuse. Among the many topics covered are **terms of abuse in standard language and argots, nicknames, historical aspects from the Middle Ages to Goebbels and the *Bundestag*, prejudice, national character, animal metaphors, insults in literary works, and terms of endearment derived from insults.**

• Another German scholar, Professor Wilfried Seibicke, teaches a *Proseminar* on curses and insults at the University of Heidelberg. Topics include **blasphemy, dialect terms of abuse (Alemannic, Bavarian, Franconian, Palatinate, Silesian, Sudeten, Swiss, etc.), political insults, animal metaphors, threats, children's terms of abuse, as well as insults in Bohemian, Dutch, English, French, and Latin.**

• The Rev. Hermann Hochegger, Director of CEEBA (Bandundu, Zaïre) recently directed the 19th colloquium on Congo folklore and society, in which two French-language presentations dealt with **maledictions and benedictions.**

• Paul Dickson, author of *Words* and *Jokes* (P.O. Box 80, Garrett Park, MD 20896) is now collecting **family words.** These are words used by the members of one family and normally not understood by outsiders; cf. Allen Walker Read's "Family Words in English," *American Speech* (1962). Most are non-offensive, but there are a few goodies: **G.M.P.O.T.**, pronounced *gimpot*, "Guest Making Pigs Of Themselves," used for the better-known **F.H.B.** "Family Hold Back," to signal that food is running low. **X.Y.Z.** "Examine Your Zipper" means that one's fly is open. **Clara** (known by Waukesha youngsters as **wedgie**, according to my daughter Susan), is used by a family to indicate that someone's pants or skirt is stuck between the buttocks. Another family uses **7734** for "hell" (read upside down).

• Professor Gerald Cohen, a Slavic linguist (Ph.D., Columbia University, 1971) untiringly edits and publishes his *Comments on Etymology.* This series of working papers is mainly devoted to etymology and Indo-European morphology, treating such varied topics as English slang (**shyster, shmuck**), Greek lexical borrowings from Semitic, Missouri place names, syntactic blending (*time and again*), and British thieves' cant. Since its inception in 1971, many leading linguists have contributed to this scholarly publication appearing roughly monthly, from October to May. Subscription cost for individuals is $5.00 annually, or $10.00 for libraries and other institutions. Order from: Prof. G. Cohen, Dept. of AACS, University of Missouri–Rolla, Rolla, MO 65401-0249.

# queries

Queries by members and research suggestions by the Editor. The numbers refer to volume and running number. Most responses will be published in **FEEDBACK**.

### 8.1 FRATERNITIES AND SORORITIES

From his undergraduate days, Frank Nuessel remembers *Alpha Omicron Pi* (sorority) as **A O Pussies**, *Delta Kappa Epsilon* (fraternity) as **Dicks**, and *Sigma Nu* (fraternity) as **Sigmanure**. Gail Reaves and Michael Smith have submitted a paper on University of Tennessee sorority insults to us. If you remember any, please send actual name of sorority or fraternity, nickname, if used by males or females, university or college, and any explanation if not obvious.

### 8.2 TERMS FOR UGLY FEMALES

Bruce Rodgers recently heard teens use **faggot** for "ugly girl." In his youth, an ugly girl used to be called a **bear** or **toad.** In Upper Michigan, I heard **two-bagger**: the girl is so ugly that *she* must wear a paper bag during sex, and *you*, too — in case hers comes off during the action. What terms have you heard?

### 8.3 VERBAL CASTRATION

Ms. Nirvana, a modern Californian, gets rid of obnoxious males with such lines as: **You, scumbag, go slam your dick in a door!** and **Want to see your nuts fly out of your nose, asshole?** She wonders what verbal weapons other ladies use to repel undesirable men.

### 8.4 GOOD NEWS–BAD NEWS INSULTS

For lack of a better term, I have used the above classification for the special type of insult where the first part is a flattery and the second part is the insult proper. By first flattering your opponent, you make him or her more vulnerable. I have examples from three languages: (1) Black American English: **I hate to talk about your mother, she's a good old soul — but she has a ten-ton pussy and a rubber asshole.** (2) Chilean Spanish: **Tu madre es una santa — pero tú eres un hijo de puta.** ("Your mother is a saint — but you are a son-of-a-whore," disregarding the slur on mother in part two). (3) Yiddish: **Zi hot a punim vi a malke — un a pirge vi a floym.** ("She has a face like a queen — and a cunt like a plum.") Yiddish is especially rich in this type of insult, e.g., **May you become famous — they should name a disease after you!** or **May you inherit three shiploads full of gold — and it shouldn't be enough to pay for your doctor's bills!** Does anyone have other examples from these and other languages?

### 8.5 TERMS FOR ELIMINATION

Denison H. asks what euphemisms other people use for "urine" and "to urinate," and "feces" and "to defecate," providing these examples: his proper Bostonian female relative used **go tryhard** for "defecate." A Jewish lady asks her children to **make a kug** ("ball, round pile," from Yiddish *kugl*). Relatives living on a farm used to defecate in the fields, **making a snekkie** (from the snake-like appearance of the well-coiled feces). Mrs. Portnoy (*Complaint*) used to ask her son whether he made mostly **poopies** or mostly **water.** As a child, his wife used **to hark** (urinate) and **make a gruntie** (defecate). He recalls reading that those people were psychologically most screwed up who were taught to tell their parents that they had **to make a yuckey.**

As for my own terms for "urinate," I use **tinkle** when among strangers, **take a leak** among friends and at home, and **piss** when I want to annoy certain proper people. I'm aware of the "vulgarity" of **to piss** in English, as compared to German *pissen* which, like French *pisser*, is just colloquial, not vulgar. As to "defecate," I always use **I have to lay an egg**, probably influenced by the German *Ich muß ein Ei legen*. What terms do you use now, and what euphemisms did you use as a child?

### 8.6 CHINESE TELEPHONE CALLS

Dr. Tim Healey wishes to know what **making Chinese telephone calls** means, allegedly a professional specialty of female prostitutes in Marseille, France.

### 8.7 JEWESS

Nowadays, many people avoid the words *Jew* and *Jews*, using instead the "less derogatory" *Jewish (gentle)man* or *Jewish lady/woman* and *Jewish people*. Even before the fem libbers scolded us for using the "sexist" suffix *-ess*, **Jewess** seemed to sound more pejorative than **Jew**. Does anyone have any ideas why?

### 8.8 BLOWJOB

Several readers have asked about the origin of **blowjob** (fellatio) and **to blow** (to fellate), neither of which involves much, if any, blowing. A *Hustler* editor wondered whether it was derived from the result, the man "blowing his wad" (to ejaculate). Any better ideas?

### 8.9 COURSE NAMES

Students often have their own names for courses. Martha Cornog remembers that students at Brown University called "The Sociology of Deviant Behavior" *Nuts and Sluts*. Alleen and Don Nilsen collected some, e.g., "Urban Local Government" called by students *Slums and Bums*. Paul Eschholz and Alfred Rosa published "Course Names: Another Aspect of College Slang" in *American Speech* 45 (1970), pp. 85-90, with many humorous examples, such as *Priest and Beasts, Cuts and Guts, Maps and Naps, Choke and*

*Croak*. We would like to get more of these, listing the actual course title, the students' version, institution, and year used.

### 8.10 FOOD NAMES

The Army's **shit on a shingle** or **S.O.S** for creamed chipped beef on toast is well known. Joe Fishbein sent a few less-than-appetizing nicknames for food used by college students at Michigan Technological University during the early 1970s: **blood** and **sorority sauce** for ketchup, **M.D.'s** or **monkey dicks** for link sausages, **H.C.** or **horse cock** for ring bologna, **cum-gum** for chewing gum with liquid centers, **garbage barges** for tuna boat sandwiches, and **stroke-me-off** for beef Stroganoff. Any more such food names?

### 8.11 FUCKING THE DOG

Does anyone know the origin of **fucking the dog**, "to goof off"?

### 8.12 ABUSIVE WILLS

Judith Corbett wonders whether anyone has collected any verbal aggression and abuse in wills. As this is one's last chance to blast one's relatives, there ought to be some good verbal abuse in testaments.

### 8.13 GAMBLERS' CUSSING

Howard Schwartz, editor of the Gambler's Book Club in Las Vegas, would like to hear of cussing and swearing by gamblers and race track betters. Gamblers, being in a high state of affect, surely blast out a few blue ones when losing. One could collect such material with a concealed tape recorder.

---

A guy walks into a drugstore and asks the lady behind the cash register: "Do you keep stationery?" She answers, "Yes, right up to the last moment. But then my toes curl up, and I turn into an animal!"

# REACTIONS

Readers' responses to anything but **QUERIES**: corrections, additions, comments. Longer **REACTIONS** may be published separately as articles.

## AASAA – 3:309

We didn't receive many reactions to my proposed **AASAA** – Aman's Annual Super Asshole Award. Perhaps there are too many assholes in this world, or your frustration threshold is higher than mine. The following are this year's recipients for this award:

• The Newspaper Enterprise Association, New York, for charging $125 for the rights to reprint a single cartoon.

• The Course & Curriculum Committee, as well as the "chairperson" and dean of a midwest university, for allowing such trash to be taught as "Feminism, Sexism & Fairy Tales" in a German language department. The prof who teaches this crap is too far gone to know what he is doing, but the students will learn all about glorious Marxism instead of how to put together a correct sentence in German.

• The Philadelphia folks who put out an advertising flier for a transliterated dictionary of the Russian language. In their advertisement, they show a list of Cyrillic characters and the corresponding Roman alphabet, and give this example to show how easy their method is: *ilektron* (in Russian) which, when using their table, is transliterated to – *tadá!* – "Leningrad."

• The National Endowment for the Humanities for supporting this grant: "A Social Historical Study of Marriage and Morality Patterns of Young Girls in 15th-Century

Florence." The Chicago prof who pulled this one received $74,993 to do his thing, no doubt in part for having such an exact budget.

• The federal Law Enforcement Assistance Administration for giving a female prof at Asshole U in Milwaukee a grant of $177,700 to interview 500 boys and 500 girls to find out what conceptions and myths teenagers have about rape.

• Various Washington bureaucrats for spending some $750,000 on another female researcher's project to study child pornography in several so-called mens' magazines. (Don't submit further examples of such wastes of taxpayers' money. The cretins who waste our money make me puke.)

• All those ignorant reference librarians at university and public libraries, as well as the many bookdealers who, when asked by their patrons, were unable to find our address or information about our journal, books, or the Society, even though they are listed in *Books in Print, Directory of Associations*, and in dozens of other standard reference works.

• This "chairperson," clearly a manifest asshole, who sends out the following standard reply to professors inquiring about a job opening (submitted by a colleague):

> I am writing to acknowledge receipt of your lines of [date], pertinent to the possibility of obtaining a teaching position in our German division commencing in the fall of [year], and to inform you with regret that I do not here and now anticipate any openings in the area of your linguistic specialization for the ensuing academic year. I have made it a point, however, to call your letter to the attention of [name], Assistant Administrative Head of the section concerned, who will contact you directly on my behalf should unforeseen circumstances prompt changes in our currently envisaged hiring posture. You may be assured, in any case, that we will be more

than happy to give your application every comparative consideration consistent with our needs. Thanking you for your aforementioned inquiry, as, indeed, for your manifest interest in [university], I am [name].

• The promotion and publicity departments of publishers who are *too cheap* to supply review copies to us (but send out tons to newspapers, who could not care less about books), and especially those publicity flunkies who don't have the decency to reply or who *lie* that they are "out of review copies," even though the book was published short time ago. Notorious among such uncooperative cheap-ass publishers are **Oxford University Press** (New York office) and **Longman** (New York and London offices). It costs them about five dollars for the book and postage to get a plug in *Maledicta* read by thousands of potential buyers and in libraries around the world, but these anal-retentive, ignorant sluts can't grasp this. The books of these publishers are great, but their promo people suck!

• As to lawsuits, Zbigniew Kindela of *Chic* magazine informed me of the libel laws pertaining to calling someone an asshole: only those who seek public notice can be called "asshole" without risking a lawsuit. He also sent me a list of "Asshole of the Month" awards handed out by *Hustler* magazine; they range from Gerald Ford and Jimmy Carter to Aleksander Solzhenitsyn and Ayatollah Khomeini.

### SHIT – 1:173 and 3:195

On page 19 of the April 1, 1985 issue of *Screw* magazine, Bric 'n' Brac, two bizarre figures in 6 cartoon panels entitled "Well I'll be dipped in shit and hung out to dry!" utter the following dialog: "Man, I was so scared I shit in my pants!" "I was scared shitless!" – "I shit a brick!" "I shit a ton of bricks!" – "I was shittin' pills!" "I shat where I sat!" – "I shit a pile this high!" "You're full of shit!" – "Oh yeah?! Well you got shit coming out of your ears!" "You've got shit fer brains!" – "I've got shit on my shoe." "Holy shit!" – "And he ain't shittin'!" comments the artist, Peter 'Shithead' Bagge. (Contributed by Don Haarman)

### FART – 7:149

The database of the forthcoming *Dictionary of American Regional English* contains question number 0853, "words for breaking wind from the bowels." There are 183 terms and variants of *fart* and euphemisms for it, the most frequent response being *fart* (603 times). Other frequent terms with up to 10 responses from throughout the U.S. are *poop, poot, breaking wind, gas, toot, passing gas, windbreaker, passing wind, break wind, pass gas, stinker,* and *fizzle*. It was probably the fieldworkers' fault that 140 informants did not respond to this question (even though they fart like you and me). The responses indicate the geographic location, but are not separated into nouns and verbs. Among the unusual, single-response terms are *belch in reverse, blowing off at the bung-hole, cut a melon, easy slider, frog jumped in the pond, he done fizzled, shootin' Germans, shot a duck, singing hymns,* and *whiffer*. (Contributed by Len Ashley)

### SPOONERISMS – 7:31 and 34

David Hibbard contributed these Polish spoonerisms:

**Stój, Halina! / Hój stalina.**
Stand, Helen! / Stalin's cock.

**Mądra Jola / Jądra mola**
Clever Yola / mole testicles

**Pradziadek przy saniach**
**Sra dziadek przy paniach**
Great-grandfather beside the sleigh
Grandfather shits in front of the ladies

# REFLEXIONS

The British spelling variant, reflexions, is an appropriate heading for this department featuring short personal anecdotes, stories, comments, remembrances about x-rated and other "bad" words: physical or verbal chastisement by parents, teachers, neighbors, peers, superiors and others for having used offensive language. Also, anything about swearing and vulgarities: how and why you use (or don't use) swearwords and taboo words; how you feel about high-ranking or educated people or elegant ladies using x-rated words; how you deal with your students or children when they use offensive language; how you react to name-calling; and the like. Please indicate your age, sex and profession. All contributors will be quoted semi-anonymously.

Here is a sampling of Reflexions received over the years from our readers:

★ In *Benedicta!* 1, you mentioned various synonyms for "vulva." Ever since my first contact with *pussy* (written in four-foot letters on a blackboard in a third-grade after-school program in Harlem, NY, where I was a student teacher), I have thought of it as extremely vulgar. *Cunt* is my preferred word to use with a lover. If a lover refers to my genitals as *pussy*, I correct him and tell him I have no *pussy*; what I have is a *cunt*. I do the same with the word *vagina*. I have a *vagina* at the gynecologist's office, but not in bed. For a lover to say *vagina* is a turn-off—he sounds clinical and prissy, as though he wouldn't like to touch it without rubber gloves. *Twat* seems cute and harmless to me, having first met this word in the "TWA Tea" joke. *Beaver* is new to me. I saw it first six years ago. *Bearded clam* is the latest synonym I heard. When I asked around, a seventy-year-old executive told me that it was quite current in his office. It must be in widespread use now: the other day my younger son came home from college sporting a baseball cap that bears the name of his team, **THE BEARDED CLAMS**. (Elizabeth, teacher, ca. 45)

★ With my friend Lona, I discuss all kinds of sexual matters, and I read *Maledicta* without problems. But I can't get myself to say "cunt" or even "pussy." So I use the term "moistness" when I discuss my private parts. (Mary, librarian, 35)

★ While discussing terms of abuse with a young professor of mathematics and his wife, at a university in Wisconsin, I asked her what the nastiest term was her hubby would call her. She said *washerwoman*. Surprised about this relatively harmless insult, I asked her about much nastier terms. She said, "He can call me a 'cocksucker' any time. That doesn't bother me, because I *am* a cocksucker—I suck his cock. But I do get furious when he calls me a *washerwoman*, because I'm *not* a washerwoman." (Editor)

★ When I listened to your lecture on verbal aggression, I didn't mind all the sexual and scatological examples you used. But when you used blasphemous curses from English and other languages, I became upset and got sweaty palms. I'm not a religious person, so I don't understand my negative emotional and physical reaction to blasphemy. (Janet, professor, ca. 35, commenting to the Editor after his lecture)

★ My father was a native speaker of Russian, and he used to enjoy making puns in English. He would have changed your *cacademic* to *cock-eyed-demic*, a crew he thoroughly hated. He was an artist, painter, and pianist, with deep contempt for academics of all kinds. (Timothy, professor, ca. 40)

★ When very angry, my mother used to say *Yetolosangua!* I'm not sure of the spelling, but it's Italian and means "May all your blood fall out!" Another of her favorites was *That sonamabitch two time ana half!* (Vincent)

★ My parents did not say *shit* around the house. Once my mother came close to it, when she tried to say "Fiddlesticks!" to my brother, but said *Shiddlesticks!* instead, because she had forgotten to put in her teeth. (Fred)

★ The information on *chingar* in Zlotchew's article (3:121-122) was interesting to me because of my name, Ching. I teach high school and have Mexican-Americans in my classes who smile enigmatically over my name but who are far too polite to reveal the source of their amusement, saying that it is "private." The name is not Oriental, but English and Irish. (Evelyn)

★ I do an Elderhostel course on American humor — I really just make the old farts put on a performance with song, dance, and witty repartee. It's fun, and I have found that intimidation can be a strong motivator. Last year an old lady was complaining about having to perform, saying she had arthritis, her circulation wasn't good, etc. She wanted sympathy, but I gave her some real shit, saying, "Look, honey, you're already 75 and you're not in good health. This may well be your *last* chance to appear on stage." It worked. Our show was better than much prime time TV variety shit. (Robert, ca. 45)

★ I taught a short course at the Open High School in which I urged the students to use more creative language in vilifying one another, with copious quotes from MAL. We cannot put up with the present state of affairs where people face one another and yell "Fuck you!" "Oh, yea? Fuck you!" "Oh, yea? Fuck you!" (Joanne, teacher)

★ Once when my dad said "fuck," my mother jumped down his throat. He replied, "If they can say 'Republican' on TV and radio with impunity, I sure as hell can say 'fuck' in my own home." (Tom, professor)

★ My uncle Jacques had an engaging method of teasing his eldest brother at dinner. At an opportune moment, Jacques would clap his hands repeatedly, about two inches in front of his brother's nose, while chanting a litany: *Jesu Christ! Petit Baptême! Maudit esprit de Tabernacle! Câlice d'hostie! Calvaire!* and so on. Uncle George is not amused by these blasphemies. He's monsignor of the village church. (Norman, Québec)

★ In my youth, I served with a Swedish volunteer outfit in the Finnish Army. As is common among soldiers, a lingo developed. Our greeting upon meeting was "Penis, penis," and our parting was "Vagina, vagina." We called the Russian-made rifle *rysshora*, "Russian whore," and the bread sticks *hundskit*, "dog turd." (Lennart)

★ Last winter, while wheeling my mother out of the hospital, the director came by. He asked me why my face was so red. I told him that I had just walked 20 minutes in record-breaking cold weather, adding, *"Heute ist es so kalt, daß ich mir fast die Nebenhoden abgefroren hätte."* ("Today it's so cold I almost froze off my epididymides.") The surgeon guffawed and appreciated my urogenital precision, but mother, always a lady, was embarrassed by her boy's crudity. (Editor)

★ My mother emigrated to the United States from Latvia as a very young woman, and I recall her maledictions, or more often counter-maledictions to ward off Evil Eye threats to her children, always quietly under her breath and presenting a smile on her face to the purported evildoer. Oh, that I had listened carefully instead of turning away in embarrassment at her foreign tongue! (Edna, CA)

★ We work with special preschoolers for a mental health agency in Pennsylvania. We can't curse around the children, so we resort to phrases like "Jiminy Cricket!", "God Bless America!", and "Sugar Honey Iced Tea!" [S.H.I.T.] We long for more novel and sophisticated phrases to use openly amongst ourselves without administrative censure. (Nadine, Charles)

★ I do not like to listen to nor do I like to see the "four-letter words" in print nor in the movies. I'm a great-grandmother and no one uses those words around me. I have asked the others to stop using them, and they respect me. I'm of the old school, and the four-letter words that I know and appreciate are **WORK** and **CASH**. (Margaret, CA)

# biBLioGRApby

Compiled and annotated
by Reinhold Aman

This bibliography is divided into three parts: (1) publications dealing with maledicta-related matters, (2) dictionaries, and (3) other works received. See also *Announcements* for other general and maledicta-related books published or in progress. Unless otherwise noted, all books are hardbound and typeset.

Adams, James N. *Latin Sexual Vocabulary*. London: Duckworth, Baltimore: Johns Hopkins University Press, 1983. 272 pp., $27.50. – Hundreds of Latin terms for sexual organs and activities, with synonyms and metaphors, derived from literary and other sources. Copious quotations in Latin and Greek (untranslated, alas). Shows diachronic changes and weakening of obscene words into general terms of abuse. Excellent.

Afonso, Belarmino. "Facetas da alma transmontana: Bruxarias e maldições." *Brigantia: Revista de cultura* (Bragança) 3/3 (1983):419-38. – Portuguese sorcery poems and single curses to inflict illness, poverty, etc. Also, demonic and Gypsy curses.

Allen, Irving Lewis. "Male Sex Roles and Epithets for Ethnic Women in American Slang." *Sex Roles* 11/1-2 (1984):43-50. – Inventory of derogatory names for women of ethnic out-groups (i.e., all but WASPs), with some black slurs against white women. The slurs derogate the women's sex and ethnic roles.

———. "Personal Names that Became Ethnic Epithets." *Names* 31/4 (1983):307-17. – Over 100 ethnic slurs used in American popular speech (past and present); given names mainly, and a few surnames. Discusses social causes, cultural clashes, and allusions.

———. *The Language of Ethnic Conflict: Social Organization and Lexical Culture*. New York: Columbia University Press, 1983. 162 pp., paper $9.50, cloth $20. – A very useful study of nicknames for ethnic groups used in the USA, with historical, sociological, and philological analyses. Etymology and earliest date used shown where known. Discusses conflicting etymologies.

Allport, Gordon W. *The Nature of Prejudice*. Reading, MA: Addison-Wesley, 1982. Paper, 537 pp., $5.95. 25th Anniversary Edition. – The best introduction to this field, with ample material on racial and ethnic differences, stereotypes, rejection of out-groups, scapegoats, theories and acquisition of prejudice, tolerance, and much more.

Aman, Reinhold. "*Dingbat, Dungheap,* and *Dunce*: Metaphoric Terms of Abuse in English and Other Languages." In *Whimsy II*, ed. by Don and Alleen Nilsen, pp. 196-200. Tempe: Arizona State University, 1984. – Discusses 7 classes of metaphors by word formation, pejorative suffixes, and Spanish derogatory animal metaphors.

——. "Interlingual Taboos in Advertising: How Not to Name Your Product." In *Linguistics and the Professions*, ed. by Robert Di Pietro, pp. 215-24. Norwood, NJ: Ablex, 1982. – On interlingual and intercultural taboos, and the dangers of using trade names (product or company name) that have an obscene, ridiculous or otherwise negative meaning in other languages.

Arango, Ariel C. *Las malas palabras*. Buenos Aires: Legasa, 1983. Paper, 223 pp. – Psychoanalytic study of taboo words, with many quotes from world literature, philosophers, and Freud. Topics include sexual organs, fellatio, defecation, urination, cruelty, homosexuality, masturbation (with case histories). Full-blooded "bad" words are better than cold clinical terms.

Baldinger, Kurt. "*Cucuruco* und *panpayrona*: Von den gehörnten Spaniern bis zu den (un)bescholtenen Jungfrauen in Perú." In *Umgangssprache in der Iberoromania*, ed. by G. Holtus and E. Radtke, pp. 303-14. – On "cuckoo," "cuckold," and loose women in ancient Peru. With many citations, notes, and Quechua examples.

——. "Homonymie- und Polysemiespiele im Mittelfranzösischen." *Zeitschrift für Romanische Philologie* 100/3-4 (1984):241-81. – Wordplays and riddles in 15th-century France based on homonyms and polysemy. Many examples from Bruno Roy's *Devinettes françaises du moyen âge* (Montréal, Paris 1977). Copious citations and notes. Index of words.

Barrick, Mac E. "Texas Chicken." *North Carolina Folklore Journal* 27/3 (1979):88-91. – Ethnic slurs and other examples of *blason populaire* in American English, such as *Mexican breakfast, Spanish supper, Irish turkey, Texas oysters*, and *South Carolina icecream*.

Baumann, Winfried. "Grenzüberschreitungen: Erzähltes Ostbayern in tschechischer Sprache." *Ostbairische Grenzmarken* (1985). In press.

– On translating Bavarian exclamations, insults, and scatological terms into Czech.

——. "Švejk und die Frage der nationalen Stereotypen." In *Hašek-Symposium, Bamberg 1983*. Frankfurt/M., 1985. In press. – Sociological, linguistic, and literary aspects of national stereotypes of Hungarians, Germans, Austrians, and Russians found in Hašek's *Švejk*.

——. "Verbale Aggression in den 'Mertvye duši' Gogols." *Sborník prací filozofické brněnské univerzity* (1984-85). In press. – On various kinds of verbal aggression in Gogol's *Dead Souls*.

*The Bean Report*. New York: Warner Books, 1984. Paper, 176 pp., $5.95. – This illustrated "thorough airing of society's last taboo," published anonymously by Sean Kelly, is an amusing and instructive collection of *Fartiana*: the anatomy of crepitation and flatulence; medical, folk, and French terms; the famous French *Pétomane* (Louis Pujol); farts in literature; a version of Twain's *1601*; fart poems, riddles, jokes. Also, from this journal (5:209), a version of our No Farting poster.

Belgrader, Michael. "Fluch, Fluchen, Flucher." In *Enzyklopädie des Märchens*, ed. Kurt Ranke, vol. 4/4-5 (1984), pp. 1315-28. – A survey of "curse, swearing, blasphemer" in antiquity, the Bible, church, modern writings, legends, fairy tales, etc.

Bolinger, Dwight. "Metaphorical Aggression: Bluenoses and Coffin Nails." Paper read at the Georgetown University Round Table on Languages and Linguistics 1979.

Brandes, Stanley H. "Los gitanos y la autoimagen andaluza: Analisis psicocultural." In *La Antropología Médica en España*, ed. by Michael Kenny and Jesús de Miguel, pp. 103-20. Barcelona: Anagrama, 1980. – On the self-image of Andalusian Gypsies, jokes about Gypsies, and stereotypes.

Bronner, Simon J. "Saturday Night in Greenville: An Interracial Tale-and-Music Session in Context." *Folklore Forum* 14/2 (1981):85-120. – A fully transcribed and annotated edition of an audio tape featuring a (dirty) joke-telling competition between a white and a Mississippi black. Rare in-context document of joking behavior among men. Other prudish folklore journal editors and printers refused to publish this material.

Brosig, Elly. "Sociolinguistic Aspects of US Army Slang." M.A. thesis, Universität Stuttgart, 1984. Paper, 106 pp. – The author, who has for many years worked with U.S. servicemen stationed in Germany, analyzes the function of Army slang: general, artillery, medical corps, signal units, and by ranks. Linguistic, sociological, and psychological aspects. Usage and attitudes. Methods and questionnaire.

Burke, J. Ashley. *The X-Rated Book: Sex and Obscenity in the Bible.* Houston: J.A.B. Press, 1983. Paper, 223 pp., $8.95. – Sixty short chapters, citing book, chapter & verse of the Bible, preceded by a poetic version and comments. Reveals little-known Scriptures (highlighted in bold) on prostitution, rape, cannibalism, fornication, hemorrhoids, nocturnal emissions, flatulence, etc.

Cardozo-Freeman, Inez. *The Joint: Language and Culture in a Maximum Security Prison.* Springfield, IL: Charles Thomas, 1984. 579 pp., $52.75. – In collaboration with Eugene Delorme and the technical assistance of David Maurer and Robert Freeman, anthropologist and ethnographer Cardozo presents the results of her fieldwork (1978-80) at the Washington State Penitentiary in Walla Walla. Description of prison culture as seen by the inmates (via many interviews), resulting in an objective corpus of (vulgar) folk speech in its natural context, the most valuable and largest part of this work. Inmates of various ethnic and social backgrounds discuss interaction, subsistence, sexuality, territoriality, etc. The Glossary of some 800 words and expressions contains much general (street) slang known to all but the most sheltered, e.g., *acid head, asshole, bad, bitch, blade, bogus, booze, bozo, bum, chump, give head...yahoos, yes-man, zonked.* The product does not match the publisher's quality boast on the copyright page: unlike the equally overpriced books by Gale and Garland, this valuable work is printed cheaply on cheap white paper, and is merely glued. For $52.75, one can expect sewn signatures, especially in a book that will be consulted frequently.

Claire, Elizabeth. *What's So Funny? A Foreign Student's Introduction to American Humor.* New Rochelle Park, NJ: Eardley, 1984. Paper, 151 pp., $7.95. – A useful guide for teachers of English to foreign-born students, with hundreds of funny jokes. The reasons for not understanding a joke (wordplays, cultural differences, etc.) are patiently explained. With exercises.

Cohen, Gerald Leonard. *Origin of the Term "Shyster."* Bern, Frankfurt/M: Peter Lang, 1982. Paper, 124 pp., sFr31. Forum Anglicum 12. – Twelve suggested etymologies of *shyster* are presented and documented with citations. Newly discovered material from 1843-44 is introduced. Early attestation and activities of New York politicians and journalists are discussed. Bibliography.

——. *Origin of the Term "Shyster": Supplementary Information.* Bern, Frankfurt/M: Peter Lang, 1984. Paper, 114 pp., sFr 26. Forum Anglicum 13. – The life and character of Mike Walsh, who's who for the *shyster* story, glossary.

Colombo, John Robert. *René Lévesque Buys Canada Savings Bonds & Other Great Canadian Graffiti.* Edmonton: Hurtig, 1983. Paper, 96 pp., Can.$5.95. – A visually very appealing collection of graffiti, illustrated by David Shaw. Introduction; material from throughout Canada, with location and date. Funny stuff: *veni, vidi, wiwi* while reading it.

Conniff, Richard. *The Devil's Book of Verse: Masters of the Poison Pen from Ancient Times to the Present Day.* Dodd, Mead & Co., 1983. 269 pp., $15.95. – Arranged into 12 categories, these satirical-to-nasty poems attack rulers, writers, artists, professions, the sexes, and neighbors. The editor comments where needed. Due to a dispute with the prudish Bible-selling parent publisher, who wanted the author to tear out two pages with offensive words, the author now sells it directly: Deep River Books, P.O. Box 64, Deep River, CT 06417, $17.30 total.

Dagrin, Bengt. *Kakamoja.* Norsborg: Privately printed, 1983. 160 pp. – Facsimile edition of an anonymous 1872 anthology of Swedish scatological graffiti, riddles, and poems. With extensive notes and bibliographical commentary. [All books by Mr. Dagrin are available from the author, Brages Väg 5, 6 trp., 14569 Norsborg, Sweden. Write to him in English for prices.]

——. *Klotter.* Falun: B. Wahlströms, 1982. Paper, 80 pp. – Swedish graffiti, with sources. Examples from Pompeii to the present, with some English, Latin, and German samples. Organized by topic.

——. *Mera Klotter.* Falun: B. Wahlströms, 1983. Paper, 80 pp. – Over 500 new Swedish graffiti, with sources, organized by topics. Includes some English graffiti from New Zealand.

——. *Ännu Mera Klotter.* Falun: B. Wahlströms, 1984. Paper, 80 pp. – Still more Swedish graffiti, organized by topics and illustrated.

Di Pietro, Robert, ed. *Linguistics and the Professions.* Norwood, NJ: Ablex, 1982. 272 pp., paper $16.50, cloth $29.50. – Twenty articles on the language and communication problems in the medical professions, law, commerce, advertising, and bureaucracy. Includes R. Aman's article on interlingual taboos.

Dickson, Paul. *Jokes.* New York: Delacorte, 1984. 236 pp., $13.95. – 28 categories of jokes, puns, riddles, including Tom Swifties,

Shaggy Dog, Knock-Knocks, What's the Difference, Do It's, and other genres. Ethnic jokes are told under *Funistradans*, a fictitious nationality, pp. 162-67.

——. *Words: A Connoisseur's Collection of Old and New, Weird and Wonderful, Useful and Outlandish Words*. New York: Delacorte, 1982. 366 pp., $13.95. – 52 thematic sections of words (with definitions) for nearly everything, including Curses, Loutish Words (terms of abuse), Sexy Words, Soused Synonyms (2,231 words and phrases for "drunk"). Illustrated. A word lover's delight.

Dreizin, Felix, and Priestly, Tom. "A Systematic Approach to Russian Obscene Language." *Russian Linguistics* 6 (1982):233-49. – On vulgar (obscene) Russian infixes and *"mat* PRO-nouns," with many examples in Russian and English translations.

Drogin, Marc. *Anathema! Medieval Scribes and the History of Book Curses*. Totowa, NJ: Rowman & Allanheld, 1983. 138 pp., $15.95. – Actually two books in one beautifully illustrated volume: the life and work of medieval scribes producing and caring for their books; and a treatise on book curses meant to protect the valuable productions. Over 80 book curses, many in the original languages, beginning with a 7th-century B.C. Babylonian tablet curse. A glossary of medieval book terminology complements this informative work.

Dundes, Alan. "Misunderstanding Humour: An American Stereotype of the Englishman." *International Folklore Review* 2 (1982):10-15. – The English, when trying to retell a joke, allegedly misunderstand wordplays, etc., and bungle it.

——. *Life is Like a Chicken Coop Ladder: A Portrait of German Culture through Folklore*. New York: Columbia University Press, 1984. 174 pp., $17.50. – A *turd de force* folkloristic-psychological study of "German national character" based on the alleged German preoccupation with shit. Discourses on Germans and Jews. Valuable collection of source materials, but ignores the tremendous differences among the German tribes who are at least as different as the Scots are from the Australians. My objections to such "national stereotypes" are not caused by ethnic chauvinism but are based on intimate first-hand knowledge of German tribes, which Dundes lacks. Support of his theories by left-wing Germans can be disregarded, as those reds like to defile everything, especially their own country; this kind of anti-German Germans can be compared to Non-Jewish Jews (*see* Prager). Further, the fact that there are so many sources (songs, verses, etc.) of scatological material in German is not necessarily proof of its importance to Germans; there is much scatological material in other cultures, too (remember Bourke's *Scatalogic Rites of All Nations?*), but pedantic German scholars — many of whom were Jewish, by the way — faithfully collected and studied such material, including much on sex and homosexuality, while scholars of other languages ignored the "offensive" material. Either the "German national character" has changed or Professor Dundes is wrong: of the approximately 350 jokes in the *Temmler Ärzte-Kalender 1984* (a calendar with jokes contributed by non-prudish physicians, nurses, and medical students), some 300 deal with sex and marriage, and only one with *scheißen,* "shit."

Eberhard, Wolfram. "On Some Chinese Terms of Abuse." *Asian Folklore Studies* 27/1 (1968):25-40. – An excellent study, based on the material collected by Frank Huang, but without any Chinese originals (only translated examples). Most abusive expressions consist of 2-6 words. Metaphors of animals, plants, supernatural beings, objects, people, and body parts.

Faruki, Zuhdi T. "Reflections on the Etymology of 'Clitoris' in Arabian Sexual Lore." In *The Clitoris*, ed. by Thomas Lowry, pp. 183-90. St. Louis: Warren H. Green, 1976. – Metaphors and synonyms for *clitoris* from the Arabic-speaking world, from Morocco to Persia.

Frank, Francine, and Anshen, Frank. *Language and the Sexes*. Albany: State University of New York Press, 1984. 130 pp., paper $7.95, cloth $24.95. – Essays on naming, women's talk, derogatory terms for females; research projects, guidelines for non-discriminatory and non-sexist language, bibliography.

Gjurin, Velemir. "Interesne govorice sleng, žargon, argo." *Slavistična Revija*, Ljubljana (Jan.-March 1974):65-81. – Discusses the relationship of slang, jargon and argot, and standard, informal and regional dialects. Shows the influence of foreign languages on Slovenian. Analyzes drug users' lingo. Many examples.

Gottlieb, Alma. "Village kapok, Forest kapok: Notions of Separation, Identity and Gender among the Beng of Ivory Coast." Diss., University of Virginia, 1983. – Contains Appendix I, "Sexual Insults."

Gregersen, Edgar. *Sexual Practices: The Story of Human Sexuality*. London: Beazley, 1982; New York: Franklin Watts, 1983. 320 pp., $18.95. – A superior treatise by an anthropologist, of the history and evolution of sex, techniques, attractiveness, clothing, marriage, and prostitution throughout the world. Beautifully illustrated with useful photos, drawings, and maps.

Greive, Artur. "Bezeichnungen für 'Geld' im Spanischen und anderswo." In *Umgangssprache in der Iberoromania*, ed. by G. Holtus and E. Radtke, pp. 351-57. – On colloquial, slang, and metaphorical terms for "money" in Romance languages, with references to German.

Hoareau-Dodinau, Jacqueline. "La violence verbale dans les lettres de rémission du trésor des chartes (XIVe-XVIe siècles)." Thesis, Université de Limoges, 1982. Paper, 234 pp. – Detailed study of legal aspects of verbal abuse, threats and blasphemy in royal letters of pardon in 14th-to-16th-century France. Texts, classifications, penalties. Excellent indexes and bibliographies.

Holtus, Günter, and Radtke, Edgar. "Der Begriff 'Umgangssprache' in der Romania und sein Stellenwert für die Iberoromanistik." In *Umgangssprache in der Iberoromania*, ed. by G. Holtus and E. Radtke, pp. 1-22. – On the concept "colloquial language" in Romance languages and its relation to other language levels.

———. *Umgangssprache in der Iberoromania: Festschrift für Heinz Kröll zum 65. Geburtstag*. Tübingen: Gunter Narr, 1984. – Essays in German, Spanish, and Portuguese on various aspects of colloquial language in Romance-language countries.

Holzinger, Herbert. "Beschimpfung im heutigen Französisch: Pragmatische, syntaktische und semantische Aspekte (Korpusauswertung literarischer Texte." Diss., Universität Salzburg, 1984. Paper, 292 pp. – An excellent study of pragmatic, syntactic, and semantic aspects of French insults found mainly in novels of contemporary writers but also used in cartoons. Presents common structures (*enfant de, fils de, espèce de, tête de*). Detailed study of common terms and their synonyms by types of shortcomings or semantic fields (*salaud, con, fou, putain, pédé*). Also lists insults found in the *Petit Robert* dictionary.

Kennedy, X. J. *Tygers of Wrath: Poems of Hate, Anger, and Invective*. Athens: University of Georgia Press, 1981. 282 pp., $16. – Twelve sections of maledictive outpourings directed against family members, contemporaries, cities, nobility, statesmen, poets, scholars, and the self, mostly by well-known writers.

Kiener, Franz. "Die Fluchtäfelchen." Unpubl. article, 18 pp. 1983. – A survey of cursing tablets (*defixionum tabellae*) from Roman and Greek cultures. Illustrated.

———. "Zwei Halbkugeln, die miteinander spielen." Unpubl. article, 10 pp. 1984. – On anatomical, folkloric, and psychological aspects of female buttocks and clothing.

———. *Das Wort als Waffe: Zur Psychologie der verbalen Aggression.* Göttingen: Vandenhoeck & Ruprecht, 1983. Paper, 304 pp., DM 34. – The first comprehensive study of verbal aggression in German, stressing psychological and linguistic aspects, classification of utterances, formal aspects, situations, intensifiers, euphemisms. Features examples from Bavarian and many other languages.

Klintberg, Bengt af. "Folkliga hotelser." *Svenska Landsmål och Svenskt Folkliv* (1984):91-117. – An introduction to vernacular threats in Swedish, with 121 examples in context, collected mainly through an appeal in the Stockholm *Expressen* newspaper. Traditional threats have been added. An abundance of slang and formulaic exaggerations of physical violence are typical.

Koukoulès, Mary. *Loose-Tongued Greeks: A Miscellany of Neo-Hellenic Erotic Folklore.* Paris: Digamma, 1983. Bibliophilic loose-leaf edition in 303 numbered and signed copies. Introduction by G. Legman. Bilingual Greek and English edition, translated by John Taylor. 182 pp., in case, $30. – A fascinating collection of 320 Greek bawdy songs, verses, poems, proverbs, insults, threats. Good glossary of Greek insults, sexual and scatological terms, with translations. [The last six copies are available from us.]

———. *Neoelliniki Athyrostomia.* Athens: Nefeli, 1984. Paper, 134 pp. – A Greek-only version of her *Loose-Tongued Greeks.* Without the glossary, but with an index.

Kruck, William E. *Looking for Dr. Condom.* University, AL: University of Alabama Press, 1981. PADS No. 66. Paper, 105 pp. – Painstaking research of *condom* from 1705 to the present, trying to establish its etymology. With texts, massive notes and bibliography. Where Kruck left off, Zacharias Thundy continues trying to find the etymology; see *American Speech* 60/2 (1985):177-79.

Kutter, Uli. *Ich kündige! Zeugnisse von Wünschen und Ängsten am Arbeitsplatz.* Marburg: Jonas Verlag, 1982. Paper, 127 pp., DM 18. – Photocopy humor in words and pictures, original German material and adaptations of American sources, much of it obscene or scatological. Very good introduction, especially on the reasons why such materials circulate at work: the fears and anxieties of the working man who seeks release from frustrations caused by coworkers and superiors. Some 20 pages are reproduced poorly or reduced illegibly small. A new edition is planned.

Laycock, Don. *The Best Bawdry.* North Ryde, Australia: Angus & Robertson, 1982. 310 pp., Austr.$14.95. – Lyrics of 153 bawdy songs (but no melodies), from "The Street of a Thousand Arseholes" to "Eskimo Nell." Introduction, bibliography, indexes. Comments about sources and occasional changes made precede most songs.

Légaré, Clément, and Bougaïeff, André. *L'Empire du sacre québécois: Étude sémiolinguistique d'un intensif populaire.* Québec: Presses de l'Université du Québec, 1984. Paper, 276 pp., Can.$16.95. – An excellent and detailed study of French-Canadian blasphemies used widely and mainly as intensifiers. Morphology, syntax, semantics, functions.

Legman, G[ershon]. *No Laughing Matter: An Analysis of Sexual Humor.* Bloomington: Indiana University Press, 1982. Reprint. Vol. 1 (*Rationale of the Dirty Joke*), 811 pp., $37.50. Vol. 2 (*No Laughing Matter*), 992 pp., $37.50. (Both volumes have been offered for $60). – An immense collection of well-told, unexpurgated jokes & stories, analyzed and with much bibliographical information and personal commentary. Chapter 14 (vol. 2), "Dysphemism & Insults," pp. 672-809, is particularly useful.

Levy, Leonard W. *Treason Against God: A History of the Offense of Blasphemy.* New York: Schocken, 1981. 414 pp., $24.95. – Scholarly survey of blasphemy (heresy) of the past 3,000 years, from Moses to the 18th century. The religious foundations, continental precedents, and England to 1700. Copious citations from religious, historical, and legal works, all thoroughly annotated.

Ljung, Magnus. *Om Svordomar i svenskan, engelskan, och arton andra språk.* Stockholm: Akademilitteratur, 1984. 125 pp., sKr 69. – A popular book on swearing, with many examples from 6 Germanic, 3 Romance, 3 Slavic languages and a few examples from several others. Except for the long English section, about one third of the material is taken from *Maledicta*, without much credit: the Egyptian donkey curse, the swearing apes; most of the Russian, Serbo-Croatian, Italian, Spanish examples are straight out of our journal; listing our articles in the bibliography is not enough to indicate inspiration and sources. This amounts to "adorning oneself with borrowed plumes." Professor Ljung, who had a grant from the American Council of Learned Societies for his research, claims that his book is the result of ten years of research; to me it seems more like a couple of years, and several years of reading *Maledicta*. The book contains several errors, including the silly etymology of Yiddish *schmuck* (which is NOT from German *Schmuck*, "jewelry"), and weird examples of American "swearing": *Peel me a grape! Eat cat! Eat light bread and duck butter!*, etc.

Lötscher, Andreas. *Lappi, Lööli, blööde Siech! Schimpfen und Fluchen im Schweizerdeutschen.* Frauenfeld: Huber, 1980. Paper, 156 pp., sFr 22.80. – A popular, well-written treatise on insulting and swearing in Swiss-German dialects, with many examples.

Lowry, Thomas P. "Some Notes on the Etymology of the Word 'Clitoris.'" In *The Clitoris*, ed. by Thomas Lowry, pp. 163-82. St. Louis: Warren H. Green, 1976. – Contains many terms for *clitoris* from dozens of languages worldwide, transliterated or in the original scripts. With references and list of informants.

Lowry, Thomas P., and Lowry, Thea Snyder, eds. *The Clitoris.* St. Louis: Warren H. Green, 1976. 255 pp., $26.50. – This medical reference work (anatomy, neurophysiology, pathology) also contains essays by collaborators on female genital mutilations, cultural psychology, and a valuable contribution on the etymology of *clitoris* and synonyms in many languages worldwide (T. Lowry), as well as Zuhdi Faruki's contribution on terms for *clitoris* in Arabian sexual lore. 28 stereoscopic color slides of clitorides are enclosed, on four disks. (Viewing these slides before breakfast is not recommended, unless you are a *Hustler* fan.)

Maher, J. Peter. "The Dethroning of Sir Thomas Crapper." In *The How, Why, and Whence of Names*, Papers of the North Central Names Institute, 4. Ed. by Edward Callary and Laurence Seits, pp. 125-35. DeKalb: Illinois Name Society, 1984. – Dispels the ever-popular folk etymology, and discusses the difficult etymology of *crap*. More on this in his "Out of the Closet" in vol. 5.

Martling, Jackie. *Just Another Dirty Joke Book.* New York: Pinnacle, 1982. Paper, 156 pp., $1.95. – Long and short uncensored, funny jokes by a practicing New York comic.

———. *Raunchy Riddles.* New York: Pinnacle, 1984. Paper, 184 pp., $1.95. – Funny, offensive ethnic and sexual riddles, and multiple-answer-type jokes.

———. *The Only Dirty Joke Book... You'll Ever Need.* New York: Pinnacle, 1984. Paper, 149 pp., $2.50. – Some short but mostly longer ethnic, sexual, and scatological jokes; many are "personalized" by using the names of real people (R. Aman is doing something uncouth in his driveway, pp. 102-03).

Massou, Issa. "Imprecations and Invocations in the Bethlehem District." *International Folklore Review* 3 (1983):88-92. – Cursing and blessing in Arabic, with many examples in Arabic and English translations. Classification, formulas. Example: "May God let the devil take you away!"

Meerloo, Joost A.M. *Curriculum Vitae and Bibliography*. Purmerend: Nooy's Uitgeverij, 1976. Paper, 56 pp., $12. – Shortly before his death in 1976, Prof. Meerloo published 100 copies of this bibliography of his writings, listing nearly 1,010 books, articles, and notes he had published in Dutch, English, German, and French, on psychological and psychoanalytical topics, such as violence, suicide, war, drugs, toxomania, hallucinations, suspicion, brainwashing, koprolalia, anal magic, evil eye, alcoholics, gerontophobia, etc. [We have the last 9 copies for sale.]

Merrill, Norman W. "Cicero and Early Roman Invective." Diss., University of Cincinnati, 1975. Paper, 202 pp. – Chapters on the terminology of Roman invective, pre-Ciceronian invective, and Cicero's invective in relation to his predecessors.

Meter, Helmut. "Die Metaphorik der Vagina im Italienischen: Ein Beitrag zur Diskussion über die Metapher." In *Sprachtheorie und Sprachpraxis: Festschrift für Henri Vernay*, pp. 215-43. Tübingen: Gunter Narr, 1979. – Italian metaphors for *vagina*. Classified by senses (visual, smelling, tasting, etc.), animal metaphors, metonymy. List of dialect and standard synonyms.

Mieder, Wolfgang, ed. *Proverbium: Yearbook of International Proverb Scholarship*. Vol. I, Matti Kuusi Festschrift. Columbus: Ohio State University, 1984. Paper, 350 pp., typescript, $10. – Articles, studies, research reports, book reviews, and bibliographies in several languages for the proverb scholar.

——. "Das Wort 'Shit' und seine lexikographische Erfassung." *Sprachspiegel* 34 (1978):76-79. – An overview of which American and English dictionaries have the entry *shit* and some reasons why most don't.

——. *Anti-Sprichwörter*. Wiesbaden: Verlag für deutsche Sprache, 1982. Vol. I, paper, 235 pp., DM 37,80. – 1,500 parodied, satirized, or twisted German proverbs, arranged alphabetically by key words. With introduction, sources, bibliography. By intelligent wordplays and other means, the people and writers of advertising love to twist proverbs into witty, ironic, or sarcastic take-offs. This entertaining book alone disproves the ignorant stereotype of Germans having no sense of humor.

——. *Deutsche Sprichwörter in Literatur, Politik, Presse und Werbung*. Hamburg: Buske, 1983. 230 pp. – On German proverbs in literature, politics, newspapers, magazines, and advertising.

——. *International Bibliography of Explanatory Essays on Individual Proverbs and Proverbial Expressions*. Bern: Peter Lang, 1977. Paper, 146 pp., sFr 34.70. – On the origin, history, and meaning of proverbs, indexing 2,000 investigations from the 18th century to the present.

———. *International Proverb Scholarship: An Annotated Bibliography*. New York: Garland, 1982. 613 pp., $66. – 2,142 critically annotated entries, emphasizing English and German secondary materials. Extensive indexes of names, subjects, and proverbs.

Mulcahy, F. David. "Gitano Sex Role Symbolism and Behavior." *Anthropological Quarterly* 49/2 (1976):135-51.

———. "Los valores sexuales de los gitanos: Los ritos flamencos." In *La Antropología Médica en España*, ed. by Michael Kenny and Jesús de Miguel, pp. 309-19. Barcelona: Anagrama, 1980. – On sexual values of Spanish Gypsies and the flamenco rites and ceremonies. Some scatological insults.

Müller, Johannes. "Zur Form der Obszönität im Nürnberger Fastnachtspiel des 15. Jahrhunderts." Universität Zürich, 1983. 120 pp., typescript, paper. – A study and interpretation of the sexual metaphors found in 15th-century Shrovetide plays of Nuremberg. Detailed analyses of metaphors for vagina, bosom, penis, testicles, lust, coitus, and related topics. Text in German and MHG.

Newall, Venetia J., ed. *International Folklore Review: Folklore Studies from Overseas*. London. Vol. 2 (1982). Paper, 168 pp., *£8.00, Irish £11.70, U.S. $12*. – A quality publication in appearance and contents, illustrated, covering wide-ranging topics: British stereotype, Little Red Riding Hood adaptations, Born-Again Christians, Bulgarian Funeral Laments, Jewish Textile Printers, Rodeo in Kansas, and Russian Midday Spirit (*poludnica*). Book reviews. This volume is dedicated to the late Richard M. Dorson. Order and subscription address: Fourth Estate Ltd., (Int. Folklore Rev.), Leo's House, 100 Westbourne Grove, London W2 5RU, U.K. – Editorial address only: Dr. Venetia Newall, 14 Sloane Terrace Mansions, Sloane Terrace, Belgravia, London SW1X 9DG, U.K.

Nilsen, Don L.F., and Nilsen, Alleen. *Whimsy I: The Language of Humor – The Humor of Language*. Tempe: Arizona State University, 1983. Paper, 412 pp., $10. – Proceedings of the 1982 WHIM Conference, with (extensive) summaries of papers presented on American, British, and children's literatures, bilingual humor and translation, education, foreign languages, feminist studies, etc.

———. *Whimsy II: Metaphors Be With You: Humor and Metaphor*. Tempe: Arizona State University, 1984. Paper, 320 pp., $10. – Proceedings of the 1983 WHIM Conference, with (extensive) summaries of papers presented on American and foreign literatures, linguistics,

education, philosophy, popular culture, psychology, and religion.
———. *Whimsy III: Contemporary Humor*. Tempe: Arizona State Unversity, 1985. Paper, 287 pp., $10. – Proceedings of the 1984 WHIM Conference, with (extensive) summaries of papers on literature, fiction, poetry, education, linguistics, popular culture, psychology, religion, riddles, sex roles, and several foreign languages. Indexes, useful addresses, etc.

Nuessel, Frank. "Linguistic Distortions and Stereotypes of Asians." *Thinker* 8/2 (1984):66-77. – Ethnic slurs and stereotypes (looks, behavior, attitudes) as found in the media and literature, with suggestions on how to portray Asians fairly.

Ojoade, J.O. "African Sexual Proverbs: Some Yoruba Examples." *Folklore* 94/2 (1983):201-13. – 104 examples, in Yoruba, with English translations, commented where appropriate.

Oschlies, Wolf. *Lenins Enkeln aufs Maul geschaut: Jugend-Jargon in Osteuropa*. Köln: Böhlau, 1981. Paper, 216 pp. – Interesting and useful German study of the colloquial language and slang of East European youth: Russia, Poland, Czechoslovakia, Rumania, Bulgaria. Many examples, lists, with philological commentary. Terms are given in the original languages, plus literal meaning and translation. Additional essays on thieves' cant, prisoners' lingo, psychological aspects, major topics (school, money, sex). Very useful for any Slavicist.

Paros, Lawrence. *The Erotic Tongue: A Sexual Lexicon*. Seattle: Madrona Publishers, 1984. Paper, 241 pp., $9.95. – More an encyclopedia than a lexicon, with 12 chapters of sexual and erotic terminology of body parts, activities, and participants, presented in an entertaining, witty style. Many illustrative verses, songs, and excerpts. The forbidded seven words are sanitized with two asterisks, making the point that the prudish reader still knows what the camouflaged offensive word is. Needs an index and better documentation of sources. [Several copies are available from us.]

Peñalosa, Fernando. *Introduction to the Sociology of Language*. Rowley, MA: Newbury House, 1981. Paper, 242 pp., $13.95. – On taboos and euphemisms, pp. 56-59. Very good introduction to this field, with material from many cultures. Detailed bibliography.

Pops, Martin. "The Metamorphosis of Shit." *Salmagundi: A Quarterly of the Humanities & Social Sciences* 56 (Spring 1982): 26-61. – On toilets through the ages, with literary excerpts and a two-page appendix, "Excremental Language."

Prager, Dennis, and Telushkin, Joseph. *Why the Jews? The Reason for Antisemitism*. New York: Simon & Schuster, 1983. 238 pp., $14.95. – The reasons for the enduring antisemitism, in this brilliant, provocative book, include Hatred of Judaism, The Chosen People Concept, the Higher Quality of Jewish Life, and the radical Non-Jewish Jews (e.g. Trotsky, Marx, Chomsky). Several other theories are explained. The second half of this book presents historical evidence: antisemitism [their preferred spelling] in antiquity, Christian, Islamic, Enlightenment, Leftist, Nazi, and anti-Zionist antisemitism. Notes and bibliography. Excellent.

Radtke, Edgar. "Die Übersetzungsproblematik von Sondersprachen – am Beispiel der portugiesischen, französischen und italienischen Übertragungen von Christiane F. – *Wir Kinder vom Bahnhof Zoo*." In *Umgangssprache in der Iberoromania*, ed. by G. Holtus and E. Radtke, pp. 63-80. – On the difficulties of translating teenagers' jargon, including drug and sexual slang.

———. "Il lessico sessuale nei gerghi come problema lessicografico (con particolare riferimento alle voci gergali nel 'Dizionario del dialetto veneziano' di Boerio)." In *Linguistica e dialettologia veneta*, ed. by G. Holtus and Michael Metzeltin, pp. 153-63. Tübingen: Gunter Narr, 1983. – On sexual terminology and lexicographical problems of Italian jargons and slangs.

Rancour-Laferriere, Daniel. *Out from under Gogol's Overcoat: A Psychoanalytic Study*. Ann Arbor: Ardis, 1982. 251 pp., $25. – A study of 35 aspects of Gogol's masterpiece, stressing sexual and anal themes. Extensive bibliography.

Raskin, Victor. *Semantic Mechanisms of Humor*. Dordrecht (Holland) and Boston: D. Reidel, 1984. 284 pp., $44. – A very scholarly treatise of humor research, linguistic and semantic theories. Chapters on sexual, ethnic, and political humor. Many of the 625 jokes (dated, origin; often Russian) are not necessarily funny but illustrate the script-based semantic theory.

Read, Allen Walker. "An Updating of Research on the Name 'Podunk.'" In *Names, Northeast*, ed. by Murray Heller, pp. 86-99. Saranac Lake, NY: North Country Community College Press, 1980. – *Podunk*, an American Indian place name, now stands for any small, dull, rustic, backward, unenterprising, isolated town. Many citations are given.

Richlin, Amy. *The Garden of Priapus: Sexuality and Aggression in Roman Humor*. New Haven: Yale University Press, 1983. 289 pp., $28.

– A thorough study of Roman satire, invective, and sexual humor, using literary, anthropological, psychological, and feminist approaches in analyzing graffiti, epigrams, and the works of Catullus, Ovid, Juvenal, Petronius. Detailed notes, indexes, bibliography.

Rothwell, J. Dan. *Telling It Like It Isn't: Language Misuse & Malpractice – What We Can Do About It.* Englewood Cliffs: Prentice–Hall, 1982. Paper, 242 pp., $6.95. – Includes essays on verbal taboos, the language of violence, the killing power of words, and the language of racism and sexism.

Salemi, Joseph S. "*Priapus* by Pietro Bembo: An Annotated Translation." *Allegorica: Texts and Documents for the Study of Medieval and Renaissance Literature* 5/1 (Summer 1980):81-94. – The beauty, wit, and craftsmanship of *Priapus* are not appreciated by readers offended by its pornography. Original Latin, with English translation and notes.

——. "Selections from the *Facetiae* of Poggio Bracciolini." *Allegorica* 8/1-2 (1983):77-183. – About 40 of the 273 short jokes, witticisms, and stories, in Latin with facing English translations; notes, variants, corrections. Terms of abuse, sexual vocabulary; attacks on ignorance and the clergy.

Schmitt, Christian. "Spanisch ¡caramba!, ¡carajo!, ¡caracoles!" In *Umgangssprache in der Iberoromania*, ed. by G. Holtus and E. Radtke, pp. 359-66. – Etymological study of the interjection *¡carajo!* (prick!) and its euphemisms, and on *penis* metaphors in Spanish, Italian, and other languages.

Séphiha, Haïm Vidal. "Néologie en Judéo-Espagnol: Les euphémismes (1)." *Iberica III* (Paris: Sorbonne, 1981):113-23. – On euphemisms for *God, black, toilet* in Ladino and other Jewish languages, Spanish, French, and others.

Sgroi, Salvatore C. "Riflessi dell'interdizione linguistica nella lessicografia francese." *Studi italiani linguistica teorica ed applicata* 10/1-2-3 (1981):403-21. – A quantitative and qualitative analysis of sexual terms in standard French dictionaries, showing which works suppress taboo terms, thus castrate the living language.

Simmons, Donald C. *Extralinguistic Usages of Tonality in Efik Folklore.* University, AL: University of Alabama Press, 1980. 150 pp., typescript, $15. – A scholarly study of tonality in drum signals, tone riddles, and tone poems of this Nigerian language and its possible influence on the black *dozens*. Over a dozen obscene, erotic or scatological examples are given.

——. *Dead Baby Riddles*. Hartford, CT: Privately printed, 1981. Paper, 13 pp. – Introduction, 13 riddles, bibliography. The author, a folklorist, anthropologist, professor, and attorney, published this booklet "In Commemoration of the One Hundredth Anniversary of The University of Connecticut, 1881–1981," but the cacademic powers were not amused.

Sornig, Karl. "Alltagssprache: Konnotationen der Vertrautheit / Strategien der Distanzierung." *Jahrbuch für Internationale Germanistik* 14/2 (1983):127-44. – On the use of dialect and colloquial language; teasing, irony, scolding, metaphors.

——. "Beschimpfungen." *Grazer Linguistische Studien* 1 (1975):150-70. – Formal, semantic, and pragmatic aspects of scolding and other verbal abuse. Terms of abuse used as terms of endearment, and vice versa. Examples from several languages.

——. "Emphatische Intentionen – Intensivierende Formen." *Grazer Linguistische Studien* 22 (1984):201-30. – On the use of emotive, expressive, and affective language by means of particles, exclamations, prefixes, stress, capitalization, syntax, etc. Examples from several languages.

——. "Persuasive Sprachstrukturen." *Grazer Linguistische Studien* 17-18 (1982):239-77. – Linguistic structures used to persuade, including semantic means, phonetic alterations, neologisms, metaphors, foreign terms, epithets, etc., found in literature, advertising, political writings, journalism.

——. "Soziosemantische Allergien." *Klagenfurter Beiträge zur Sprachwissenschaft* 9 (1983):242-61. – On ethnic slurs from antiquity to the present, from several languages.

——. "Strategien literarischer Namengebung." In *Proceedings of the 13th International Congress of Onomastic Sciences*, pp. 447-58. Kraków: Akademie, 1982. – When creating personal names in literature, writers use phonetic, morphological, and other means to characterize the person negatively or positively.

——. *Lexical Innovations: A Study of Slang, Colloquialisms and Casual Speech*. Amsterdam: John Benjamins, 1981. Paper, 117 pp., typescript, $14. – Includes material on intensifiers, metaphors, taboo, pejoratives, body parts. As in his other publications, Dr. Sornig uses examples from many languages and organizes his material very precisely.

Taylor, John. "Kaliarda Revisited." *The Cabirion / Gay Books Bulletin* 11 (Fall-Winter 1984):10-11. – On Greek homosexual argot words collected in Elias Petropoulos's *Kaliardá*, emphasizing compounds formed with French-derived *soúkra* and those of formerly unknown etymology now traced to Romany (Gypsy) by Prof. Gordon Messing.

Thibault, Johanne. *Les Intensificateurs en français montréalais.* Maîtrise, Université de Montréal, 1977. Typescript. – On blasphemous and other intensifiers in Montréal French.

Thibault, Johanne, and Vincent, Diane. "Le sacre en français montréalais: Aspects fonctionnels et dynamique expressive." *Le français moderne* 49/3 (1981):206-15. – French-Canadian blasphemies used as interjections and intensifiers. With an appendix of 7 common blasphemies, their derivatives and uses as verbs, adjectives, and adverbs.

Thiel, Axel, Thiel, Maria M., and Beyer, Jürgen. *Sprüche und Kommunikationen aus Damen- und Herrentoiletten.* Kassel: Privately printed, 1982. Paper, unpaginated [70 pp.], typescript, DM 9,50. – Mostly obscene and scatological graffiti, political messages, and primitive facsimile line drawings copied from toilet walls of the University of Kassel and a large industrial plant. Axel Thiel is the leading collector of visual and verbal graffiti in West Germany. [H.–Pierson Str. 6, 3500 Kassel, FRG]

Timroth, Wilhelm von. *Russische und sowjetische Soziolinguistik und tabuisierte Varietäten des Russischen (Argot, Jargons, Slang und Mat).* München: Otto Sagner, 1983. Paper, 196 pp., DM 28. – Historical survey of Russian argots and jargons from the prerevolutionary period to today. Analysis of related terms. Extensive treatment of Russian obscenities (use, frequency, morphology, etc.).

Turner, Glenn. *Fairy Tales: A Treasury of Gay Jokes.* New York: Pinnacle Books, 1985. Paper, 119 pp., $2.25. – Longer jokes and Question-and-Answer quickies told by, or ridiculing, homosexuals. Some of these were originally straight jokes, transformed into gay jokes.

Vincent, Diane. "Norme, langage expressif et sacre en français montréalais." In *Langages et collectivités: Le cas du Québec,* ed. by Jean-Marie Klinkenberg et al., pp. 73-92. Montréal: Lémeac, 1981. – On people's attitudes toward blasphemies (aesthetic and psychological condemnation, tolerance, recognition of their expressive value). Appendix with French-Canadian blasphemies.

——. *Pressions et impressions sur les sacres au Québec.* Québec: Gouvernement du Québec. Office de la langue française, 1982. Paper, 143 pp. – Linguistic analysis, definitions, attitudes toward French-

Canadian blasphemies, historical aspects (France and Canada), social and sexual stereotypes of blasphemers. Bibliography, questionnaires. Excellent.

Wayne, Tom. *Nastiness Grown Pensive*. Milwaukee: Bench Press, 1983. With a foreword by Roger W. Phillips. Paper, 97 pp., $7.65 ($8.00 foreign). – Thousand witty, biting, cynical aphorisms by an undiscovered wit comparable to Mencken and Wilde. Attacks on cacademia and other deserving targets. [2113 E. Wood Place, Shorewood, Wisconsin 53211]

——. *Pressing Ahead*. Milwaukee: Bench Press, 1984. With a foreword by Roger W. Phillips. Paper, 96 pp., $7.65 ($8.00 foreign). – 823 new biting aphorisms about culture, art, cacademia, religion, virtue, death, society, the sexes, friendship, guilt, and other topics.

Wehse, Rainer. *Warum sind die Ostfriesen gelb im Gesicht?* Frankfurt/M: Peter Lang, 1983. Paper, 193 pp., typescript, sFr 49. – A folkloric-ethnographic study of the jokes of German-speaking teenagers, 11-14 years, with texts, analyses, many statistics, and questionnaires. Additional essays by seven collaborators on the role of woman in jokes, research methods, etc. Bibliography.


## DICTIONARIES

Abel, Ernest L. *A Dictionary of Drug Abuse Terms and Terminology*. Westport, CT: Greenwood Press, 1984. 188 pp., $29.95. – Older and newest terms of drug buyers, sellers, and users. Short definitions; longer explanations of drugs and chemicals. List of synonyms of major terms, e.g., 165 synonyms for *marihuana*.

Bergeron, Léandre. *Dictionnaire de la langue québécoise*. Montréal: VLB Éditeurs [Victor Lévy Beaulieu], 1980. Paper, 575 pp. – Excellent monolingual dictionary of Canadian French spoken in Québec. Some 17,500 words and 5,500 expressions. Very useful thematic synonym lists on body parts, disliked individuals, blasphemies, sexual activities, drugs, etc.

——. *The Québécois Dictionary*. Toronto: Lorimer, 1982. Paper, 207 pp., Can.$17.95. – An unexpurgated French-Canadian bilingual dictionary, condensed from the monolingual *Dictionnaire de la langue québécoise*, with pronunciation and bilingual usage examples. Contains many English words, some of which have a different meaning in French-Canadian.

Courouve, Claude. *Vocabulaire de l'homosexualité masculine*. Paris: Payot, 1985. Paper, 248 pp., 99 FF. – An alphabetical collection of 74 essays on key words, ranging from antiquity (*amour grec*) through the Middle Ages (*bougre*) to the most recent (Camus's *achrienne*). After the etymology follows the history of the word. Richly documented with some 1,000 source citations.

*Duden – Deutsches Universalwörterbuch*. Ed. by G. Drosdowski et al. Mannheim: Bibliographisches Institut, 1983. 1504 pp., DM 58. – A new one-volume dictionary of German. 120,000 entries, with much grammatical, semantic, and usage information. As all Duden publications, highest quality in appearance and contents. (However, the silly definition and usage example of Bavarian *Bazi* must have been written by a North German meathead.)

Dynes, Wayne R. *Homolexis: A Historical and Cultural Dictionary of Homosexuality*. New York: Gay Academic Union, 1985. Paper, typescript, 177 pp., $6.95. Gay Saber Monograph No. 4. – A series of essays on historical semantics. Discusses over 600 terms but is more a contribution to the history of ideas and words than to lexicography. Very interesting and informative, discussing for example the vulgar *fistfucking*, the more acceptable *handballing*, and the new medical term *brachiproctic eroticism*. The historical changes shown include Greek *lesbizein*, "to give a blowjob," named after the skillful fellators of Lesbos, which later became the source for *lesbian*, "female homosexual." The German **175er**, "faggot," is not obsolete, however; the law is gone, but not the insult. Indexes, well-annotated bibliography. [GAU, Box 480, Lenox Hill Station, New York, NY 10021]

Elting, John R., Cragg, Dan, and Deal, Ernest. *A Dictionary of Soldier's Talk*. New York: Charles Scribner's Sons, 1984. 383 pp., $35. – Definitions and etymologies of Army language, official and slang, from the Revolution through Vietnam. A short appendix of Naval and Marine terms. A very valuable source of information on military lingo with lucid explanations.

Franklyn, Julian. *A Dictionary of Rhyming Slang*. London, Boston: Routledge & Kegan Paul, 1975. 202 pp., $16. – Excellent introduction to, and dictionary of, rhyming slang from the English-speaking world (not just Cockneys). Introductory essay, list of meanings, texts, index. Each entry is dated, source given, and well explained.

Goldenson, Robert M. *Longman Dictionary of Psychology and Psychiatry*. London: Longman, 1984. 816 pp., $39.95. – This quality reference work designed by Walter Glanze contains nearly 16,000 (encyclopedic) article entries, including 550 entries for syndromes and diseases, 93 manias, 61 neuroses, 72 psychoses, 36 complexes, and 500 phobias (but not yet *maledictaphobia*, the childish fear of so-called bad words; see **MISCELLANY**).

Grambs, David. *Words About Words*. New York: McGraw–Hill, 1984. 409 pp., $17.95. – A dictionary of 2,000 words about the styles, devices, and defects of prose writing. Definitions and illustrative quotations. 20 valuable special sections on libel, headline jargon, mixed metaphors, Irish Bulls, rhetorics, weasel words, and other linguistic or literary topics.

*Harrap's Slang Dictionary English–French / French–English*. London: Harrap, 1984. Paper, 476 pp., £9.95. – Marks & Johnson's dictionaries completely revised and updated by Jane Pratt. 50,000 words and phrases of colloquial to vulgar slang from the English-speaking world, France and Canada. Bilingual usage examples (3 columns on *foutre*), rhyming slang and *verlan*. Thematic synonym sections on expletives, body parts and functions, prostitution, prison, etc. *Femme* lists some 50 synonyms; *sex* a whole column. Examples of the changes (additions, deletions, new translations) from the former to this edition include *zyeute-moi ça!* "Just have a dekko at that!" (1970) and "Get a load of that! Get an eyeful of that!" (1984); and there was no synonym list for "to have anal sex" in 1970, but this 1984 edition lists two dozen synonyms. Excellent.

Heestermans, Hans, van Sterkenburg, Piet, and van der Voort van der Kleij, John, eds. *Erotisch Woordenboek*. Utrecht: Het Spectrum, 1980. Prisma-boeken 1928. Paper, 263 pp. – An excellent Dutch dictionary of erotic and sexual language, with some 2,000 defined entries, citations, and sources. Good bibliography.

Jacobs, Sidney J. *The Jewish Word Book*. Middle Village, NY: Jonathan David, 1982. 356 pp., $12.50 – A simple but valuable dictionary of Yiddish and Hebrew words and phrases. The entries are briefly translated and followed by spelling variants. The only major flaw is the author's writing system: not a transliteration but how the words sound to an American, resulting in odd-looking creations, such as *Mawgein Dawvihd* and *Muhgn Duhvihd* for *Magen David*.

*Langenscheidt Condensed Muret-Sanders German Dictionary: German-English*. Ed. by Heinz Messinger. Berlin: Langenscheidt, 1982. (Distributed to U.S. libraries exclusively by Gale Research, Detroit.) 1,296 pp., $70. – This superb dictionary, with 140,000 entries, covers the entire range, from highly technical to vulgar language. 10 appendixes on biographical, geographical and given names, abbreviations, weights and measures, etc. (I have been using Langenscheidt dictionaries in about 30 languages for some 35 years now and have almost always found what I was looking for.)

Mager, N[athan] H., and Mager, S[ylvia] K. *The Morrow Book of New Words: 8500 Terms Not Yet in Standard Dictionaries.* New York: Quill, 1982. Paper, 284 pp., $6.50. – Many terms, drawn from all fields of knowledge, meanwhile have been entered in updated editions of standard dictionaries, but specialized ones will be found only here. A fair number are long-known words.

McConville, Brigid, and Shearlaw, John. *The Slanguage of Sex.* London: Macdonald, 1984. – Said to be largely a derivative of earlier dictionaries, especially Bruce Rodgers's *The Queens' Vernacular,* and lexicographically incompetent.

*Petit Larousse illustré 1983.* Paris: Librairie Larousse, 1983. 1906 pp. – The first half of this superb reference work is the dictionary proper, the second half is an encyclopedia, both richly illustrated, and many maps. Since its last edition, 283 new entries have been added and some 1,100 updates and changes have been made. Just as the German *Duden,* the *Larousse* now lists *gay.* Whereas the 1964 edition ignored *foutre* ("to fuck"), the 1983 edition features *foutaise, foutoir, foutral, foutre, foutrement, foutrique,* and *foutu. Con* ("cunt; creep; fool") is now also included.

Rawson, Hugh. *A Dictionary of Euphemisms and Other Doubletalk: Being a Compilation of Linguistic Fig Leaves and Verbal Flourishes for Artful Users of the English Language.* New York: Crown, 1981. 312 pp., $15.95. – Some 1,500 positive and negative euphemisms, precisely dated, well explained, and amply illustrated with anecdotes and citations from literature and the media. Excellent introduction. Euphemisms from all areas, especially the notorious doubletalkers: business, education, government. Informative and very readable.

Robinson, Sinclair, and Smith, Donald. *Practical Handbook of Quebec and Acadian French – Manuel pratique du français québécois et acadien.* Toronto: Anansi, 1984. Paper, 302 pp., Can.$14.95. – Organized by topics from Nature to Sports, including swearwords, body parts, love and sex. Three columns, with Québec French, European French, and English, showing many words that don't exist in the others, or have different meanings in the two varieties of French. Grammar and pronunciation hints for Canadian and Acadian French (spoken in Louisiana and the Maritime Provinces). Short glossary of Acadian vs. European French. Text bilingual throughout. Excellent.

Sirlin, Lazaro. *Diccionario sexologico*. Buenos Aires, 1973. [Not seen.]

Spears, Richard A. *Slang and Euphemism: A Dictionary of Oaths, Curses, Insults, Sexual Slang and Metaphor, Racial Slurs, Drug Talk, Homosexual Lingo, and Related Matters*. Middle Village, NY: Jonathan David, 1981. 448 pp., paper $12.95, cloth $24.95. – Some 17,500 entries and 40,000 short definitions, culled from dozens of U.S., British, and other sources; from the 800s to the 1970s. Dozens of useful synonym lists hidden under silly entries: find "copulation" synonyms under *smockage*, "slovenly woman" under *trollymog*. Superficial introductory essays on slang, euphemism, taboo, verbal aggression, etc. Other flaws, but a very useful first resource.

Vinyoles i Vidal, Joan J. *Vocabulari de l'argot de la delinqüència*. Barcelona: Millà, 1978. Paper, 191 pp., 500 ptas. – Catalan dictionary of underworld slang. Entries are precisely dated, with sources and citations. Useful introductory essays on the evolution of argot, *caló*, and other marginal languages. Also discusses characteristics, such as foreign influences, infixes, suffixes, metaphors. Bibliography.

Vinyoles i Vidal, Joan J., and Ferran i Serafini, Joan. *Llenguatge subterrani de la política*. Barcelona: Millà, 1982. Paper, 232 pp. – Catalan dictionary of the underground language of politics. With comments on historical political argots, thematic classifications, list of initials of political parties and subgroups.

## OTHER

Aronson, Howard I. *Georgian: A Reading Grammar*. Columbus, OH: Slavica Publishers, 1982. 526 pp., typescript, $22.95. – A thorough, scholarly grammar of this South Caucasian language.

Barbaud, Philippe. *Le choc des patois en Nouvelle-France: Essai sur l'histoire de la francisation au Canada*. Québec: Presses de l'Université du Québec, 1984. Paper, 204 pp., Can.$22.95. – A historical and sociological study of the 30 French provincial dialects as the sources of modern French-Canadian. Tables, maps, statistics, questionnaire.

Borneman, Ernest. *Rot-weiß-rote Herzen: Das Liebes-, Ehe- und Geschlechtsleben der Alpenrepublik*. Wien: Hannibal, 1984. Paper, 293 pp. – A collection of 39 essays and lectures originally written between 1974 and 1984, dealing mainly with sexuality, birth control, children, sexual therapy, and psychoanalysis in contemporary Austria.

Colombo, John Robert, ed. *Years of Light: A Celebration of Leslie A. Croutch.* Toronto: Hounslow Press, 1982. Paper, 194 pp. – Four short stories and facsimile reproductions of Croutch's work, and 7 appendices on Canadian Fantastic Pulp magazines and fanzines compiled by the editor.

Doering, Henry, ed. *Book of Buffs, Masters, Mavens and Uncommon Experts.* New York: World Almanac, 1980. Paper, 342 pp., $6.95. – Contains "Reinhold Aman: Profanity & Cursing," pp. 304-305, a general article on him and *Maledicta.*

Gross, Ronald. *The Independent Scholar's Handbook: How to Turn Your Interest in Any Subject into Expertise.* Reading, MA: Addison-Wesley, 1982. Paper, 261 pp., $8.95. – A useful guide for the intellectually curious not affiliated with academe: where to do research, finding collaborators, funds, sources. Contains "Reinhold Aman's Pursuit of the Meaning of Abusive Language," pp. 206-209.

Gross, Ronald, and Gross, Beatrice. *Independent Scholarship: Promise, Problems, and Prospects.* New York: College Entrance Examination Board, 1983. Paper, 68 pp., $7.95. – A study of researchers not affiliated with a university, with practical advice on how to deal with their problems with libraries, funding, and the academe.

Karlen, Arno. *Napoleon's Glands and Other Ventures in Biohistory.* New York: Little, Brown & Co., 1984. 277 pp., $15.95. – Integrating medical, behavioral, social, and environmental sciences, the author investigates in 9 chapters the illnesses afflicting Napoleon, Goya, Poe, and looks at mummies, skeletons, biocataclysm, and human super-sexuality. Partially annotated bibliography.

Kearney, Patrick J. *A History of Erotic Literature.* London: Macmillan, 1982; New York: Bookthrift, 1982. 192 pp., £12.95. *A Dutch edition by Agathon, Bussum, was published in 1983.* – An intelligent survey from the 17th to the 20th centuries, illustrated with titles pages and erotic pictures. Mainly French and British.

——. *The Private Case: An Annotated Bibliography of the Erotica Collection in the British (Museum) Library.* With an introduction by G. Legman. London: Jay Landesman, 1981. 1000 copies printed. 360 pp., £45. – A descriptive catalog of some 2,000 titles dealing with erotica, pornography, and sexuality.

Mitchell, Greg. *Cats, Chocolate, Clowns, and Other Amusing, Interesting and Useful Subjects Covered by Newsletters.* New York: Dembner, 1982. Paper, 189 pp., $7.95. – The chapter *Words, Words, Words* contains "Foul Play," a general article on R. Aman and *Maledicta,* pp. 37-38.

Monteiro, George, ed. *In Crete with the Minotaur and Other Poems*. Providence, R.I.: Gávea-Brown, 1980. Paper, 77 pp., $6.00. – A bilingual Portuguese-English edition of the poems of Jorge de Sena, translated and prefaced by the editor.

Schilders, Ed. *De voorhuid van Jezus en andere Roomse wonderen*. Groningen: Xeno, 1985. Paper, 93 pp. – Several essays on eroticism in Catholicism and religious art, discussing The Foreskin of Jesus (as a relic and fetish), How to Skin a Saint (adoration of martyrs), Mary's Mother's Milk and breasts, Mary's Conception, and Other Roman Wonders. Illustrated.

Zehetner, Ludwig. *Das bairische Dialektbuch*. München: C.H. Beck, 1985. 302 pp., DM 38. – An excellent and comprehensive study of the Bavarian dialect of Bavaria proper (excluding Austria), including its variants, history and literature (from the 8th century to the present), grammar (phonology, morphology, syntax), contemporary usage and problems. Bibliography, indexes.

The Wizard of Id

Jay Ames composed the following rhyme from last names found in the Toronto, Ontario, telephone directory:

**Jacques An Gill Wenn Tupper Hill**
**Toff Etchell Pailey Waters,**
**Gill Kaim Back**
**Widder Gory Crack**
**Butt Knott Frumm Carrion Woders.**

# NOTES ON CONTRIBUTORS

**REINHOLD AMAN**, born in Bavaria in 1936, received his Ph.D. in Medieval Literature and Germanic Philology from the University of Texas in 1968. He typesets, edits, publishes and ships MAL to 64 countries. In addition to the monikers bestowed upon him earlier (see MAL 7), he is also known as the *King of Curses, High Priest of the Insult, Doctor of Damnations, Swami of Swearwords*, and *The Noah Webster of Verbal Aggression* (*Chicago Tribune*). However, his own favorite handle is the delightful "Dr. Dildo." (More information in earlier volumes)

**MAC E. BARRICK** is Professor of Spanish at Shippensburg State College, Pennsylvania. Dr. Barrick has published widely on folkore and is President of the Pennsylvania Folklore Society and a consultant to the *Encyclopedia of American Beliefs and Superstitions*. (More information earlier)

**RICHARD O. BARTON**, who sustained a degree in Political Science from the University of Michigan, works as a respiratory therapist in San Francisco. He is presently writing a book on pulmonary rehabilitation. Earlier, Mr. Barton tried to compile a volume on The Wit & Wisdom of San Francisco Politicians but could find no source material.

**RICHARD CHRISTOPHER***  holds a Ph.D. in English and teaches in New Hampshire.

**NORMAN CUBBERLY**, a ship captain and Master Mariner, lives in Grafton, Virginia. Capt. Cubberly graduated from the U.S. Coast Guard Academy in New Haven in 1954 and now does underwater research for the U.S. Navy. He has published book reviews and articles, mainly on navigation, in various professional publications. He states that marine cursing is unimaginative.

**JOSEPH DORINSON**, born in 1936, received his M.A. at Columbia University. He is an associate professor and the chairman of the History Department at Long Island University's Brooklyn Center, where he has taught for the past 18 years. *A.B.D.* Dorinson writes for *Jewish Currents, The Journal of Psychohistory*, and with Joseph Boskin just published "Ethnic Humor: Subversion and Survival" in *American Quarterly* 37/1 (1985):81-97.

**JOSEPH G. FOSTER**, A.B., University of Chicago and M.A., Pennsylvania State University (1954) in Romance Languages, taught French language and literature at Grinnell College, at the University of Nebraska, and at Penn State University (McKeesport) from 1959 to 1981, when he retired in Mifflinburg. Prof. Foster translated René de Obaldia's comedy *Wind in the Branches of the Sassafras* (produced at Pitlochry and Dallas), as well as works by Claudel, Glissant, Alexis, and Manet.

---

*Pseudonym

**CHARLES CHI HALEVI**, on a Talent Scholarship, received his B.A. in Creative Writing from Northeastern Illinois University in 1972. As a publicist and writer living in Chicago, he occasionally writes features for the *Chicago Tribune* and the *Chicago Sun-Times* and works as a stringer for *Time* magazine.

**ADAM JAWORSKI** lives in Poznań, Poland, and has taught at the University of Florida in Gainesville.

**EDGAR C. KNOWLTON, Jr.**, has been teaching in the European Languages Department at the University of Hawaii since 1948. (More information earlier)

**GERSHON LEGMAN**, born in Scranton, Pennsylvania in 1917, lives on the French Riviera. He is the world's leading expert on erotic folkore and literature, on the dirty joke and the limerick. (More information earlier)

**DOUGLAS LINDSEY**, M.D., is a surgeon at the University of Arizona in Tucson. During three wars and 30 years of service with the U.S. Army Medical Corps, Dr. Lindsey was awarded two Purple Hearts and two Silver Stars. He practices surgery and teaches at the U. of A., where he has been elected "Best Clinical Teacher" by four graduating classes. Nineteen publishers turned down his book *Simple Recipes for Simple Surgical Emergencies* because of his irreverent approach to the activities of a noble profession, but ARCO finally published it so that you, too, can learn How to Cut and Sew for Fun and Profit.

**MUKUMAR MPANG** is a teacher and associate researcher at the Center for Ethnological Studies in Bandundu, Zaïre. In addition to Dinga and French, he speaks Kongo, Lingala, Lori and Swahili.

**JOEL A. NEVIS** is a Ph.D. candidate in Linguistics at Ohio State University. During 1983-84, he researched Baltic Finnic morphology and clitic phenomena at the University of Helsinki, as the recipient of the Finnish Fund Fellowship and a Fulbright-Hayes travel grant. Mr. Nevis holds a B.A. in Linguistics from the University of Florida (1979) and an M.A. in Linguistics from Ohio State University (1981).

**FRANK H. NUESSEL**, Ph.D., University of Illinois (1973), is Associate Professor of Spanish and Director of the Program in Linguistics at the University of Louisville, Kentucky. (More information earlier)

**ROGER W. PHILLIPS** is Professor of Russian Language and Literature in a midwestern university. Dr. Phillips has written critical articles notably on Dostoevsky, translated numerous works from the Russian, and is the author of a Russian review grammar. Prof. Phillips's research also includes verbal aggression in Russian. Currently he is compiling a thesaurus of sexual and scatological vocabulary in English, which he claims will be altogether *sui generis*.

**JOSEPH SALEMI** recently completed his Ph.D. in Renaissance literature at New York University. His translations of Catullus, Horace, and other Roman lyric poets have appeared in journals throughout the country. Dr. Salemi teaches at Nassau Community College (SUNY) in Garden City, Long Island.

**CASPER G. SCHMIDT**, M.D., is a Namibian who is in private practice as a Child Psychiatrist in New York City. Dr. Schmidt is Associate Director of the Institute for Psychohistory in New York. He grew up under censorship and thus appreciates *Maledicta*'s candor. He dabbles in *belles lettres* and clay.

**SIR MAURICE SEDLEY***, *Baronet*, received his Doctor of Education degree from UCLA. He is a school administrator in Nevada.

**HANNES STUBBE** received his Ph.D. and *Diplom* in Psychopathology and Ethnology from the University of Freiburg, Germany. He now teaches in the Psychology Department at the University of Rio de Janeiro, Brazil. Dr. Stubbe's articles have appeared in *Etnologia Americana, Social Psychiatry, Jornal Brasileiro de Psiquiatria, Medizinische Welt* and elsewhere. He has also published *Der depressive Mensch.*

**SUE TURE*** is a Surgical Head Nurse working in metropolitan Milwaukee hospitals.

By courtesy of the Bibliothèque Nationale, Paris

"Les Fleurs du mal, Les Shmeurs du mal! There's nothing like **Les Joies du MAL**. So, order your copy of MAL 9 now, *grippe-sou.*"

— Chuck "Bo" de L'Air

Baudelaire, photograph by Étienne Carjat, 1863.